HERO LIVING

HERO LIVING

Seven Strides to Awaken Your Infinite Power

RUDY REYES

with ANGELA SMITH

Foreword by Evan Wright

A CELEBRA BOOK

Celebra
Published by New American Library, a division of
Penguin Group (USA) Inc., 375 Hudson Street,
New York, New York 10014, USA
Penguin Group (Canada), 90 Eglinton Avenue East, Suite 700, Toronto,
Ontario M4P 2Y3, Canada (a division of Pearson Penguin Canada Inc.)
Penguin Books Ltd., 80 Strand, London WC2R 0RL, England
Penguin Ireland, 25 St. Stephen's Green, Dublin 2,
Ireland (a division of Penguin Books Ltd.)
Penguin Group (Australia), 250 Camberwell Road, Camberwell, Victoria 3124,
Australia (a division of Pearson Australia Group Pty. Ltd.)
Penguin Books India Pvt. Ltd., 11 Community Centre, Panchsheel Park,
New Delhi - 110 017, India
Penguin Group (NZ), 67 Apollo Drive, Rosedale, North Shore 0632,
New Zealand (a division of Pearson New Zealand Ltd.)
Penguin Books (South Africa) (Pty.) Ltd., 24 Sturdee Avenue,
Rosebank, Johannesburg 2196, South Africa

Penguin Books Ltd., Registered Offices:
80 Strand, London WC2R 0RL, England

First published by Celebra,
a division of Penguin Group (USA) Inc.

First Printing, October 2009
10   9   8   7   6   5   4   3   2   1

LIBRARY OF CONGRESS CATALOGING-IN-PUBLICATION DATA
Reyes, Rudy.
    Hero living: seven strides to awaken your infinite power/Rudy Reyes, with Angela Smith;
foreword by Evan Wright.
        p.   cm.
    ISBN 978-0-451-22810-9
    1. Self-realization.   2. Self-actualization (Psychology)   3. Heroes—Psychological aspects.
I. Smith, Angela, 1962–   II. Title.
    BF637.S4R47 2009
    158.1—dc22   2009020379

Set in Perpetua
Designed by Spring Hoteling

Printed in the United States of America

IN MEMORY OF FIRST SERGEANT EDWARD
"HORSEHEAD" SMITH, WHO LIVED
AND DIED A HERO TO ALL

CONTENTS

FOREWORD

BY EVAN WRIGHT

Late in the afternoon of March 24, 2003, I was digging a hole by a bridge over the Euphrates River in Iraq. I was a reporter embedded with a platoon of Marines in the elite 1st Reconnaissance Battalion. We had been under rocket and machine-gun fire for several hours. The bridge was a key crossing point for the American invasion and was hotly contested by several thousand Iraqi paramilitaries firing on our position from three sides. More than a dozen Americans had already paid for this bridge crossing with their lives. The Recon Marines I accompanied—the Special Forces of the Corps—had been ordered to hold a position beside the bridge and wait. An armored assault across the Euphrates was due any time now, and the Recon Marines were standing by to rescue the crews of any armored vehicles disabled by enemy fire. In classic military tradition, the assault had been repeatedly delayed. Now, as night approached, the Recon Marines were ordered to dig in. Machine-gun fire raked the palm trees overhead. To avoid the bullets I excavated my hole from a kneeling position. Weighted down with forty pounds of body armor and gear, I felt myself wheeze each time I pitched my shovel into the earth and scratched out more clay. I was midway through this exhausting task when I felt a steely hand grip my arm, then heard a voice: "That's it, brother. Work those biceps."

Sergeant Rudy Reyes stood over me, offering an encouraging smile. It seemed Rudy had chosen this moment to continue the fitness instruction program he had begun—without my ever asking—when we had met a couple of weeks earlier, prior to the invasion. Eyeing the progress of my excavation on this combat-filled afternoon, Rudy pounded my back and added, "You see, brother. Just a little bit of fitness every day is all you need." Pausing to allow an enemy mortar to explode in the field to our rear, Rudy concluded, "Keep this up, you'll be in shape in no time."

Rudy was one of twenty-three men in the platoon I would follow to Baghdad and beyond for two months and profile in my book *Generation Kill*. Recon units are the most mentally and physically demanding of the Marine Corps, and as such attract some of the most indelible characters you'll find anywhere in the military or out. Trained to fight independently in small teams behind enemy lines, Recon units are filled with young men of indomitable spirit, with ferocious intellects and the physical power of pro athletes. In a platoon of fierce individualists Rudy stood out as the oddest.

I first met Rudy in his platoon's tent in the desert holding area where the U.S. invasion force was gathering for war. Rudy was shirtless, reclined on the plywood floor, reading Oprah's magazine. When I sat beside him to conduct the initial interview, Rudy spoke of the "artistry" of being a warrior, and his fervent desire to stay true to his Tao. In the midst of this, he studied my posture while I took notes, and he observed that I leaned slightly to one side. He correctly guessed that I was nursing a long-standing back injury. With artillery booming at a nearby test range and Cobra attack helicopters thundering overhead in practice formations, Rudy leaned in close and informed me: "At seventeen hundred hours I am teaching a yoga class. I suggest you join me, so we can work on redirecting your prana—your life force—which I would guess, dog, is the true source of discomfort in your back."

In Rudy I was confronted with an unlikely Marine. The first few times we spoke, I halfway wondered if someone was playing a prank on me. He struck me as the kind of wheatgrass-sipping, New Age–spouting phony you see around gyms in my hometown, Los Angeles. His physique was so ridiculously perfect, I assumed he must be one of those guys who has lived on workout machines and has acquired no other skill but the ability to majestically flex his pectorals. I imagined that if the bullets ever truly started to fly, Rudy might be the first one to curl into a fetal position. Let me be clear: There wasn't anything about Rudy that suggested phoniness. But when I initially encountered him I was a very skeptical reporter, and all my experience in life suggested that Rudy was simply too good to be true.

I quickly learned that other Marines held Rudy in high regard, especially for his hand-to-hand combat skills. The other men I spoke to in the platoon judged him the best martial arts fighter in the unit, if not the entire battalion. In the Marine Corps, martial arts training is undertaken with a gladiatorial spirit. Troops don't practice martial arts to earn belts. They prepare to fight to the death. Rudy's reputation as the best fighter in the group wasn't something he could merely walk around feeling proud of. At least once a day, a brother Marine would test him by trying to take him down in a sneak attack. The most vicious test I observed took place one afternoon when Rudy stood unaware in his corner of the tent, changing out of his pants. As he stood on one leg, sliding his other foot out of his pants, a brother Marine—one who had an advantage of several pounds and a couple of inches on Rudy—charged him across the tent. Before he could be tackled, Rudy somehow slid to one side and flipped his attacker on his head, which landed on the plywood floor with a loud crack. Rudy immediately helped his bewildered assailant back onto his feet, while expressing his deepest apologies for putting a knot on the guy's skull. "I didn't mean to hurt you, brother," Rudy repeated. When the Marine regained his footing, Rudy—always the sensei—spent several minutes reviewing the attack, explaining how next time he might succeed in taking him down.

By the time Rudy offered his encouragements to me during combat at the bridge over the Euphrates, I had come to accept he was for real. I also knew him well enough to understand that his offering fitness advice in the midst of an enemy attack was a manifestation of his humor, as well as his generosity of spirit. Rudy was doing his best to allay the fear in the midst of that firefight. Though we were in the midst of the most horrific kind of violence, Rudy was trying to keep his own prana properly directed by being of service to someone else. For Rudy, this was a form of spiritual self-discipline.

During the next two months in Iraq, Rudy and his fellow Marines endured through ever-harsher combat conditions and increasingly trying—often irresolvable—moral dilemmas. Within a year, Rudy would come home, briefly, then return to Iraq for the battle of Fallujah. On the battlefield, Rudy occasionally joked that as a child he had always wanted to be a superhero, and for him his military fatigues were the equivalent of a Caped Crusader's costume. Like so many others in his generation who have chosen to serve in uniform, Rudy acquitted himself as a hero, though I would argue more in the tradition of Achilles than Spider-Man.

If you spend time with Rudy, you know he does talk frequently of his childhood love for superheroes. Before martial arts, the Tao, and yoga, he had Superman. Growing up in a boys' home, fending for himself and his younger brothers, superheroes were his first positive role models. For him they weren't just fodder for escapist fantasy. Rudy will tell you he actually hoped to become one.

Rudy will also tell you that as a kid he was not just physically weaker than the predators who ruled his universe, but he was also filled with fear and its corollary, hatred. It was, he has told me, comic book superheroes who first inspired him to reimagine himself as an entirely different sort of human being. Had he not striven for a radical shift in his mental and spiritual outlook then, odds were favorable he would grow up to be a menace, no better and perhaps worse than the monsters on the streets who plagued him. As Rudy matured his role models changed, but one thing didn't: his bold use of imagination and will to change himself for the better, even in the face of impossible circumstances.

Rudy essentially told this narrative about himself in the first weeks after we met in 2003. At the time it was a great story, but no more real to me than a generic tale of hope and inspiration he might have read out of Oprah's magazine. His story became far more real to me after he returned from his third combat tour and left the Marine Corps.

Though he departed with awards in recognition of his bravery and service, I saw him as a shattered man. Whether a particular war is considered just or unjust, a battlefield offers inescapable, crushing lessons in the cruelty of the human condition. Such lessons are prone to break victorious and vanquished alike. I saw Rudy wrestle with his return to civil society as many other young men and women of his generation are now forced to, and witnessed as he essentially rebuilt himself from the ground up, again using imagination, willpower, and what I can only describe as spiritual discipline. I saw Rudy on some very bad days pull himself up, plant his feet on the ground, put his face in the sun, and train—and invariably try to help somebody else. Despite his Herculean effort, he confessed on a few occasions, "It's still not going well inside, but at least I'm out there hooking and jabbing, just trying to believe."

Rudy did come back. He's a different sort of warrior than the one I first met. Most of his effort today is geared toward helping those still trying to come back from a rough journey, or struggling to reimagine themselves as better human beings.

Rudy is himself a completely improbable person. He is an act of imagination and will. His physique, balance, and grace (as evident on the battlefield as when he enters a room) are all genuine. At the same time they are all just manifestations of a dream, by-products of a disciplined human being who has trained his spirit to overcome impossible realities. As such he is a profoundly inspiring person. Much as Rudy has spent the past few years perfecting methodologies for physical training—working with a wide variety of people—I personally am less interested in his study of proper breathing and muscle development than in a basic truth: What Rudy offers comes from the heart.

HERO LIVING

INTRODUCTION

Y ou are a hero.

There are moments in my life these words have seemed about others and not me. Even though I have been called a hero for battlefield exploits of war, fights won in the ring, or even for leading by example in coaching, there have been times throughout my life I've been knocked down with doubts flooding in. Moments of pain, anger, fear, insecurity, guilt, despair, depression, paralysis . . . all those things that can lead a person to question his or her self and self-worth.

I was raised feral. Truly. I was uncultivated, uncared for, and unseen. I thought of myself as a wolf child. The upside is I wasn't downloaded with many of the so-called normal systems and rules that can squash imagination, repress passion, and inhibit dreaming. The downside is I was raised in a war zone of poverty, fear, drugs, and abuse.

It's from this humble vantage that I share my story with you and begin by stating the most painful truth of my childhood, a fact that played out over and over again the first sixteen years of my life: I was not wanted. I tell you this not for dramatic effect, but for

1

relational effect. Reason being that, to some degree or another, we all yearn to belong somewhere, to someone. Even inside our own families and relationships we can feel incredibly unseen and lonely. That's how I felt. I had no home, not a stable and safe one anyway. I had no stable family system to plug into. Little structure. Zero consistency. No religion. There were times when I had no food, no clothes, and no medical care. Abuse and neglect were my family's rites and rituals. And love? Well, love was conditional and danger-ously unreliable.

My mother was seventeen when I was born, still a child herself and the victim of an abusive home. She had gotten pregnant by a man she was dating, but they didn't stay together even through the pregnancy, so I never met my biological father. Lacking options, my mother married my stepfather and namesake, Rudy Sr.

I was a scrawny little mutt. I had been born two months pre-mature and was not expected to live. My legs were bowed and my feet were turned inward. At eight months I was fitted for metal leg braces and corrective shoes, which I wore until I was three.

My two younger brothers came along within just twenty-four months of each other, just a year and a half after me. When I was still very young, my mother would spend one-on-one time with me at the mall or the park while my brothers stayed with a family member, but all of that changed when her parents passed away. The burden of three young boys and the heaviness of her sad heart seemed simply too much and she gave in to defeat. She became an alcoholic and a drug addict. She had intermittent flashes of nurtur-ance, but the abuse she had suffered wreaked such destruction that she ended up fragile, fragmented, and unavailable. The stress of poverty, the immaturity of youth, and the legacy of abuse had beat and subjugated my mother into survival mode—a kind of animal hypervigilance where she was in fight or flight most of the time. The darker her life became, the more she used and drank. And the more she used and drank, the more my brothers and I were shuffled from cousin to uncle to grandfather to stranger.

Nevertheless, at age five, the glint of possibility, the dream for more, graced its way into my life. Rudy Sr. took me to see Bruce Lee's movie *Enter the Dragon*. Without many examples of courage and compassion up to that point in my life, something on the silver screen spoke to me. I heard my first loud quiet call into Hero Living. It wasn't conscious. It was deeper than that. It was primal. It was what I needed to survive.

I watched Bruce Lee save the day and imagined, "If I could learn to be like him, maybe I could save the day too."

With my little brothers.

This one moment captured my imagination with such hope, such commitment, and such joy I plugged myself into all things superhero. Hero Living became my religion. Comic books became my scripture. And a pantheon of heroic icons—from Bruce Lee to Spider-Man to Achilles to Rocky Balboa to the Samurai—became my family.

It's not that life got better at this point. In fact, it got a lot worse. But I had a philosophy now. It was childlike and rudimentary. But it was my philosophy. It was my superpower. It was my grail.

Throughout my childhood, my two brothers and I were moved around and handed off innumerable times. We were like used, ratty clothes—boxed up and unpacked only to be boxed up and unpacked again. Every time we were handed off we spiraled into grosser poverty and more violent abuse. One of the most terrifying incidents was being beaten in and out of consciousness by my grandfather. I was four. My senses memorized this nightmare with such detail I can still smell the whiskey on his screams, I can see the ruthless monster in his eyes, and I can feel the relentless tyranny of his belt. With a hero's vantage point, I now see a sad, desperate, broken man who had given up on his own hero somewhere inside. Who had made the most self-destructive, uncreative choice a human being can make: It's too late for me; I am a lost cause.

My mother, divorced, poor, and alone at twenty, had handed me off to my grandfather. When she paid a visit and saw the shape I was in—a shuddering, bloodied, curled-up little boy—to her credit, she moved us in with my grandmother, who had divorced my grandfather years before. There, I was able to rest and thrive. My grandma didn't have much. But she had love. And food. And a continuity of being that felt safe.

During the next three years I flourished. I devoured the hero stories in my comic books. I soaked up the values of TV's Superman, Tarzan, and Spider-Man. My leg braces were off, so I practiced every kick I saw in a Bruce Lee movie. I was the strongest, fastest kid in school. I was reading, writing, painting, and drawing. I was creating action figures and monsters out of clay, using my mom's pot seeds for eyes. I was free to play. I was free to be a little boy.

This lasted until I was seven and then another spiral into a new kind of hell. My grandmother died and, a few months later, so did my grandfather. My mom never recovered from the loss. Never has, in fact. Drugs became her family, and her most intimate relationship. And as she came and went, homes came and went for my little brothers and me. We were back in the war zone.

In retrospect I think my mom died along with her mother and father. What life force she had seemed suddenly snuffed out. I believe she made the same self-destructive, uncreative choice her father had made: It's too late for me; I am a lost cause.

In Victor Frankl's book, *Man's Search for Meaning*, he recounts his three torturous years as a prisoner in Auschwitz during the Holocaust. Amidst horrific inhumanity he somehow came to this insight: "Everything can be taken from a man but one thing: The last of human freedoms—to choose one's attitude in any given set of circumstances, to choose one's own way."

This truth is the essence of Hero Living: the freedom to choose one's attitude, to choose one's own way. Why my mom chose an attitude that would swallow her up and deaden her life force, I don't know. Why I chose an attitude that would buoy me up and enliven my life force, I don't know. It's the mystery of mysteries. But what I know for certain is the choice to move into Hero Living is present ever and always. In every instance of unfairness, in every moment of victimization, it's there. Now. And now. And now . . . Extending its wise old hand. Beckoning every one of us into more life.

I experienced my first taste of this transformative truth when I was eight. My mom had emotionally combusted. That afternoon she had scraped together enough courage to ask her man, the man of our house, for some money to buy clothes for my brothers and me. In turn he knocked her around with his iron fists and words, saying he didn't want us. This man from whom I desperately wanted love and acceptance declared my mommy was nothing and her three kids were meaningless.

I had been playing Shogun Warriors with my little brothers, imaginations running full gear with vacuum cleaner parts as our weapons. Mommy and her man fought often enough, but this time she emerged from the kitchen with eyes shot full of tears and dazed like a kicked puppy. Dazed and broken, she was intoning, "*Mijos,* boys, we must leave . . . we have no home . . . we must leave." She was sobbing, "We have no home . . . we HAVE TO GO . . . we have to go." And so we went. With vacuum cleaner parts in hand, her three little *mijos* filed out the front door and piled into the silvery green old beater Buick.

But we didn't go. She was behind the wheel, my little brothers were in the backseat shell-shocked, and I sat up front watching the numbers "1818," the address high on the dark brown wood panel of our home, loop in and out of view again and again. My mother was driving around our cul-de-sac in circles. She was frozen at the wheel of her life. Literally. It was terrifying. What little ground-

With my little "Shogun Warrior" brothers.

Courtesy of Reyes family

Courtesy of Reyes family

With my little brothers.

ing my brothers and I had in this person called a mother, we watched her unravel circle by agonizing circle. She kept droning, "I have nothing . . . we have nowhere to go . . . I have nothing," as she kept turning left and left again. My mother was trapped in a downward spiral.

I consider this moment my first tiny hero mission. My little Shogun Warriors were clasped together on the backseat scared and crying, while my mom sat on the paisley green velveteen upholstery of the front seat going nowhere. I thought, "I have to help. We're going to need food and blankets and pajamas, and Mommy's hurt. Mommy just needs some help."

In that moment I stood up. I anchored my butt against the cracked vinyl dashboard, looked at my mom, and put my little hand on hers. "Mommy, we can go to cousin's house. We can go!" But she kept driving past 1818 for the nth time.

"Mommy, listen to me! We have to go to the street. We can go to cousin's house."

For the first time since the cruelty of her man's iron hand and hate had broken her, she looked me in the eye. Like a little girl she breathed, "Okay, little Rudy. We go to cousin's house. Cousin will take us." And although I was too young to drive, I directed my mom out of the cul-de-sac, down the street, onto the freeway, and ultimately into the driveway of a cousin's home.

Movement. Without it, nothing is possible but impossibility. Without it, my family, my little brothers, were becoming victims of nowhere, victims of 1818 over and over again.

In Eastern philosophy this is called samsara—the loop of suffering. We've all lived portions of our lives in this dead-end cul-de-sac. Looping through the same old stories and betrayals day after month after year. Circle long enough and life shuts down. Circle long enough and we become victims of nowhere. Trapped and caged.

By the time I reached eleven, survival mode was all I knew— poverty, drugs, beatings, and the daily fight for life. My teeth were rotting, leading to unbearable headaches, and the smell of the rot was like garbage. My hair hadn't been cut for over a year. I had lice. But still . . . Still I had my Hero Living. My philosophy. My superpower. My grail. My lifeline.

Yet even that would be threatened. I was too young at the time to know that a direct attack on one's essence is an archetypal event in the hero journey. It happens in some shape-shifting form to all of us—the existential event that shakes us to our core.

For me it was the day a family friend sexually molested me. Of any other trauma before or since, this detonated a cold-blooded rage in me. I felt blown into a million worthless pieces. I could feel my identity slipping away dream by dream, and I descended into a vortex of revenge. I was certain everyone in my life—family, teacher, neighbor, or stranger—was plotting to kill me. Just like my mom in our cul-de-sac three years before, terrified and frozen at the wheel of her life, I circled my circumstances like a caged rabid animal. I was trapped in samsara. I would either fight for my

life or I would conclude what my mother and grandfather had mod-
eled: It's too late for me; I am a lost cause.

Here I was, just eleven years old, and I was trapped in my own
samsara of stagnancy and paralysis.

The fact that I'm sitting in front of a computer writing this
book is a miracle. Something inside me fought for my life. It refused a future of violence, addiction, and crime. Although knocked
down so many times, it refused to give up. It wanted more life than
that.

What I've come to realize is these are the telltale markers along
the hero's path, along everyone's path. Often it's from the depths
and darkness of experience that I've found and cultivated my rich-
est assets, my sharpest tools and implements. As I've learned to
read the signs and hone my skills, I understand more and more
there are no limits to possibilities. I understand this as much from
the role models in my life as from my own experience. My heroes
are real-life people I have known or look up to, as well as the icons
of bigger-than-life stories that reside in books and movies and my
imagination.

It's those mythological heroes that belong to everyone, because
they are the archetypal stories of everyone's potential—yours and
mine. Being a hero doesn't mean being all things to all people, nor
being excellent or perfect at everything. Even Superman has his
kryptonite. If you think about the classic heroes of stories and myth,
they're not perfect. That, in fact, is what makes them heroic. They
see their way through their problems, overcoming their own weaknesses and foibles to stand up for themselves, others, or what's
right.

So in this sense I am a hero. I am not perfect; I struggle and
stumble, yesterday, today, and tomorrow. I am a hero because I am
hero *living*, simply walking with awareness in deep footsteps of

those heroes traveling before me on the path. And believe me, if I can do it, anyone can.

Throughout this book, I will share with you how I kept moving. I'll share with you how I worked through the molestation, how I survived an all-boys' school, how I emancipated myself and raised my brothers, how I sought out living heroes, how I became a kung fu world champion, how I trained and served as a Reconnaissance Marine, and how, to this day, I continue to move and breathe and grow through Hero Living. I will share my lessons, my blunders, my accomplishments, my fears, and my epiphanies. My journey, you will see, is your journey, because what we have in common is the hero's journey.

For that reason I want to turn the attention to you. I want to be sure you're not diminishing or dishonoring your story by comparing it to mine. You can't quantify trauma. You can't measure struggle. Hurt hurts. Period. So be kind to yourself. Respect your story by starting where you are. Get involved in your life and consider what you want. Consideration is movement. It is the first tool of Hero Living.

This isn't always easy, I know. I've been there, and *still* find myself there at times. There have been periods in my life when the call to myself sounded so muffled, so confusing, even dangerous, it was like wandering through a minefield at night. But as I moved with consideration, with choice, with breath, and with the dream for more, as I worked with my mind, my body, and my emotions, I began to experience the pure, creative, transformative power of Hero Living.

So I share my story with you not as sage or guru, but as fellow sojourner—as your hero brother. Together we have a pantheon of heroes to reference, from fictional to actual, and infamous to unsung. We have the here. We have the now. We have our breath. And we have our choice.

So listen up, my fellow traveler. Listen to the loud quiet call of Hero Living. There's an important truth to remember here. Perhaps you know it already, right here, right now. Or perhaps it has slipped your grasp, or fades in and out like a weak broadcast signal. But the truth is, the very simple truth is, you are a hero.

You are a hero.

You might not feel that way in this moment. Your definition of the word might not include you. Your current challenges or actions might disagree. In fact, you might even feel a bit put off by the idea, concluding this is just another self-help book for selling feel-good clichés.

But before you dismiss the idea entirely, before you discount the word so often attributed to mythological icons, legendary champions, and acts of hair-raising courage, consider this: These grandiose figures and feats are ultimately just symbols for a magical journey each and every one of us is on, whether we are conscious of it or not.

And so I repeat: You are a hero.

How do I know this with such certainty? You are here. *You. Are. Here.* That's no insignificant happenstance. Whether you're a creationist, an evolutionist, or undecided, the beat of your heart, the flex and flow of your lungs, the electrical currents of your brain, and the desires of your spirit all conspire on your behalf to gift you moment after mind-blowing moment. You are here. Now. And now. And now . . .

In this moment, this mysterious, fleeting, quantum moment in which a universe of possibility awaits your direction, I invite you to tune in to the loud quiet call within—to breathe more, to consider more, and to dream more. I don't mean more in terms of distance covered. I mean more in terms of your own life force discovered. I mean small, gentle, intentional movements that add up to a hero's revolution.

The question is, will you answer the call and stride into your own hero journey, or will you squelch the call with fear, doubt, anger, depression, difficult circumstances, or any number of other obstacles? I want to be clear. It's not that obstacles are bad. Obstacles are essential to Hero Living, with the capacity to slingshot us into new possibilities, but only if we're willing to work with them in that way. I've found in my own journey that I regularly ask, "Am I using obstacles to trap and cage me or to compel me into growth?" They can be barriers or opportunities. It's a matter of perception, and the choice is mine every moment of every day.

If you feel cynical, so be it. Embrace it and move. If you're pissed off, that's a powerful energy. Express it in constructive ways and get moving. If you're afraid, tap the fear and move. If the most you can do is half-assed, perfect. Move halfway. The point is to be compassionate with yourself. Don't give up. Believe in the possibility of yourself. Easy to say, I know. But by all accounts one of the most important skills the hero learns and practices.

In short, start with yourself not as you wish yourself to be, but just as you are. No judgments. No apologies. Move and breathe and practice and dream. That is enough because you are enough—because you are right here, right now.

You might be wondering, "If I accept the call into Hero Living and the journey into more life, where am I headed?" The truth is, I can't tell you the destination. I can't do it for my journey, and I can't do it for yours. That is counter to the rhythm of Hero Living, which by nature is dynamic, organic, and iterative.

What I can do is offer a working guide made up of three parts—a compass that helps you navigate the landscape of Hero Living, a mirror that facilitates contemplation and reflection, and a lantern that illuminates the shadowy path into brilliant discoveries. That is the intention of this book, informed by years of traversing emotional, mental, and physical terrain. Some of it so terrifying I wasn't sure I'd survive. And some of it so transforming I found my power, my joy, my creativity, my safety, and my prayer, all of which I will share and embellish throughout this book.

From my perspective this book is your book because it's about Hero Living, and I can't own that mysterious journey any more than I can own your journey. So to the extent you identify with and plug in to what is offered, that is the extent this book becomes your own autobiography.

For that reason I have organized my philosophy, our philosophy, of Hero Living into seven distinct strides, one per chapter. Why strides instead of steps or stages? Because the word, whether used as noun or verb, connotes movement, each stride intimately entwined with the others, just like inhaling and exhaling.

Think about it: At what point does inhaling begin and exhaling end? Take a moment and pay attention to your breath. Can you identify the exact moment when inhaling begins and exhaling ends? Try it and you'll see there is no point of separation. Not unless you hold your breath. The two are in mutual, cyclical agreement to keep you alive. And moving. Breath has no hierarchy. No regret about past breaths. No fear of future breaths. No breaths are embarrassing. None are more impressive than the others. They all matter because each and every one connects to the next. Stop breathing and life begins to shut down.

It's exactly the same with Hero Living and the seven strides in this book. No stride is more important than another. But dynamic movement within each stride and, likewise, cyclical movement between strides are not only typical of the hero's journey, but essential. Stop moving and life begins to shut down.

So welcome to the Seven Strides of Hero Living outlined below and fleshed out in hero-living color chapter by chapter.

As you review each of the strides outlined below, feel free to leap forward into any stride you resonate with. There's an accompanying page number just for that purpose. Hero Living isn't tidy and sequential. It's a jazz piece, a cool improvisation you get to play, practice, and play the rest of your life. If you decide to leap forward into a specific stride, do so with enthusiasm. If you decide to stay put and move in sequence, likewise, do so with enthusiasm. Either way, get interested and show up for yourself. After all, you are the masterwork. You are capable of more range, more rhythm, more voice, more harmony, more groove, and more fun. As the great jazz musician Louis Armstrong put it, "What we play is life."

THE SEVEN STRIDES OF HERO LIVING

Stride 1—Stagnancy & Paralysis (page 20)

The feeling: "I feel trapped. I feel stuck. I don't want to stay here, but I don't know how to make things better. I don't even know if it's possible."

The gist: Sometimes circumstances have thrown you such repeated, ongoing blows, you need to catch your breath and take a rest. Feeling stuck is normal. But you don't want to stay trapped in this stride too long because nothing is possible here but impossibility. When you're ready, turn your stay into a visit and gently begin to move. How? By simply considering that the painful things that have happened to you in life are not, in fact, you. You are not flawed, you are not hopeless, you are not a lost cause, and you are not trapped.

Stride 2—Moment of Movement (page 42)

The feeling: "Somewhere inside I feel the glint of more possibility. I hear the loud quiet call into Hero Living. I see there might be a way out of my pain."

The gist: Breath is the ultimate metaphor for more life. Stop breathing and you die. Keep breathing and you move toward new possibilities. Breathing truth into your journey is in and of itself a heroic act. Look honestly at the facts of your life. Dig deep. Give voice to your emotions. Connect to your body. Dream new dreams. Get visceral, get real, and get it all out on the table. Start with yourself just as you are and the hero inside will sit up and take the lead. You don't have to move much in order to move far.

Stride 3—Fighting & Surviving (page 83)

The feeling: "I'm tired of being beaten down. I'm mad. I'm hurt. And I'm afraid. But I'm going to show up for myself even if no one else will. I'm going to fight for myself."

The gist: There are two ways to view the painful obstacles that plot and plan to foil your hero journey: as your enemies, or as your guides. It's human, healthy, and archetypal in this stride to draw your battle lines and to take on your enemies with angry counterattacks and menacing aggression. To which I say, fight. Fear and doubt be damned. Show up for yourself, get pissed off, grapple, scream, work with your resistance, get guttural about what you want, win a few, lose a few, and fight for your right to more life.

Stride 4—Tools & Skills (page 118)

The feeling: "Instead of fighting and resisting my obstacles, perhaps I should treat them as new sources of information for me. Maybe there's a way to use my mind, body, and emotional life to create new possibilities."

The gist: You will fight and fight until one day you consider a new possibility: Obstacles are just guides in disguise. They are muses for teaching you skills and opportunities for revealing newfound tools. When obstacles are allowed to instruct, they gift you with vision, hope, courage, accountability, sense of humor, and compassion. Then comes the epiphany emblematic of this stride: There are no enemies outside. They are just illusory battle lines drawn on the inside. Combat dissolves and you come home, only to see that you were free all along.

Stride 5—Practicing & Honing (page 150)

The feeling: "I am ready to seek out challenges and missions that test my skills, refine my training, and integrate my life force. I am now driven by movement, not by a destination."

The gist: As your hero journey is gifted with more and more tools, you practice. And hone. And sharpen. In this stride you apply your proficiencies across the many facets of your life—career, relationship, fitness, family, money, and so forth. Mind, body, and emotions begin to integrate. Your life force tunes and tones into wholeness. Yet you have not arrived, nor will you ever. You will practice your skills and tools the rest of your life, acquiring new ones along the way and discarding those that no longer suit your journey.

Stride 6—Pure Unedited, Uninhibited Potential (page 179)

The feeling: "My life is literally coming to life because I know who I am. I am free, I am pure possibility, and I am here for something bigger than myself."

The gist: Whatever your notion of a higher power, an awestruck reverence now moves through you. Your life has become about pure potential and the limitless possibility that is available. The doing, coercive energy of the "me" is transformed by the being, openhearted energy of the "we." You are playing in the slipstream of your authenticity. And you regularly intone the most powerful prayer of all: "Thank you." In this stride you are ready to consider the sacred summons: "How will you share? How will you bring Hero Living back to the village?"

Stride 7—Reciprocity of Sharing (page 219)

The feeling: "Now that I've become my own truth, it mustn't be kept in the temple. I must share Hero Living in my unique way, because in sharing the light with others, we are all transformed."

The gist: The sacred summons to share takes form gently and intuitively. The sensation often feels like you're being plugged into something bigger than yourself—a purpose, a meaning, a calling. You have become a conduit for the message of Hero Living, and no other hero can share it quite like you. There is a poignant moment in this stride when you take stock and are humbled by the arc of your journey because, in the beginning, you could have never dreamed, let alone orchestrated, such possibility. It's at this moment the phrase "more life" is understood, not just as an experience for yourself, but as an offering to others.

As you can see, we all move dynamically through these strides, sliding back and forth depending upon where we are in life and what challenges we are working with. Later on in the book I will invite you to consider and contemplate the many facets of your life and how each facet relates to each stride. We will do that work together in the last chapter. Until then, as you read and consider each stride in the chapters to come, I invite you to tune in to what's going on with you right now, this moment. Nothing's more powerful than tuning in and working with our emotions and circumstances just as they are. Perhaps you feel good about your life on the whole, but there are a couple of areas you'd like to improve. Or perhaps you're in the fight of your life and the obstacles are overwhelming. Maybe there are past pains and traumas that keep you trapped. Or maybe new opportunities are presenting themselves, but you're not sure how to fully realize them. As I said before, the Seven Strides of Hero Living are yours. Use them as compass, mirror, and lantern. Use them to breathe, to help you fire on all cylinders, and to move you stride by stride into more life.

Throughout each stride you will see opportunities to take stock and reflect using contemplative prompts I refer to as the Hero's Whetstone. Named after the whetstone used by the great samurai warriors as a tool to sharpen their sword, these contemplative prompts are intended to help you cut to the truth of yourself. True heroes seek themselves first and foremost. They look honestly into their obstacles, their strengths, their needs, and their journey. They flex great courage in their determination for more life.

The hero also understands the interconnected nature and importance of body, mind, and spirit, and actively exercises and nourishes all their faculties for use along their journey. Over the years my practice of physical training, along with my inquisitive search for learning and knowledge—paying attention to movement and nutrition for the body, tending the garden of the mind, and feeding the spirit with overall health and hope—has been and continues to be part and parcel to my own hero's journey. While the purpose of this book is not to provide instruction on your physical health, I do want to make the point up front that as you step into more of yourself on the hero's path, paying special attention and taking care of yourself in this way is a natural and essential element to getting more out of your life.

So in this moment I invite you to choose to show up for yourself. In every way. It's no accident you've picked up this book. It's a synchronous nudge, because my story is your story. In this mysterious, fleeting, quantum moment I invite you to heed the loud quiet call of the hero within and to really experience what you've always known: "Things are only impossible for me until they're not."

As I write this, as I reflect on my own journey and the Seven Strides of Hero Living, I'm overwhelmed with awe and gratitude. Without Hero Living, the odds were stacked against me. I had every opportunity to squelch the loud quiet call within and to choose a life of violence, addiction, crime, and self-destruction. But with my pantheon of heroes and the philosophy of Hero Living at my side, the odds rejiggered and conspired on my behalf with such amazing order, they lifted me up and out of hell into opportunities I didn't know existed. Hero Living taught me anything is possible.

Given where I come from, given what I come out of, it makes no sense I would be writing this book—that is, until I acknowledge the enduring presence, push, and parenting of Hero Living day after week after month after year. And then it makes perfect sense. Divine sense. Hero sense.

STRIDE 1
Stagnancy & Paralysis

The feeling: "I feel trapped. I feel stuck. I don't want to stay here, but I don't know how to make things better. I don't even know if it's possible."

I was thirty-three years old at the time. There I was, a Recon Marine, the best of the freaking best, the toughest of the tough, trained to survive the most death-defying missions, trained to gather intelligence against all odds, trained to be a professional killer, and I felt like a scared, traumatized little boy. I wanted to hide under a table. I wanted to hide from the icy despair in my stomach. I was frozen with the feeling that the whole universe was pressing in on me, crushing me with shame and fear. I felt totally powerless. Was it the sniper missions? The close air support missions? The insurgents in Fallujah? The bloody fights for my life? No. It was my marriage. It was falling apart.

I had survived the arduous training grounds of reconnaissance indoctrination—a training regime so elite and intense eighty percent don't make it. I mastered every skill for amphibious raids, underwater demolition and infiltration, weaponry, surveillance, intelligence, scuba, paratrooping, hostage survival, and escape. I survived one tour in Afghanistan and two tours in Iraq. But I did not have the preparation or the experience to survive a divorce.

I can remember being underwater in Combatant Diver School where I held my breath for three minutes while a team of Recon Instructor Sharks simulated a violent attack. That I understood. That I could survive. But on the day I realized my marriage was ending, I was gasping for air. Completely ambushed. Totally destroyed.

In hindsight I can see how my marriage was unraveling long before the divorce. I had entered Recon training at twenty-six, already married. For the next seven years our relationship consisted of a few days or months together. Then I would be gone for long periods of time in training missions and ultimately in combat. During my first deployment to Afghanistan I couldn't get my wife out of my head. I missed her. I hurt to be with her. I was walking around like a zombie. My team leader, a rangy, tough mountain man from North Carolina, saw me writing a letter to her. "Get your head out of your hole," he warned. "I didn't invest all this time in you to have you end up a turd. Put that crap down. It will be waiting for you when you get back. Right now we got business to handle." I don't fault him for that. He was right. If you're not focused, you die. So I poured my energy, my devotion, everything I had into my recon platoon and our missions. I was fighting the hardest fights of my life. I fought for my team. Some of them died for me. You can't put a language to the bonds you forge when you're responsible for people's lives.

Duty is a slippery thing. It can save lives but it can also kill a marriage. Everything I was going through in my job I was going through for both of us. But she needed more. I needed more. We needed our connection. It's sad to me that neither of us knew how to really talk and support each other. It was tragic to me the day I had a chance to phone her from the field to only have bombs suddenly coming in from the enemy with loud explosions blasting in the background of the call. She could hear the sounds of war over the line and started distressing, "Baby, what is that? Are you okay? What's going on?" I could hear the worry in her voice and it troubled me to hear her upset, so right then and there I decided to not call her anymore. I told her I had to go, there was business to handle. I hung up the phone and let go of our connection.

And so I did my duty. I worked hard and sent home a paycheck. Every time I came home on leave, there was more and more distance. And so I'd return to combat, do my duty, and keep sending paychecks. Seven years later, by the end of my final tour, I was empty—emotionally, mentally, sexually, and spiritually. I had nothing to give her. And she had nothing to give back. I had grown to hate the cage that had become my marriage and I blamed myself for its failure. The battles on the field were now being mirrored by the battles in myself. I was unhappy, depressed, and in shock. I kept thinking, "It's my fault, I don't deserve anything better."

All the traumas and betrayals of my youth were exponentially

With my wife while in the U.S. Marine Corps.

Courtesy of Reyes family

magnified by the trauma of losing my marriage and the traumas I experienced in battle. I was already fractured on the inside. I had worked hard in my career to make something of myself. To glue the pieces back together. But those fractured pieces turned to powder when my marriage dissolved.

Even though I was thirty-three years old, a grown man and an elite warrior, I felt eleven again. I felt like the little boy who was molested twenty-two years earlier by a family friend—the little boy who was being used and disposed of; whose very essence was being assaulted; who felt blown into a million worthless pieces; who paced the cage of his life in shame and fear; and who wondered: Is it too late for me? Am I a lost cause?

Honestly, I felt I wanted to die. I felt doomed to a futile existence. Trapped in stagnancy and paralysis.

If there's any sentiment that sums up stagnancy and paralysis, I think it's simply this: "I don't know who I am, I don't know what I want, and I don't know where I'm going." That's how I felt.

Your Story is My Story

It doesn't matter whether the facts of our stories are similar or different, everyone can relate to the crushing demands of family, duty, career, relationship, money, and surviving day-to-day. Many of us can relate to the terror of childhood neglect and abuse. And most of us can relate to periods when we've felt lost, afraid, alone, and worthless. Wherever you're at in life today, if you feel any amount of stagnancy and paralysis, I hope you can feel me when I say, "I'm with you." I know it's big. I've been in the same muck and mire. I know it feels insurmountable. But believe me, it's not. If my story is your story you can move. If stagnancy and paralysis is integral to the hero's journey you can rattle the cage. You can take a tiny step, utter a new word. If I can do it, you can do it too. I'm not talking about coping. Coping is acceptance of the cage. It may keep your heart beating and your lungs breathing, but it's not life. It's resignation. It's not Hero Living. No, I'm talking about dismantling the cage bar by bar. I'm talking about tuning into your feelings. I'm talking about telling yourself the truth. I'm talking about coming to know who you are, what you want, and where you are going.

Fyodor Dostoyevsky, the Russian author, philosopher, and forerunner of existentialism, said, "Taking a new step, uttering a new word is what people fear the most." When we feel trapped, caged, imprisoned, stuck, or mired in quicksand, we're in fight or flight. Sometimes the fear manifests as a steady anxiety, a continual insecurity we can't seem to shake. But sometimes the fear is so primal and raw that movement of any kind feels life threatening. Either way, we desperately want out of our situation, but it can feel unachievable, even death defying, to consider anything but the bars to our cage. To use an old idiom, it really is a living hell.

Some of us resign ourselves to this hell. We can't see a way out no matter how hard we try. Some of us think we deserve it, as if we have to pay some kind of penance. And some of us get so used to the cage we don't even know we're in it.

Stagnancy and paralysis can be disorienting because of its ability to sneak up and ambush us. Before we know it we can't remember the dreams we used to dream; we can't put a finger on why we're so angry; we can't make sense of our unhappiness when we have so much; we can't let go of past traumas and regrets; and we can't figure out why life keeps dealing us blow after unfair blow.

Some philosophers call this an existential crisis—the point at which our life feels lost; our obstacles feel insurmountable; our day-to-day responsibilities feel pointless; and the meaning of our life feels purposeless. You may not relate to all of this, but if your lungs are breathing, your heart is beating, and your neurons are firing, you can relate to some of it. You are a human. You are a hero. And we heroes know a little something about hell.

Think about Sisyphus. Poor Sisyphus. What a life. The gods in this iconic Greek myth really did a number on him. They weren't particularly charmed by his overweening pride and cockiness, so they cursed him. He now spends eternity pushing a massive boulder to the peak of a steep hill, only to have it mash over his toes and roll down to the bottom. He dutifully descends, bloodied and bruised, to start the uphill battle all over again, day after week after year after eon. Talk about stagnancy and paralysis. Talk about a loop of suffering. Talk about hell.

Whether Sisyphus deserves this punishment or not is a whole other book that has nothing to do with Hero Living. In Hero Living there is always the possibility for freedom. Always the loud quiet call to move into the next stride. But Sisyphus doesn't know this. He doesn't know he has made a silent agreement with his circumstances, a dead-end pact with his suffering. So he fixates on his obstacle; he obsesses over the damage it has done to his life; he wallows in the pain of his broken back and broken spirit; he replays the innumerable times the boulder has hurt him; he regrets every uphill attempt and sees only the downhill failures; he resigns himself to the boulder and, in the process, forgets what he loves and dreams. He forgets who he really is and squelches the loud quiet call within.

Albert Einstein is credited for saying, "The definition of insanity is doing the same thing over and over again but expecting different results."

Who hasn't experienced this insanity at some point in their life? More accurately, who doesn't make and unmake their own Sisyphean agreements day in and day out? I certainly do and, my guess is, you do too.

The Sisyphean Agreement as It Applies to Real Life

Life can throw us some serious blows. The traumas we survive, the hardships we're in the middle of right now this very moment, wow—the stuff we endure. At least my man Sisyphus knows exactly what he's dealing with. He doesn't get ambushed day in and day out with a new set of problems. No bills to pay. No career to create. He's not raising kids or trying to make a relationship work. There's no cultural system telling him what to believe. He's not jockeying for a position in the world. He doesn't have body issues. He wasn't neglected or abused as a child. Comparatively speaking, when you think about it, a boulder ain't so bad. At least it's just one problem to worry about instead of a stormy confluence of many. It's this superhuman juggling of life that makes me proud of the heroes I get to meet and work with every day.

One of the great opportunities of my life is training fellow heroes just like yourself in my fitness program. They may see themselves as average people, but I see them as courageous standup warriors who have heard the loud quiet call inside and show up for an hour to push beyond their stagnancy and paralysis. You can bet we whoop it on. It's a total mind, body, and spirit overhaul. At the end we're so transported by the journey, so drenched in sweat, it's like a baptism into new possibilities. Imagine that experience three times a week—three baptisms into new possibilities.

One of my fellow heroes in fitness is Kim, a soulful forty-year-old woman who has been haunted by low self-esteem her entire life. Kim told me, "I'm not really sure why this has been such an issue for me. I grew up with a lot of friends, I excelled in school, and I had a family that supported me. But I always compared myself to others. I weighed more than my friends. I stressed about being successful in my job. And I was afraid of not being accepted. I just never felt good enough for anyone. And I kept asking myself a question I could never answer, 'Good enough for whom?' "

Another friend, Lee, a successful advertising executive, told me about his particular brand of stagnancy and paralysis. "For years

I split myself into different roles—husband, father, executive, son, and churchgoer. I was parsing out my life force like currency and so I really wasn't able to show up one hundred percent in anything I did. No wonder I felt zapped all the time. No wonder I didn't take the opportunity to play, to have fun, to do the things I really love to do. It's a new idea to show up authentically as myself in everything I do."

My hero sister Madeline felt trapped in her marriage. The pain caused by an unfaithful husband drove her into despair, which resulted in gaining a lot of weight. "My weight protected me so I couldn't be hurt anymore. For a while I thought if I got fit, it would be a sign I was moving on. It would be my way of forgiving him. But moving on wasn't ultimately about losing the weight. It was about me wanting more for myself. Until I got that, I was stuck."

My man Geoff, a consultant and fellow warrior in Hero Living, spent years on a roller-coaster ride with money. His mother was single when he was born, raising three kids on just $200 a month. When his mother married a multimillionaire, Geoff's identity shifted from a poor kid to a rich kid. Then in his mid twenties his stepfather lost it all, including Geoff's inheritance. Geoff describes his relationship with money as a turbulent one. "Money took on a kind of abusive energy metaphorically. Sometimes it was good to me, sometimes it wasn't. I thought it had an agenda for me and so I distrusted it. I unconsciously looped in that space for fifteen years. Money would show up and then disappear, show up and disappear. Talk about a cage."

We all have a story. In fact, most of us have several stories going simultaneously, each one a seemingly immovable bar in our cage. The problem with our stories is they're not very supportive of what we really want. They keep us afraid, disoriented, and feeling alone. Sometimes they can even play mind tricks on us. Take the mom who works so hard to be the most amazing mother ever. Who loves and supports her kids in every way but somewhere along the line loses her sense of self. Or the son or daughter who, regardless of how hard they try, always feel like a disappointment to their parents. Or the mother or father who goes off to work to support their family but is disheartened because they feel so disconnected from the people they love the most. Duty without passion, responsibility without getting your needs met, soon turns into resentment and guilt—a big cage for many of us.

Growing up, I read and reread all the books in the Frank Herbert classic science fiction saga *Dune*. In the first book he set down the Litany Against Fear. I love the word "litany." It is by definition a prayer—a recurring invocation for courage and purpose. How beautiful it is to have a prayer that invokes possibility for more life. If you know the book, you know the character Paul Atreides intones the litany when the Reverend Mother Gaius Helen Mohiam challenges him to a test. This test employs severe physical pain in order to prove Paul's humanity. What's interesting is that Atreides' petition isn't one against pain, even though he knows that intense pain is part of the approaching ordeal, instead his supplication is to turn his attention to an even greater threat. Fear.

As a basic survival mechanism, the emotional response of fear can serve to keep a person safe from immediate danger. But fear can have a way of taking hold, of tacking on past the point of needed protection and billow into nervous panic or paranoia, or it can seep in with a numbing power to slow the pace or stop a person dead in their tracks, to mesmerize and overwhelm. It is in such moments that fear crosses over from a helpful guardian into an enemy and destroyer of the mind and dreams. In voicing the Litany Against Fear the petitioner opens to possibility with the words:

"I will face my fear.
I will permit it to pass over me and through me.
And when it has gone past I will turn the inner eye to see its path."

Inferred in this prayerful prose is that our cage can be opened and we can be set free, and in seeing the wake of fear's path, we find ourself revealed. It could be said our stagnancy and paralysis work the same way. The truths that are hidden in our pain are, in fact, the keys to our freedom. In other words, if Herbert is right, if facing my fears, if permitting them to pass over me and through me, is the key to freedom, then the possibility of opening the cage door is available every moment. Now. And now. And now . . .

How exactly? The key to the cage door is right in front of me, right inside me, and it's described in those transformative words, "the inner eye."

The French archaeologist and historian Paul Veyne said, "When one does not see what one does not see, one does not even see that one is blind." What power this statement has. When I fully grasp the truth that everything I need is inside me, my inner eye instinctively begins to look. And search. And seek possibilities. New questions then invite me into new ways of seeing. And I consider: What feelings have I refused to acknowledge? Why do I allow myself to be treated poorly? What do I get out of staying attached to the past? Why am I so afraid to make a change? What would a better life feel like? Why do I agree to situations that aren't good for me?

Go looking for your truths, my brother and sister. Use your inner eye to seek, to find, to excavate, and to reveal. Your inner eye is your hero's eye. It will never lie. It will never betray. It will always lead you stride by stride through the hero's journey. Use your inner eye to go looking for your truths and then name them. Identify them. See them for what they are. What you'll find is that, in time, the frozen lock to your cage loosens. The truths you identify become your keys to newfound freedom. And the cage itself dismantles and dissolves. As Herbert says in the Litany Against Fear, "Where the fear has gone there will be nothing. Only I will remain."

THE HERO'S WHETSTONE:
TUNING IN

As I mentioned in the introduction, throughout this book I will be providing contemplative prompts for you to take stock in your life; to tune in to your mind, body, and emotions; and to give full attention to your hero within. As a reminder, remember to start with yourself just as you are, right now, this moment. No judgments. No apologies. The value of these prompts is the powerful information you will get about yourself. Whoever said, "Ignorance is bliss," I guarantee you they were not in bliss. They were in stagnancy and paralysis. Lack of knowledge about your self is the cage. Information about your self is the key.

Why do I call these contemplative prompts whetstones? I began my studies in Shaolin kung fu when I was eighteen. As you can imagine, the warrior philosophy of the Oriental martial arts corroborated everything I had learned from my comic books heroes and from my hero of heroes, Bruce Lee. The whetstone I reference is what the twelfth-century samurai used to sharpen their sword. As taught in the Bushido, the samurai's code of conduct, the sword represents the soul—the authenticity, strength, and power of the soul. So the whetstone is the means by which the samurai sharpens his or her soul so they can cut to the truth. Use the Hero's Whetstone throughout this book and the truths of your life, your power, your authenticity, your dream, and your destiny will begin to reveal themselves. They just will.

As we move through each whetstone, you may find it helpful to keep paper and pen at hand. It's not necessary, and it's up to you, but you may find power in seeing words on paper versus just in your head, something that could make a difference to your journey. If this resonates with you, take a moment to gather your writing tools.

Now, before we begin with the first Hero's Whetstone, take some deep breaths. Before you read on, take a few moments to give your full attention to your breathing. Take three deep inhales through your nose and three full exhales through your mouth. Go ahead. Breathe life in and out for three moments.

As you sit in the breath of life, think of a friend. Think of how you sometimes see them struggle or stumble along life's path. When they do, see how you support them. With a listening ear, kind advice, compassion and understanding, sympathy, a hug, or perhaps even telling them like it is when needed. Now consider whether you give yourself as much compassion, understanding, sympathy, and empathy when you see yourself struggle and fall. Generally, I believe it's most common that people are more generous and kind with others than they are with themselves.

So this is an important aspect to consider in moving through each Hero's Whetstone prompt. As you contemplate each one, I want you to do so while seeing yourself not as *you*, but as a good friend. To the extent that you can, detach and see yourself from a friendly, compassionate, forgiving, empathetic, kind, and wise, outside perspective. Even if you must pretend like a child would, be an unbiased third-party observer to your self. And one that loves you.

So now with your friendly self and perspective intact, let's begin. This first Hero's Whetstone starts with a question: As you scan the list below, what feelings do you resonate with most? What feelings best describe what you're going through right now? Don't overthink it. Just note what feelings you identify with. Be careful not to judge or justify, to excuse or deride. Just tune in to your feelings. That's all you have to do. The samurai's whetstone is never abrasive. It doesn't have an agenda for the sword. It works with the sword just as it is. It's the same with the Hero's Whetstone. It works with your soul just as it is. So be honest but be gentle as you scan the list below.

Right now I feel . . .
Disappointed in my life
Angry all the time
Caged by my responsibilities
I'm never enough, no matter how hard I try
Ashamed of my body
Neglected by my partner
Generally okay, but I want more
Afraid people will see how vulnerable I am
Everything is my fault
Controlled by my addiction
Physically exhausted and emotionally spent
Trapped in a passionless relationship
Guilty about things I've done in the past
Sexually undesirable
Stuck in a dead-end job
On top of the world
As if something important is missing, but I don't know what
Unresolved about my past
Like I'm coasting along in a rut
Betrayed by those I love
Worried and stressed all the time
Fully satisfied
Embarrassed for being unhappy, given everything I have
Like my childhood was taken from me
Powerless to make a change
Totally alone

Like I can't be myself and be loved
That I never have enough money
That I don't deserve success
The constant pressure to be superhuman at everything I do
Trapped by the traditions of family and/or religion

As you scan this list, be sure to note any additional feelings that come up. As you identify the feelings you resonate with, whether on the list or not, the first thing to remind yourself is that you are a human. The second is that you are a hero. All feelings, whatever they are, can be integral to the hero's journey if you will work with them. They can be clues to the bars of one's cage. How intensely you feel is an indicator of how stagnant and paralyzed you are. I want to be clear this is not bad news about your self. This is, in fact, brilliant transformative news. Because in identifying your feelings, in using your truth-saying whetstone to give voice and attention to what is trapping you, you begin to rattle the cage. And the hero within begins to wake up.

The Silent Agreement

When you think about it, an agreement is basically a pattern. For example, if we make an agreement at work, we agree to a certain pattern of thought and behavior. When we partner with someone, we agree to a specific pattern in our relationship. It might be healthy or it might be dysfunctional, but we agree nonetheless. If we didn't, we wouldn't be there. The same applies to any of the agreements we make day in and day out, whether it's with our emotions, our bodies, and our spirituality, or whether it's with family, friends, career, religion, or culture. We agree to certain patterns of thought and behavior every moment of every day. The question is, using your inner eye, "Are you conscious or unconscious of the agreements you are making?"

Consider the fairy tale "The Emperor's New Clothes," written by the Danish poet Hans Christian Andersen. Talk about a silent Sisyphean agreement made first with himself as emperor and then with his dutiful kingdom. Remember the unspoken agreement they all have? Clothes matter most. So when two swindlers promise the emperor the finest suit made of invisible cloth, he pretends that he can see the suit. As do his ministers. As do his people. Everyone agrees to this pattern of thought and behavior as he marches in a procession amongst his throng of adoring people. Except for one child. It's the child, the pure, guileless truth-saying symbol for the inner eye, who simply declares, "He has nothing on."

Silent agreements are the bars to our cage. They are set patterns of thought and behavior we have agreed to, sometimes consciously but oft times unconsciously. The boxing trainer and commentator Teddy Atlas actually coined the expression, "Silent Agreement." He used it to describe the moment when two boxers hold on to each other and silently agree not to fight. For fear of being knocked out, for fear of fatigue, for fear of the unknown, both agree to trap themselves and each other. Or, to phrase it in terms of Hero Living, they both agree not to move. They are stagnant and paralyzed in a set pattern of thought and behavior. Nothing is possible until one of them breaks the silent agreement and frees not only himself, but the other. Now, anything is possible. Regardless of who wins, both are winners because both are free to move.

In *Dune: House Atreides*, by Brian Herbert and Kevin J. Anderson, we are reminded, "The worst sort of alliances are those which weaken us. Worse still is when an Emperor fails to recognize such an alliance for what it is."

You are emperor, warrior, hero, and sage of your journey. Your inner eye is your truth sayer. And Hero Living is your compass, your mirror, and your lantern. If you are willing, now's the time to look honestly at your silent agreements; to recognize your alliances for what they are; and to see what your cage is made of bar by hidden bar. Of course, you will want to hang on to the agreements that support and inspire you. It's the agreements that weaken and entrap you that I'm interested in.

THE HERO'S WHETSTONE:
USING YOUR INNER EYE

I love the fact that it's a child that frees an entire kingdom in "The Emperor's New Clothes." Some may choose to ignore the truth and continue their silent agreement. But those who listen and consider will be forever changed. Your inner eye is akin to the way a child tells the truth. A child isn't judgmental, coercive, or ashamed. A child just tells it like it is—as information, as fact. The biologist T. H. Huxley describes it this way: "Sit down before fact like a little child, and be prepared to give up every preconceived notion." That's it. That's all you have to do. Just go looking for your truths. Get them out on the table. Name them. Identify them. Own them. Scream them if you have to. But whatever you do, don't resist them. See them for what they really are. Simply information you can use to pick the lock of your cage, to set yourself free, and to create something different. The truths of your suffering cannot survive the light of your awareness—the brilliant, transformative, childlike gaze of your inner eye.

If this truth saying process sounds magical, it's because it is. There will be plenty of things for you to do later on in your hero's journey. But for now, in this stride of stagnancy and paralysis, all you have to do is engage your inner eye and tell yourself the truth with childlike candor. That's it. That is enough because you are enough.

So are you ready for your next Hero's Whetstone? I'm here with you, by your side. You can do this. Let's sharpen your soul— your authenticity, strength, and power. Start with your breath. I will be asking this of you often. Breath is life. Breath is movement. Breath relaxes and grounds. So tune in and take three deep inhales and then three full exhales.

Now, I'm going to invite you to engage your inner eye. This is the hero's most powerful tool for exposing the silent, Sisyphean agreements you have made with your suffering. Without judgment, let's go looking for your truths. You can answer the following prompts in whatever way you want. The important thing is that you take the time to really consider and that you allow any and all information to reveal itself.

1) Given the list of feelings you considered earlier in the chapter, which ones did you resonate with most? Which ones did your body and emotions have the strongest response to?

2) Which of these feelings have become the hidden bars to your cage? As you contemplate this, are there any new feelings that come up? Are there any new bars your inner eye is seeing for the very first time?

3) Now turn your inner eye to each bar of your cage. What is your silent agreement with each bar? What is your pattern of thought and behavior associated with each bar? What do you get from the agreement? How do you benefit from keeping a silent agreement with each bar?

4) Now that you see your cage bar by bar, agreement by agreement, what does your cage look like? What form does it take? Get a vivid image in your mind's eye. What material is the cage made of? How many bars are there? Is there a lock or a combination? What are you doing in relation to the cage? Are you curled up in the corner? Pacing? Shaking the bars? Climbing? How long has the cage been with you? When did the cage get built? Who built it? Let your imagination go and create a vivid image of the cage and your relationship to it.

5) Now that you have tuned in to your feelings, identified the bars
    of your cage, exposed your silent agreements, and have a vivid
    image of your relationship to the cage, consider this: What's
    the one thing you could do right now that would make the big-
    gest difference in your life?

Seeing the Cage for What It Is . . . Is An Act of Freedom

After the third day of no sleep and over a hundred pounds on my
back on the last few days of grueling patrol week in the Amphibious
Reconnaissance School at A.P. Hill, Virginia, I was faltering. I felt a
horrifying desire to give up. I boosted my courage by volunteering
for a mission in an icy river but I failed that assignment, and upon
failing I was sent into the mental numbness of severe hypothermia
and spiraled into sluggishness and the black-hearted terror of being
found out as a quitter.

Inside, I knew I had quit a lot of times as a boy. Not long after
my grandmother had passed away, my gifted and talented fourth-
grade teacher and her husband, Mr. and Mrs. Gordon, started
reaching out and took me under their wing. I didn't know it at the
time, but I imagine she could see that my home life was falling apart
and for whatever reason they were compelled to extend their loving help. I used to spend a day on the weekend with them listening
to music and going to the museum and building model rockets.

Then at some point I found out the news that Mom was plan-
ning to move my brothers and me to my uncle's home in Dallas.
Mom felt Grandma had quit on her by dying, and now Mom was
quitting on herself and on my brothers and me, and sending us
away. I felt punched in the gut with the wind despondently knocked
out of me as uncared for and unwanted. The thought of being
sent away, leaving my home, of leaving my school and others I
loved just crushed me. I thought of the Gordons and really wished
they could have been my parents in those moments, but I felt they

didn't deserve to have a child so unwanted as me. I figured I should just quit.

And so on the inside, I did. I didn't even say good-bye.

I stopped going to the Gordons, and about a week before the road trip to Texas I stopped going to school. I just stayed in my room during the day while my little brothers were at school and Mom was downstairs watching her TV programs checked out in the haze of marijuana and the grief of the loss of her parents. I sat in my room and silently cried. I didn't even hang out with my best friend Sean Blakemore anymore. I just quit.

So that same kind of quit was creeping and bubbling up from me as my proud body was being destroyed by Amphibious Reconnaissance School. On the fifth day of constant operations I started to hallucinate images in my heart not in my head. I felt as though I was being lost in a wave of Marines a thousand strong and I was completely insignificant. I felt unimportant and not needed. I was certain the stink and rancor of quit was all over me and that my teammates could smell it. The weight of my ruck felt like a thousand pounds, but the weight of my heart and its regret seemed a million tons. The ruck straps cut into my clavicles and trapezius like razor wire, but it was nothing compared to the naked shame I felt.

There at the root of my drive and success was the black kernel of fear and shame, the agreement that I was a coward and weakling for what I had done in the past. As a mechanism for coping, duty and its bedfellows of discipline and power had helped me overcome the darkness of my most broken and vulnerable child self, but the drawback was that if I was not fighting forward or accomplishing missions, my confidence waned. My center of strength and light faltered.

My duty as a warrior and protector gave me that continuous

impetus to accomplish and quest. So I built my body and the strength of its muscle as part and parcel of this duty. To make myself attractive to not be thrown away. To make myself strong to repel the enemies' assault. To be exceptional to mask my shame of cowardice. I felt my savior would be my accomplishments and accolades, but underneath the armor and weapons I felt myself a coward and a weakling. And for some reason I could not understand that it's completely normal to be hurt and angry and feel paralyzed with fear as a seven-year-old boy being tossed as litter to the wind. In my heart I didn't understand it wasn't my fault that my mom had quit. Somehow I missed that her sending me away and not wanting me was actually on her and her inability to care for me. Although rational to the mind, my heart instead held onto my agreement to seeing myself as unwanted, undeserving, and a quitter.

When my marriage fell apart at thirty-three, I was overwhelmed by worthlessness and guilt, emotions that were magnified by fears and shame of being unwanted and a quitter, amplified by the cold-blooded rage of the eleven-year-old inside who had been molested. I had never felt so imprisoned. My cage was small and cramped, like a kennel. It had so many bars it was pitch dark. It was subzero cold, turning my veins into ice. And it pressed in on me like a vise cranking tighter and tighter as I sunk into deeper and deeper despair. It was crushing my life force, emotionally, spiritually, mentally, and physically. Until I gave voice to my feelings; until I engaged my inner eye; until I saw the cage for what it really was: Rich information about the life I wanted and the freedom that was available.

When you turn your inner eye to what you feel, to what you've silently agreed to, and to what traps you, you see the transformative truth that animates Hero Living: I am not my cage and I am not my suffering. I want you to really take this in, really internalize it: I am not my cage and I am not my suffering. You are more than your suffering simply because you want more. You are hardwired with the freedom to choose your perception, to choose your own way. You have your feelings to guide you and your inner eye to tell you essential truths. You can unmake the silent agreements that imprison you and make new conscious agreements that liberate you. You can throw the lock and open your life. You are not your cage. You are not your suffering. You are a hero.

For me, this has always been my way out of stagnancy and paralysis. When I find myself trapped in a cage of fear and pain, when I find myself looping with negative thought and cruel self observations, when I retreat from the world and isolate behind the bars of my silent agreements, I engage my inner eye and return to the prompts above. Then I am able to see the cage for what really it is: Information. The cage is rich, insightful information about what I don't want and thus, rich, insightful information about what I do want. The cage is the loud quiet call to more of myself, to more life. The cage is no cage at all. Can you feel that?

I mentioned the phrase "existential crisis" earlier in this chapter. It describes those moments when our life feels lost; our obstacles feel insurmountable; our day-to-day responsibilities feel pointless; and the meaning of our life feels purposeless. By definition, the word "existential" refers to one's experience. The word "crisis" comes from the root that means to "sift out." So an existential crisis is, in fact, an opportunity to sift out that which no longer serves your experience, your life, and your dreams. It dismantles and dissolves your cage and, in the process, frees you up to receive the support you need. It hurts like hell, that's for sure. But it's worth it. Trust me, hero, it's worth it. If you doubt, note your doubt and keep breathing. Just stay with me. If I can do this, so can you.

Ultimately, wherever you're at in this stride that I call stagnancy and paralysis, whether you're living with a steady anxiety and fear, or whether you're threatened and caged from all sides, I end this chapter with its thesis: Breathe and go looking for your truths, hero. Do only this and you have already taken a huge courageous leap into your moment of movement. You have already become the change you wish to be.

STRIDE 2
Moment of Movement

The feeling: "*Somewhere inside I feel the glint of more possibility. I hear the loud quiet call into Hero Living. I see there might be a way out of my pain.*"

My mother had by her extreme apathy, illness, and injured self let her children go adrift and my youngest brother and I ended up in the filth of a poor south Texas shanty. A short time before this, she had blurted out to me one random day in an angry summer tirade that Rudy Sr. wasn't my biological father. Yet despite this "news," and the fact it had actually been years since I had seen Rudy Sr., I still felt excited to reunite with the man who had been my first hero. With his Marine dress blue uniform pictures from Vietnam, his athletic sports abilities, and football pads and gym equipment, the man I knew as my father loomed as a large icon in my imagination, and I was thrilled with anticipation to go live with him and his new family. I so wanted a home, so wanted his love and acceptance, wanted just to feel wanted.

Instead we walked into a house that was falling apart and was home to a fallen hero. Dad was an alcoholic. He had two kids with

With my brothers and my first hero, Rudy Sr.

our stepmom, but the marriage was crumbling too, and everything around us was coming apart at the seams. Dad started staying out all the time, sometimes not coming home for days, and eventually our stepmom packed up her kids and moved out. For the most part we were left to fend for ourselves, wild and feral in a strange land, in a strange school, where strange kids wanted to fight us all the time.

We were in a state of deep neglect, with little food, no medical care, a poor school system, and an infestation of cockroaches and rats that lit up the house at night with their noise of scurrying and climbing over us in search of food. We would hide in the closet and put dad's cowboy boots on our arms, so we could smash any rats coming in. At some point our electricity was cut off, and they scared the living hell out of us with their beady little eyes and big teeth glinting in the moonlight.

Somewhere along the way I started getting bad headaches and the horrible smell of rotting garbage seeped in and followed me

With my brothers

everywhere. I had such bad tooth decay and serious infections, my mouthful of crooked teeth was literally rotting out of my head, and the kids at school started calling me *boca podrida* in Spanish, or "rotten mouth." I had no friends. My brothers were my only playmates. My self-esteem dwindled into neutral. I was so self-conscious of my teeth I stopped talking, only speaking when absolutely necessary so as to not show my teeth or let out a foul puff of garbage stink. I slipped further and further into a smaller world of taking care of my brothers, and deeper into my mind and world of comic books and movie icons, Olympic athletes, and *Black Belt* magazine, where the heroes I chose to follow and emulate could be found.

Across the street from our house made of tarpaper and rotten wood and a driveway of crushed seashells, was a magnificent park. With imagination and heroes in tow, this magnificent "dojo park" was where I could make sense of things by teaching my little brothers. For hours we would practice Bruce Lee punches and kicks, host Olympic events, leap tall buildings in a single bound, train hard, and train harder again to feel ourselves strong and invigorated with physicality and the breath of life. This became my purpose, my outlet, my glint of saving grace.

Occasionally, there were people coming by the house, or we'd visit family members of my dad and stepmom. During one holiday occasion my stepmom took me and my brothers to visit with her family. Dad didn't come with us, but her family thought poorly of him so they were pretty standoffish with us boys because we were his, so we played in the alley and entertained ourselves chasing and catching lizards and looking for snakes.

After awhile one of the younger men in our stepmom's family came back and played with me and my brothers, took us to the neighborhood store to buy us candy and gum, and picked me up and carried me on his shoulders. My father had been gone for a few weeks so I was happy to have a friend that was older and "cool." Here was this young man who loved to talk and do stuff with me, it almost felt like having an older brother, maybe even a young father. Dinner came and went and I crawled into bed for the night and drifted off to sleep.

Next thing I remembered was feeling my skin crawl in my dream. A hand slipped into my dreaming under dark of night, under the covers of my bed, and I woke to slow motion moments of unwanted, unwelcome, inappropriate, lascivious, sleazy, greedy vampire touches. In those slow motion moments my world quietly violently exploded and I fell into an implosion of my now sexually abused self-wreckage.

What little self-esteem I may have still possessed became so heavy with pain, betrayal and devastation, it sank even further, so low I felt it was gone and lost, wrecked off the shore of a cold desolate island. I was alone with no one to go to, talk to, no one to protect or save me. I felt completely destroyed inside, and I started falling apart and breaking up, my mind and sense of self quickly dissipating.

In the waking hours that followed, I still moved to take care of my brothers. In the ensuing days, weeks, and months, I kept them close to me. I trained them harder and harder to protect them. Protect me.

Then, amidst the wreckage of my self, out of nowhere I made a friend. Of all things, a little white chicken that started showing up in the yard every day and hanging out. It always seemed happy to see me, and it was something I could love and protect. I would save a little of my food every day, and share it with my little white chicken friend. Man, I loved that bird, and I looked forward to seeing it every day.

Emily Dickinson wrote, "Hope is the thing with feathers, that perches in the soul, and sings the tune without words, and never stops at all." I mention it because although it may sound silly or perhaps seem strange, this bird, my friend, kept me going. Somehow or another, that little chicken was a manifestation of "the thing with feathers," my hope, presenting itself in physical form as a symbol of that melody of more possibility.

But again out of nowhere my friend, my hope, disappeared. I don't know what really happened, but one day my little chicken friend just stopped coming by the yard and hanging out. As the days passed with no chicken and little else to buoy me up, I imagined the worst possible things and convinced myself that the wild dog packs patrolling the neighborhood had eaten my chicken.

As a child I was just going on pure instinct with little guidance and mentoring for how to deal with my circumstances. So I circled them like a caged animal, trapped in my own samsara, my loop of suffering. I was so bereft and furious, I descended into a paranoid vortex of revenge. I felt everyone was against me. I felt terribly alone and terrible. I devised ways to make traps for the dogs, digging holes in the yard, utilizing spikes and stakes at the bottom, covering up the holes with camouflage so my enemy dogs would fall in, be trapped, and die. Feeling trapped and abandoned myself, my undeveloped raw instinct was to trap and abandon, to protect my self and exact revenge from my perceived persecutors.

But ultimately I filled in the holes.

Although it may not appear to be, it was a simple thing really. At the heart of it was just an uncomplicated shift in focus. In a moment I shifted to something readily available and infinitely brighter, my love and caring for my brothers. I was afraid they might stumble in the holes and get hurt, so I abandoned my traps and moved on.

I still felt in the dark with nightmares and a feeling of not being able to distinguish reality or not, but somehow I stubbornly held onto my hope and compassion and kept showing up and trying to do the right thing. Somehow I felt somewhere inside that if I just didn't give up, the dawn would come.

So even though it can be difficult and terrifying or may even feel impossible when you're in the dark, I didn't give up hope on more possibility. For months I had been trying to remember the phone number of my cousin Belinda in Kansas City, the same cousin who had taken us in when we needed help before. Dad didn't have a phone at the house, but I felt if I could just find a way to reach her, that she would do something.

Then one day out of nowhere it just hit me like a lightning bolt; my cousin's phone number came to me in a bright flash. No phone at our house, but not long after that I was at a neighbor's home that had a phone. At one point I realized I was the only one in the room, and before I knew it I moved to the phone and dialed.

"Hello," my cousin's voice hearkened at the other end.

I answered back with everything pouring out of me—about how I felt I was losing my mind, my teeth were rotting and smelled liked garbage, we were hungry and didn't have lights and electricity. It all sounded so crazy, and maybe I sounded crazy, so much so my cousin's first thought was I was on drugs. In the end she realized something was clearly amiss, so she enlisted my mother to come help on a rescue mission. Within days they both showed up at the house in my cousin's Chevy Nova, and we were moving. Moving away from Texas and the years of neglect there, not knowing for sure what lay ahead, but moving just the same.

A Swedish proverb says, "Those who wish to sing always find a song." And that's the way of hope. Even when you can't see it, hope flutters and flits and sings the tune without words, and never stops at all. I am in the camp that believes this glint of more possibility, this seed of hope, resides in each and every one of us. Hope is part of our human DNA, our genetic code of being.

Perhaps you don't believe this. Perhaps you're feeling mired without hope at this very moment. Whatever you believe or think or feel, I want to invite you to consider something. A possibility.

The possibility that by the simple fact that you're reading this sentence right here right now, is in and of itself an act of hope springing eternal. You are here showing up for yourself, right here right now. You are breathing life into hope.

And if that's a possibility, whether you feel it or believe it or not, I, for one, see you have hope.

I see that with this hope you are on the hero's path.

You are a hero.

"Hope is the dream of a soul awake," so says a French proverb. So in the moments we feel bereft of hope, perhaps looking to our dreams may hold a key to awakening our soul or rekindling hope.

When I was a kid my dreams were the stuff of heroes at the movies and in comic books. Rocky Balboa prevailed in winning hearts because he didn't give up and went all the way, even though he was labeled a "has-been" and lost the fight in the boxing ring. In doing so he inspired dreams in others. Spider-Man was an ordinary human that was bitten by a radioactive higher-power spider to become magically endowed with amazing superpowers. He could have done anything with those powers, but what he does is respond to the hero's call of "with great power comes great responsibility." Wow! I spent hours and hours reading and breathing in those great stories and images of hero, and they permeated my very being and changed the fabric of my life.

While in elementary school, my class had an assignment to say what we wanted to be when we grew up. When it was my turn to answer, I said, "I want to be Bruce Lee!" My teacher dutifully informed me that being Bruce Lee was not a job, to which I replied, "Well, then I want to do whatever Bruce Lee does for a job." I had no idea what that meant exactly, but that was my dream.

Courtesy of Reyes family

In south Texas.

And that is the power of dreams.

Woodrow Wilson, twenty-eighth president of the United States, spoke these words: "We grow great by dreams. All big men are dreamers. They see things in the soft haze of a spring day or in the red fire of a long winter's evening. Some of us let these great dreams die, but others nourish and protect them; nurse them through bad days till they bring them to the sunshine and light which comes always to those who sincerely hope that their dreams will come true."

If all big men are dreamers, I believe all children have big dreams. It's what children do, they play and they dream. It's what you did as a child, simply because you were once young. So whether you feel you've let your dreams fade or die, or that you don't even know how to dream anymore, consider this possibility. That more is possible than what you think. More is possible if you dream.

THE HERO'S WHETSTONE:
BE THE DREAMER OF DREAMS

Merrily, merrily, merrily, merrily, life is but a dream.

So goes the childhood singsong of "Row, Row, Row Your Boat," where flowing gently down the stream can seem like our little life is but a brief dream in the river of the divine. Where we are the stuff that dreams are made of. And so we dream wishes and fantasy, for fun, for joy, for merrily we roll along.

Perhaps you may feel your dreams are lost or have dissipated into thin air, or maybe you even see them on the street of broken dreams. If so, resist the temptation to ridicule or discount yourself. Instead relax and breathe and remember the feeling of having those dreams before they seemed lost or broken. Experience the feeling of hope and wonder right here right now, even if those dreams are long vacant, know this feeling is available to you at any turn in your path. This is yours to have and hold in your heart at anytime. You may find yourself letting go from time to time, but no one can take that away. That is yours.

So in this hopeful space, take a few moments and consider your dreams.

As you consider, give yourself time to fully unfold your dreams and answers in the adventurous spirit of exploration. Consider writing them down. Or find other ways to explore and express them. Draw, paint, sculpt, even PowerPoint, Dictaphone, sing a song, or cut pictures out of a magazine and make a dream board to give them shape and form. The more you can see, feel, and touch your dreams, the more they become a tangible living breathing part of you. Don't worry about how you'll get there or make them come true. For now, just let your imagination go and enjoy the ride as you contemplate the following questions.

- What were your hopes and dreams as a child? How did it feel to dream?
- When you were young, what did you want to be when you grew up?
- What do you dream of now? What do your dreams look like? What does it feel like?
- Are your dreams different today than when you were young?
- Are there dreams from your youth to revive and pursue again in your present moments?

As you give articulated shape to your dreams, it's okay to get carried away by the thrill of it. Believe me, the pendulum of life and your emotions will naturally swing its way back to balance when the time is right. As William Shakespeare once penned, "The web of our life is a mingled yarn, good and ill together; our virtues would be proud, if our faults whipped them not; and our crimes would despair, if they were not cherished by our virtues." So for now, let it be fun and go with the flow of it . . . merrily, merrily, merrily.

That is in fact the very point of this whetstone, to provide a space for the flow and energy of your dreams to exist. Give mindful attention to the hopes and wishes of your heart. Cherish your hopes

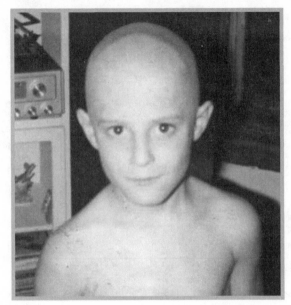

Courtesy of Reyes family

Dreaming of being Bruce Lee.

and dreams; they are the fruits of your soul and the blueprints of your ultimate achievements.

I truly believe in the power and reality of dreams.

As for my own childhood dream of being Bruce Lee, or at least doing what Bruce Lee does for a job, over the years I held fast to that vision. I took action and pursued my punches and kicks until the cows came home, day after month after year, and never let it fade away and die. I practiced and practiced, and made myself a humble servant to my dream.

There's a saying in martial arts, that when the student is ready the teacher will appear. I believe this happened for me over and over again simply by holding fast to my dream. What to me seemed of its own natural accord, my teachers began to magically appear with instruction and mentoring of martial arts skills. Under the wing of their watchful tutelage I began competing and I started winning.

First locally, and then quickly went onto regional, national, and even winning as the grand champion of international competitions.

What I have humbly learned from this experience, and other life experiments, is that by taking a step toward your dreams, they take a step toward you.

So it's from this perspective of humility, with thankful respect for my teachers, that I have been blessed with the experience of sitting in a theater long ago in awe of my silver-screen hero Bruce Lee to later going all the way and living the fruition of "I have a dream."

START WHERE YOU ARE

The highest-ranking U.S. military naval officer in the "Hanoi Hilton" prisoner-of-war camp during the height of the Vietnam War was Admiral Jim Stockdale. During eight years in prison he was tortured over twenty times living without any certainty of when he would be released or whether he would even survive at all. His daily purpose was a vigilance of using all his creative faculties and leadership to help his fellow prisoners survive their hell with spirits intact, as well as to wage his own internal war against those that wanted to break him for use in their propaganda war.

Key to dealing with his circumstances was maintaining a certain mindset balanced between positive hope and grounded reality. In his book *Good to Great*, author Jim Collins interviews Stockdale. When asked how he dealt with the brutality of being in prison for years on end while not knowing the outcome, Stockdale replied, "I never lost faith in the end of the story. I never doubted not only that I would get out, but also that I would prevail in the end and turn the experience into the defining event of my life."

When asked about who didn't make it out, his answer seemed counterintuitive—the optimists. The people who would say, "We're going to be out by Christmas." And Christmas would come and go. Then Easter would be the next goal, which would soon pass by. Then Thanksgiving and Christmas again, and after a time they would essentially die of a broken heart, unable to face the realities of their circumstance.

Stockdale's wisdom is heard in his words: "You must never confuse faith that you will prevail in the end—which you can never afford to lose—with the discipline to confront the most brutal facts of your current reality, whatever they might be."

Along with his balance of truth-saying honesty and eternal hope, Stockdale survived by acting and not waiting for some external forces to change his circumstances. When you do nothing those are the times you feel overwhelmed and powerless. Getting involved, even in a small way, even simply in your mind, can give you a sense of hope and accomplishment that come from knowing you are somehow working to make things better. Further, you feel that no matter the conditions of life, those circumstances are not the determining factor for whether or not one moves; you are the one that determines your movement, regardless of what.

Wherever you are today, no matter where you are, that is the place to start. Maybe you're reading this while at home, at school, under a tree, on vacation, in prison, at the hospital, or riding in the car or back of a Humvee. Perhaps you're feeling depressed or full of joy, scared, tearful, shy, optimistic, pessimistic, hateful or loving. Or you're married, divorced, single, widowed, unattached, in love, out of love, looking for love in all the wrong places, or tired of the whole love thing. Maybe you're even lost and don't know where you are.

It doesn't matter. Wherever you are, no matter where, that is always the place to start.

And wherever you are, there's no need to wait until you are more of this or less of that, richer, thinner, older, wiser, in luck, out of prison, happier, healthier, whatever you're waiting on, there's no need to wait to move. But no matter if you wait, no matter if you don't move this moment, the eternal gifts of Hero Living will always be waiting for you, always right here right now, and now, and now . . .

Movement is something that's done every minute of every hour of every day, week, month, year, and life. From the broadest perspective, there's really no such thing as no movement. For instance, you may be able to sit very still and hold your breath, and at a gross level of definition there is "no movement." But in the broader context, this is a very limited view of all that is. In that same moment of sitting still and holding breath, blood is still flowing, oxygen is still exchanging through cell walls, some cells are dying while others are growing, atoms are vibrating, and Earth is still spinning around the Sun, around the solar system, the galaxy, the universe. The tides move in and out as they dance with the Moon, and life moves in quantum harmony.

So movement as it relates to this stride of Hero Living isn't about whether or not you're moving at all. You do that every day. And it's not about whether you're moving correctly or in step with anyone else. You don't have to measure up, there's no pass or fail test to take. There's no particular destination or timetable. You don't even have to get out of bed or move off the couch. You can sit still and hold your breath. It's okay.

It's okay because this is *your* journey.

Even in the midst of monthly bills, family demands, poor health, disabilities, illness, death, school, work, the boss, the courts, the abuser, the weather or whatever, the *way* in which you move through *your* journey is solely up to you. Through the perceived good and the bad, how you choose to move is ultimately up to you.

And because it is up to you, understand this. You own it. This belongs to no one else. Whatever you choose, even if you do nothing, stay where you are, or feel sorry for yourself, it is your responsibility. You are accountable—to you. To your credit or blame or whatever—it is yours.

And that is an essential key to Hero Living. You accept and own your responsibility for your life right here right now and now.

When I returned from Iraq after my last tour of duty, I watched as if in surprise as my marriage failed and came crashing in. Not that I was completely oblivious to the state of my marriage in returning home, but in tucking away my concerns about it while away at war, it was as if I had fallen asleep to the realities.

Upon waking to it, I was also awakened to other aspects of my life and the years spent in subservience to my other silent agreements of duty. To my wife, who had become just a dependent for which my mission was to gain wages for groceries and rent. To my country that asked me to fight a war that made little sense by the time I left the kill zone, of having to detach all humanity away in order to kill or not go crazy while counting bodies in Fallujah. Thrown back to U.S. soil not knowing who I was or what I was good for in civilian life, all of this welcomed me home from war and came crashing in. I was in a completely disoriented state of fast falling vertigo, everything I thought was up, was now down. I fell into an abyss of rotting despair. For the first time, I was squarely faced with how my samsara of duty was working against me.

I felt overwhelmed, lost, and alone, much like when I was eleven years old and falling apart from neglect and sexual abuse. My wife had been the love of my life; to lose her faith and love, to lose our mutual trust and affection, completely devastated me. I felt like a failure, a disaster. I had so many emotions roiling it was sometimes hard to think straight. What had happened to us? What had happened to me, and to my beautiful girl?

I spiraled into depression and shut down on the inside. For a time I sank into alcohol as a way of numbing the pain and keeping a lid on all my inner turmoil. Even at that it sometimes exploded out in bursts of hot steam. I was paralyzed, cooking in my own juices. I needed to move, and in a positive way, but how?

The key to how you move is understanding where you are in relation to what you want, or where you want to go. As a Recon Marine, being lost or behind enemy lines can mean death without movement and direction. But you can't figure out where you want to go if you don't know where you are. In military terms, a resection is a method of locating one's position on a map by determining the grid angles to at least two well-defined locations that can be pinpointed on the map. This will tell you your exact location and identify important features you can use for protection, water, and other resources. A resection is a systematic way of looking back at where you've been, knowing where you've passed, and identifying features on the map that you can see with your eyes on the ground. From there you can then move toward your goals.

In life we can do the same thing. We can look at our own terrain features and truths of triumphs, trauma, joy, pain, happiness, loss, anger, those things we love, and those things that bring tears, and identify our position, our strengths, our weaknesses, and see where we are at right here right now. Taking stock can help to establish your location and provide the direction and confidence needed for you to move.

Your map contains everything you need for your journey, but unless you read the details of all your pertinent information, you could remain lost and unable to move toward your objective. For instance, if the map is in color and you're color blind, you may not see a water resource or place of safety or the lines may be confusing, so you may miss your window of opportunity to reach safety. Seeing and reading information needed to identify and provide supportive elements along your journey is an important aspect of map reading.

In my case, I did a resection. I found where I was on my map, assessed what skills and resources I had available for use in moving forward, then set a bead for where I was heading. In moving I went back to the "girl that took me to the dance" and focused on my skills of leadership, physical fitness, and martial arts, and I started teaching classes at the local boxing club. It didn't solve my marital problems, and my overall mission was still hazy and generalized, but I was moving with map in hand.

THE HERO'S WHETSTONE: READING YOUR MAP

With hope and dreams at your side, let's dive into the second contemplative prompt in this Moment of Movement stride. Remember to start with yourself just as you are, right now, this moment. No judgments. No apologies. Remember, the value of these prompts is the powerful information you will get about yourself. Be as open to your truths as possible, willing to see what's there, no matter what. And no matter what, it will be okay.

With hope and dreams at your side, let's move together by first taking three deep breaths in through the nostrils and exhaling slowly through the mouth. Close your eyes and feel the air flowing in and expanding the lungs, oxygen in and carbon dioxide out as you exhale. Each breath is part of the balance and constant cycle of life.

Now let's do a map reading using your truth-saying whetstone. Begin by thinking of a good friend, someone you know well. If no one comes to mind, think of someone you admire or respect. Now, without too much pondering about it, quickly make a list of this person's strengths and accomplishments, those things that positively enable them in his or her life. Next, list what that person struggles with or what keeps him or her trapped and held back.

Now turn your attention to yourself. Again, without too much pondering, quickly make a list of your strengths and weaknesses, accomplishments and struggles, the positives and negatives.

Next, take a few moments to honestly look at the list for your friend and compare it to the one for yourself. Think of your feelings during the process of making each list and consider the following questions.

- Was it easier to list strengths for your friend or yourself? Were there differences in making the list of weaknesses?
- What were the feelings you had while making the list for your friend? Did you have similar feelings while making your list?
- What's the balance between strengths and weaknesses on the list for your friend? What's the balance for yourself?
- Did you view your friend more positively, more compassionately, more empathically than yourself?

There are no right or wrong answers to these questions. Whatever your answers, they're simply information for your consideration. No judgments; no pass or fail.

Chances are, on the average scale of being human, you were more likely harder on yourself than on your friend—perhaps discounting your strengths, or not even seeing them, like being color blind to important details on your map, while quick to readily perceive any weaknesses. The chatter in our heads tells us we're not good enough, that we'll fail if we try, we don't deserve love, we're not lovable, why even try, and so on. I don't know why this happens, but it does, and does so often for many people.

Charles M. Schulz, creator of the beloved self-deprecating Charlie Brown, once quipped, "Sometimes I lie awake at night, and ask, 'Where have I gone wrong?' Then a voice says to me, 'This is going to take more than one night.'" So don't worry about it if that's what's happening for you; just observe it.

If you're on the other end of the scale, perhaps you struggle with seeing your pain, anger, or behaviors you feel ashamed of, addictions, obsessions, fears, things you don't want to admit, so you stay in denial perhaps not knowing what to do, or feel comfort in their familiarity.

In either case, you may be feeling stuck in a negative loop.

Or perhaps your lists seem pretty balanced and the processes similar in feeling.

No matter what your answers and processes, great! Yes, that's right! You now have more information about where you are, and how you view yourself, new insights and signposts for your journey.

Wherever you landed on the whetstone above, I want you to continue polishing away while keeping this thought in mind from Richard Bach, author of *Jonathan Livingston Seagull*: "Look in a mirror and one thing's sure; what we see is not who we are." Like seeing the tip of the iceberg with ninety percent of its mass out of sight underwater, I promise you, there is much more to you than meets the eye. And you are more and bigger and brighter than what you see in the reflection.

Revisit the list you made for yourself, and think of any difference in feeling or attitude you may have had for yourself than for your friend when making the list. Make a conscious effort to see yourself more in the way you saw your friend.

Now *only* focus on your positive strengths and add to or adjust your list with an attitude of gratitude, love, and generosity. I cannot stress enough the importance of knowing your places of strength and safety, especially when you're behind enemy lines. So go ahead and name them . . . are you kind? Loving? Courageous? Strong? Patient? A good listener? A leader? Athletic? Funny? Generous? Intelligent? A problem solver? Excellent cook? An amazing parent? Whatever you think of as a positive and a strength, put it on the list. I want this part of your map to be in bold bright colors that you can easily see.

If you did the Hero's Whetstone: Using Your Inner Eye in the stride of Stagnancy & Paralysis, where you named the silent agreements of your cage, compare it to the list of weaknesses and struggles you just made in this whetstone. If you didn't complete the other whetstone, I suggest going back to it on page 35 and doing it now; then compare it to the list from above. Note any differences between them and combine and adjust the list as makes sense for your journey. What's important here isn't a long list of "bad," only focus on those things that you feel may impede your path. No judgments. Simply recognize your information and truth.

Now combine everything together for a balanced picture of where you are right here right now, honoring the positive while recognizing the challenges, all presenting opportunities for now and the journey ahead. Your map is now more complete in detailing where you are. And wherever you are, knowing where you are is great. So well done, you're living loud on the hero's path.

Perception Is Reality

The hero's call can sound at any moment inviting you into more of yourself, more of your life, more of your dreams, no matter life's circumstances. In order to hear and respond to the hero calls that come in your life, you must be open and attuned to where you are, inside and out. So this stride is ultimately about being open and aware and making conscious choices about your movement in those moments.

The heroes in fairy tales are often called upon to slay dragons guarding a treasure or to save the village. The hero's call in real life doesn't often look like actual dragon slaying. Yet in a sense, life is full of dragons. Dragons that scare us, that ensnare and entrap, dragons at the office, dragons of our past, dragons in the closet and under the bed. Dragons can live in the shadows of our mind and heart, with the uncanny ability to elude our awareness. Sometimes it's like you need special fairy-tale prescription glasses to catch a glimpse of the dragons running circles of suffering in our lives.

For instance, life can often feel like we're trapped in the fast lane or on a treadmill of unconscious survival mode, simply running on instinct or without specific purpose, or running so fast you can't catch a glimpse of where you are or what's zipping past. And that is in fact the case when the plodding action of survival mode kicks in and starts cycling without our awareness.

More than the necessities of obtaining food and staying warm and safe, survival mode in this sense speaks to samsara—our loop of suffering—that which keeps us caged when we're acting in unconscious pursuit of an unhealthy purpose in various facets of our life. This is not to suggest that all instinctive actions are unhealthy, some are just how we're wired, or patterns we employ for staying safe, ease of decision-making, positive reinforcement, etc. Like a commute to work, the first time driving it you pay attention to the signs and turns because you're learning how to get there, but after awhile you don't even think about it and you're on autopilot. No, the instinctive and autopilot actions I'm concerned with here are those that negatively interfere with the very core essence of who you are, who you want to be, or where you want to go in life.

The thing about this type of survival or autopilot mode is it often goes on humming in the background of our perception unnoticed. Like the tree that falls in a forest when no one is around to hear it, does it make a sound? Or like the street signs on the commute, or dragons at the office, in the closet, or under the bed, have they been seen so many times they are, in fact, no longer seen? Have the senses become numb? Are you unplugged, or afraid, or out of tune? Whatever the case may be, the falling trees and flying dragons of the negative looping in your life will continue around and around, again and again, until they're observed.

While I have never seen a pair of fairy-tale glasses at the store for spotting dragons, the hero's tools of perception are readily available to everyone, already embedded in the core essence of who you are. You've probably had a moment when you've suddenly seen yourself doing the same thing over and over with the same unwanted results. This is a moment of the hero's call into awareness, an opportunity for making a choice about the next cycle.

For instance, my friend Carol told me, "I've dated several men the past ten years hoping for marriage, but the relationships always end up the same way. With me still single. But it just dawned on me that in one key aspect, all those men are alike. I've been choosing to date essentially the same guy over and over again expecting it to end in marriage, when that's highly unlikely with someone that has this certain trait. Why do I keep doing that?"

Another hero friend Ted says, "I realized the truth about why I've been overweight for so many years now. Why I've had no real success in taking off the pounds and keeping them off even though my doctor has clearly shown me the correlation to my health issues. I've been looking at food as comfort, even entertainment, and my fat as an insulation blanket to keep me at a comfortable distance from people so I don't risk getting hurt. Now that I can see that, I don't want to stay stuck here anymore. What do I do now?"

A fellow warrior Chris shared, "I have never been able to get on top of my finances. Even though I'm feeling crushed under all my credit card debt, even though I have all the clothes I could possibly need, I still find myself at the store buying more. Ringing up more debt, more guilt, more of what I tell myself I don't want. But look at what I'm doing versus what I'm saying. It's tearing me apart, but somehow spending money and buying clothes is what I keep doing uncontrollably so I'll somehow feel freedom and control. Crazy, right?"

Sound familiar? Have you had any similar experiences? Are you aware of any negative autopilot loops in your life right now? Such moments as my friends' sudden realizations of self can present opportunities to make shifts that result in movements in one's life, big and small. Paying attention to what you're sensing and how you're feeling keeps you plugged into the awareness needed for true survival of body, mind, and spirit. Different than the autopilot of survival mode where you're obliviously plodding along, these are the positive "in the moment" instincts needed to stay awake to your hero's journey. Recognizing when you're stuck in a rut of negative looping is an opportunity for movement; it's using your "in the moment" instincts for the movement of living. And let me tell you, movement is the key to truly living.

I had been in Iraq for three weeks, and the 1st Recon Marine battalion was taking over operations in Fallujah, the hottest zone of fighting, the same zone in which the Blackwater contractors were killed by insurgents and hung on the spans of a bridge. It was February with extreme temperature swings, hot and sweat during the day, and severe cold at night with snow flurries and the thermometer sometimes dropping below zero. Patrols along the Euphrates River baked a man during the day then froze his sweat soaked body into an icy popsicle at night while hiding amongst the reeds. I was bone tired and so were my buddies.

Staff Sergeant Eric Kocher was one of the most respected Team Leaders in 1st Recon. He and I had been together from the very beginning, had fought side by side through all of our training and schools, and seen combat together in Afghanistan in 2001–2, as well as two tours in Iraq. My warrior brother is a man I look in the eye as well as look up to, and I trust his instincts. He trusts his instincts as well, and because of that he has always come out on top.

That day I had been on patrol in the lowlands along the Euphrates where the paddies and fields of grass are laid out like the depressions of a waffle with the roads running high along the ridges. I came

Courtesy of Sal Alvarez

With my Marine Recon brother and friend SSgt. Eric Kocher.

in from patrol feeling bushed from the rigors of real combat day in and day out, so exchanged a few friendly words with Eric and his Assistant Team Leader, Sergeant Eddie Wright, and then hit the rack to catch some Z's. Two hours later I was roused from my comatose sleep by loud banging on the hatch and the command to get up. "We gotta go Dog! Bravo is in contact . . . heavy, heavy contact!"

Bravo platoon was in the thick of the hot zone and had pushed their lead vehicle just outside of visual and heavy gun support, leaving Eric's team Humvee dangerously skylined on top of one of the waffle ridges of the Euphrates lowlands, with a canal on one side and an impossible slope on the other. Their position, as Eric would say, was "bad juju."

Then *SWOOSH!!* The first rocket-propelled grenade, or RPG, screamed behind his head and exploded just five meters behind their vehicle.

"Roger Bravo Actual, my team is in contact!! Returning fire! Is the platoon pushing to my position or are we falling back to the platoon's position?" Eric yelled over the radio.

SWOOSH BOOM! Another RPG landed dangerously close. Then more swooshes as the cracking of small arms opened up.

Later Eric would tell me that in milliseconds in that moment there was a sudden and dynamic shift in his awareness of the precarious position he and his team were in. He entered a superheightened cognitive alert mode.

Then Eddie opened up with his SAW machine gun and within seconds the *SWOOSH* of yet another RPG slammed directly in and obliterated his weapon, hands, arms, and some of his legs. The heavy gunner up top the vehicle was supposed to be engaging with the .50-caliber gun, but it was silent. The gunner was unconscious and his groin and legs had been hit as well. Eric in the front passenger seat saw the driver next to him akimbo and unconscious. Only Eric and Eddie were still conscious, and Eddie wouldn't be here long if his massive hemorrhaging was not controlled.

"Brother, we need to get some tourniquets on you!!" Eric yelled, but at that moment an AK-47 burst fire and chewed up his right elbow and hands. He told me later that he felt something hot bite him, but it just pissed him off. When he lifted his weapon to return fire, his ulna and radius bones peered at him from his arm.

"I had a softball-sized hole in my arm and my eardrums were gone, everyone in my team was down," Eric explained later. "But Eddie was still talking and conscious, trying to keep me in the fight. Can you imagine that? Eddie, who is bleeding to death in pieces with no arms, is keeping it cool. So I thought, 'If he is cool, then I GOTTA BE COOL!'"

Eric could no longer fire his weapon with his gun hand, his hearing was gone, the radio was destroyed, and enemy was swarming all over and more RPGs were coming in. In the middle of all that chaos, in that moment of hanging in the kill zone, he instinctively came upon the simple decision that would bring salvation. "We gotta move. WE GOTTA MOVE NOW OR WE ARE ALL DEAD!"

SSgt. Eric Kocher's Humvee after making it back to base.

With his move-or-die resolution, Eric got out of the battered Humvee, took his gun in his other hand, fired and reloaded as he traversed to the driver's side of the vehicle, then pushed his driver to the back, climbed in, and tried to start the Humvee.

"Brother, I was hittin' the ignition and pressing the gas and it just wasn't going anywhere," he recounted. With his sense of hearing gone he could no longer perceive the sound of the hum and revving of the engine. Unable to plug into an awareness of what was happening in that moment, he could have just kept hitting the gas going nowhere again and again. But when his hearing didn't provide awareness, he shifted focus to another perception, his sense of sight, and he looked down to see the vehicle was in neutral. With this visual cue, he still didn't know if the engine was running or intact, but if it was, if he could get it in gear, there was at least a chance they could get moving.

With lead bullets pocking the skin of their lightly armored Humvee, it looked like a clown car with two blown tires and metal

Courtesy of Eric Kocher

SSgt. Eric Kocher after surviving the fight.

hanging off everywhere. Not knowing whether the engine was working, or if the vehicle could steer, Eric spent no time and energy worrying about that. Instead he acted on what he did know and did what he could to move. He got the stick shift shoved into gear and hit the gas. Oorah! It jerked forward! Even with blown wheels and cliffs on both sides, he got it moving and somehow turned that circus Humvee around and lumbering back toward the platoon.

"Brother, I just kept that accelerator jammed down and eyes forward to my platoon's position. I just had to make it out of that hellish kill zone. I had a thousand meters to go to get to help and hope," Eric details. "I just had to move, you know what I mean? Or else we all would have just died out there fighting to the last man. If we'd have been stuck, unable to move, that would have been sure death."

That day Staff Sergeant Eric Kocher fully plugged into his senses to be able to perceive the futile revving of an engine going nowhere, make adjustments, and move to save the lives of his whole team. He and Sergeant Eddie Wright were decorated for their heroic courage and critical decision making, but the thought of earning medals had nothing to do with the events of that day. That day was about finding a way to move when you know you must, or as Eric puts it, "Sometimes when everything is closing in or everything is falling apart, sometimes you just gotta move."

I love my Recon brothers. Every one of them goes all the way and would do anything for each other. For this and so many other reasons, Eric, Eddie, and all my Recon buddies are and always will be my heroes.

I know it's possible you may be reading this thinking that war and bullets have nothing to do with you or your life. Or perhaps you're reading this while living in the middle of a kill zone, whether on a military battlefield or in your local neighborhood. With so many possible modes of living out there, I suspect there are moments in your life that you've at least felt you're in a metaphorical war zone. Or maybe if you don't feel you're in a metaphorical war zone at all, perhaps it just feels like you keep hitting the gas with no results. Or you seem to be moving, but are going nowhere. Or you feel like your feet can't even reach the gas pedal.

Whatever it is, they all count just the same. Further, what works in moving out of or through them is the same on many levels as well.

I've typically heard the phrase "perception is reality" or "perception is everything" used to talk about the importance of attitude. I believe this is true and an essential pillar of the Hero Living philosophy, especially how it relates to movement. At the same time I also like using the term in another way as well, to call attention to the importance of using your senses of perception, your mental faculties and your physical and emotional senses, to be aware of where you are in relation to where you want to go.

When your senses are in tune, you have the tools needed to recognize when you're stuck, or see your negative loops—your circles of suffering, and use that awareness as the entry points to opening up your answers to the hero's call. In doing so, you awaken the hero inside that resonates with the very core essence of who you are, who you want to be, and where you want to go in this life.

When this happens, you are Hero Living.

Choosing Perception Is Everything and More

At eleven years old, after the rescue mission from Texas by my cousin and my mom, my brothers and I ended up being sent to live at the Omaha Home for Boys in Nebraska. Once again we were in a new place amongst strangers and not to say that life there was great, but man, things were really a lot better than when we were in Texas or living with mom. A lot better. We had stability and decent schooling, access to medical care and fresh food, clothing and haircuts. Best of all, there was the gym with weights for training, and I joined the wrestling team as well.

I had been there a few months doing well with my grades and training and work. I worked on the ground crew and in the kitchen scullery, from which I made $5 here and $5 there. We were paid sixty cents a job. Not an hour. A job. So if it took four hours to complete then that was fifteen cents an hour! But no matter, I had a little money, so I saved some and the rest I spent on comics. The new *Spider-Man*, *Secret Wars*, and all these other great books had just come out, and I just couldn't *save* all my money!

I was doing well enough in the Boys Home that I was given the opportunity to go home for Thanksgiving, plus I had phone privileges for the week due to my good conduct. I sat in the foyer on the

Courtesy of Reyes family

With my brothers.

soft worn green rocking chair and picked up the telephone re-
ceiver and turned the numbers on the rotary dial to call my mom.
I remember waiting and hearing the phone ring, feeling so full of
hope and happiness at the thought of seeing my family. I could play
and read comics and go sled riding with my brothers, and Mom
would have her special Mexican food for Thanksgiving—she was a
terrific cook!

Mom picked up the phone and I just started smiling from the
inside out. We talked a bit and I gave her the news that I could come
home for a Thanksgiving visit. "*Mijo*, that is wonderful," she says. "I
miss you and I can't wait to see you!"

The Boys Home was a solid and structured place for me, but I
thought it would be awesome to go home to a place that I knew, a
place with family and a mother. "Mommy, to come home will
cost sixty dollars for the bus ticket there and back. I only have

thirty dollars, so if there's a way you could help with the rest, I can make it!"

The phone was silent for a bit. "Mommy, you still there?"

She came back on and said, "I don't have any money, son. You can't get blood from a stone."

"Mom, could you ask cousin or—"

She cut me off. "They got their own problems, son, they can't help you!"

I felt stunned and started to cry a little, but Mom could hear it on the line. "I didn't raise no little crybabies! You better suck it up! You hear me, Rudy?"

My hope of Thanksgiving with family was falling apart, but more than the hope of a family holiday, somehow my last hopes of having a caring compassionate mother were blasting to bits. And with that, I felt I was just dying inside too. I was trying not to cry, but my heart hurt so badly.

"Two tears in a bucket, so f—it," Mom said, one of her favorite sayings. "You still crying? You need to man up and be tough! Nobody likes a crybaby wimp. Nobody."

I was paralyzed. I felt critically wounded. My still beating innocence and somewhat fairy-tale belief that somehow I had someone, had a mother, looking out for me was shown to be false. She was essentially saying, "Son, I don't have it to give; look elsewhere for what you need," and my heart dropped and slowed. For the first time I understood my truth: I knew unequivocally right then and there that I was alone and on my own.

From the depths of my letdown sorrowful soul, I grew up that day and vowed to never again rely on or ask anything of my mom. After so much disappointment, so much shuffling and abandoning, so much self-absorbed drugging and cruelty, she was now only a Mother to me in title. In retrospect I see this was a huge gift.

Although it hurt and I couldn't see past my pain in that moment, an important and seemingly instantaneous movement happened in me that day. In that moment, my insides shifted in one fell swoop to another structure of perspective. It was as if I had bolted like lightning from one stone to another to cross a swift stream and now the world was different, because I could see from another vantage point and I knew I could never go back to the other stone. It had fallen into the stream when I moved.

This was an internal shift of revolutionary honesty. A moment of me just saying to myself, "This is on you, my man; you are in charge of your own destiny. If you're going to make it, it's going to be on you. Don't expect anyone else to change it for you." And I got more serious about creating my own life. I got more firmly squared onto my own hero's path.

This notion of perspective, of choosing your perspective is such an important keystone for the hero's journey. It is the act of choosing that immediately puts the ball in your court.

Later in life as a new Marine recruit, I was at the end of a long and arduous day of a physical fitness test to try out for Recon. After a warm-up of running three miles in eighteen minutes, and then pumping out twenty pull-ups and sit-ups in two minutes, we were ready to get going.

Pick up a pack with a sixty-pound sandbag, get on your boots and combat gear, and then run the obstacle course, moving through bars and over walls and logs, climbing ropes, pumping push-ups, fluttering kicks, and more, and then take your pack and run cross-country for seven miles.

At this point I was the initiate running in first place, but all the while chasing rabbit Recon Marines through each portion of the course. I was pushing myself beyond all preconceived limits to be in front—way in front—and I had caught the lead rabbit! I was elated, but the heat and exhaustion were starting to seep into my mind.

Ahead of me navigating the hills and terrain of Camp Horno was the rabbit, Sergeant Conrey. Despite getting weaker, I would not slow down out of pride and respect as I pulled alongside him, but he knew how I was feeling because he'd been there himself and he must have seen it in me somehow.

As we paced stride for stride, my mind wilting with each step, Sergeant Conrey gently said, "Lance Corporal Reyes, are you in pain? Are you out of breath?"

I was silent, but he continued on.

"If you are, it is a problem of focus," he offered. "Focus on the light breeze on your neck, not the cuts on your feet. Focus on the sound of the birds in the trees, not the flames inside your lungs. It is all a matter of focus."

Wow! I was suddenly and immutably shifted out my exhaustion. Sergeant Conrey had compassionately nudged me to another place of perspective to observe pain and suffering with a detached lightness of being. I was transformed and grateful for lessons of Zen from this warrior master.

Such a shift of perspective can make all the difference along the journey. Regardless of the circumstance, now *you* are in control of *you* and what you do. Now you're not waiting for anybody or anything—the check in the mail, the lottery ticket, the roll of the dice, the knight in white armor. You are the one in command at this moment. This is your gift of the moment.

Keys to the Cage

Ralph Waldo Emerson once wrote, "There are always two parties; the establishment and the movement." While his comment may have been inspired by political or social affairs, I think they are just as applicable to us as individuals and the cages we construct and live in.

Anytime we seek to remove, break, transform, transmute, reform, deconstruct, or sometimes even simply look at the bars of our cage, our establishment, the very thought of change can feel like or be a moment of revolution, whether of internal shifting or external movement. And perhaps that's why we may sometimes shrink from the call to move, because of the seeming solidity of our establishment and the uncertainty we feel in making a move. If you have ever felt this way, despite that it may inherently feel lonely; there's something I want you to know.

You are not alone.

If you have ever felt yourself shrink from the hero's call to move, know that you are not the only one.

You are not alone.

Or if you have ever seen yourself not only shrink from a call to move onto the hero's path, but have instead taken a lesser road.

You are not alone.

If you have ever seen yourself further harden the bars of your cage, or even add more bars.

Still, you are not alone.

Even if you have agreed to other people's vision of bars on your cage, or attempted to place bars on someone else's cage; no matter what you have ever felt or seen or done, I want you to know you are not the only one.

I promise you are not alone.

I have felt or seen or done all these things myself. To varying degrees I have had moments of doubt and fear, insecurity, guilt, self-pity, bitterness, jealousy, revenge, laziness, or any other wave of discomfort and hesitation that has taken over and held me back from making a step, or compelled me to take a step in a lesser direction, and I know it. Somewhere inside I know that's what I've done, which in turn can set off the negative loops of chatter in my head. The loop-de-loops that rebuff and rebuke our missteps, the not stepping forward, or our backward stepping, and ask our agreement that we are "bad," not worthy, undeserving, stupid, silly, or worse.

If any of this rings true for you, you are not only like me; you are living the chapters from stories of the likes of Spider-Man and Superman, Tarzan and Rocky, Han Solo, Indiana Jones, Achilles, Spartacus, and George Bailey.

We have seen our heroes, one and all, take a misstep or question themselves. Even George Bailey, the self-sacrificing hero of the classic film *It's a Wonderful Life*, finds himself in such self-doubt he questions himself to the point of standing on a bridge in the wintry cold contemplating suicide. The point of which is if your loop-de-loops of negativity are circling, take a break, and give yourself a break of compassion. I mean, come on, if your heroes have foibles, perhaps you do as well. And if this is possible, I invite to take a moment to consider another possibility.

You are not your history.

Your experiences may hold information about where you have been or where you are, but you do not have to agree to be constrained by them. You have the choice before you to continue living in your cage as is, or to change and shift as you may see fit for your journey.

Whether or not things will change as you expect or even change for the better, I cannot say. But as an old Chinese proverb says, "If we don't change our direction we're likely to end up where we're headed." So what I can say is if things are going to have a chance at being better, there must be change. And for change to happen there must be movement.

But what if it seems the bars on your cage are immovable, or can only be rattled? What then? Perhaps what's needed is another perspective, a revolution of perspective. When we can only see the bars on our cage as things that confine us, perhaps we miss an important key to our freedom. The French philosopher Simone Weil described the concept of metaxu as "every separation being a link," illustrated by the idea of two prisoners whose cells adjoin being able to communicate with each other by knocking on the wall. The wall is the thing that separates them but it is also their means of communication. In her discussion metaxu represents an intermediary, or a bridge, with the physical world being both the barrier and the "way through" to the spiritual world. If we think of our cage as being both the barrier and "way through" to freedom, the keys are now in our hands.

For instance, there's a parable of a farmer who owned an old mule that fell into the farmer's well. The farmer heard the mule braying from the bottom of the well, but after carefully assessing the situation, although the farmer sympathized with the mule, he decided that neither the mule nor the well were worth saving.

So he called his neighbors together, told them the story, and enlisted their help in hauling dirt to bury the old mule in the well and put him out of his misery.

As the first shovelfuls of dirt fell on his back, the old mule was hysterical. But as the farmer and his neighbors continued shoveling and the dirt hit his back, out of nowhere, a thought struck him. It suddenly dawned on him that every time a shovel load of dirt landed on his back, he should shake it off and step up!

So that's what he did, blow after blow.

"Shake it off and step up. Shake it off and step up. Shake it off and step up!" He repeated this mantra again and again to encourage himself. No matter how painful the blows, or how distressing the situation seemed, the old mule fought his fears and panic and just kept right on shaking it off and stepping up.

Before long the old mule exhausted but triumphant enthusiastically stepped over the wall of the well. What seemed like something that would bury him, actually presented an opportunity for freedom simply by his changing perspective and moving in a chosen direction. The shoveled dirt became an intermediary, or a bridge, as it was both a barrier and the "way through" to the mule's freedom.

In pragmatic fashion this mule focused on what was within his control instead of dreaming that those shoveling dirt would stop shoveling, a fact he could not control. Somehow this mule instinctively knew that although he couldn't change the action of others or that he'd been thrown down a well, that if he focused optimistically on that which was in his control, his own perspective and actions, that was his opportunity for making a positive difference.

Perhaps it sounds like a Pollyannaish cliché: "When life hands you lemons, make lemonade." If so, consider that perhaps this thought is also an evolution of your internal revolution at work. Perhaps we all have a farmer and mule inside struggling over which way we go as a whole. Does one part say, "It's not worth it," and enlist the other negative loops to bury up the mule that's dreaming of freedom? While another part, the stubborn mule dreamer responds with, "Oorah! A way out!" Perhaps these are some of the battles to win in your ongoing revolution for more. More of yourself. More of your hopes and dreams.

Does this infer that everything will always be happy fanciful bliss in unlocking or transforming the bars of your cage? No, not necessarily. Consider that life is made up of all the notes on the musical scale. At different times in life they play in harmony or discord, fast or slow, high or low, in a waltz or a march. No matter what music plays as you tap on the bars of your cage, appreciate that it plays and communicates, and take a cue from the master musician Duke Ellington, who said, "I merely took the energy it takes to pout and wrote some blues."

Be the music maker of your life and the dreamer of dreams.

Choose your perspective and that will make all the difference and more.

THE HERO'S WHETSTONE:
SQUARING THE DIRECTION OF YOUR STEP

Having dreams and holding the intent of them in your mind is a powerful tool for setting direction along the hero's path. Dreams can give us the courage to move in moments we might otherwise feel paralyzed. They can inspire us to grab hold the bars and rattle our cage until free.

So with your hopes and dreams and your own youthful feeling and flowering perception, let's begin with this whetstone prompt, and start again by focusing on taking three deep breaths in and out. Take a few moments to breathe in through the nose deep into the belly, and then push from the belly slowing blowing air out through your mouth. As you breathe, close your eyes and remember your dreams from the whetstone earlier in this stride, and Be the Dreamer of Dreams.

As you feel and breathe in your dreams, turn your attention to your cage. This is your cage that represents all the silent and Sisyphean agreements, all the negative loops, everything in your life that keeps you feeling trapped, keeps your dreams and goals out of reach. The cage has bars representing each of these things, some bars may seem monumental, some easy to approach, others solidly stuck, some a little jiggly, perhaps some bars represent a physical, spiritual, or mental trap.

Although there may be many bars in your cage, for now I want you to focus on a single bar. Any one of them will do, but only pick one. Select whichever one you're drawn to—big, small, difficult, easy—it's up to you. And no worries about getting it "right"; you can always change your mind and pick a different one later. When you've settled on one, take a moment and look at this particular bar that seems to negatively impede your path or hold you back, and see it clearly in your mind's eye. Think about how it holds you back, why it's part of your cage.

Now remember the other whetstone prompts where I asked you to look at yourself as if you were an unbiased third-party observer, or see yourself as a friend would see you. Really plug into this feeling of seeing through a fresh, new, alternative point of view, another set of eyes.

Now firmly squared in your friendly self perspective, and with me by your side, take a look at this one bar in your cage as you would imagine someone else seeing it for the first time from a whole new perspective. As best you can, move into and hold this perspective as a third-party observer, as this is a powerful technique for this stride. Now consider the following.

- Does this bar appear any different to you than before? If so, how?
- Is there a way to use this bar to creatively escape and gain your freedom?
- What dreams or goals is this bar keeping you from?
- Does it seem there are benefits to having it in your cage? Even consider such thoughts as "I get to stay the victim," "I don't have to try," "I get to be lazy," "I get to feel superior," "I get to feel powerful," "I get to feel in control," etc. Are these really benefits? Why do you keep the bar there?

In doing a resection of my life after coming home from Iraq to a broken marriage and feeling lost, eventually I had to look at what was keeping me caged. I had so much energy bubbling up in the way of pain and anger, for a while I could only think about ways to keep a lid on it because it felt too big and overwhelming. But when I got real with myself I saw the problem wasn't how much energy I had, the problem was with how I was handling it. So instead of trying to keep a lid on it anymore, I let it flow and redirected it into my training and coaching. As the energy dissipated into positive activities, I was able to then look at the other issues behind my pain and anger. And that was the way out of my cage. My new perspective and movement.

So if the bar you first selected feels unwieldy or difficult in this exercise, try another one, or another, until you can find one to work with. Or if it seems easy, feel free to do the same exercise with other bars in your cage. Spend hours at it, or set it down for now and come back to it at some point when you can. Be gentle with yourself but don't let yourself off the hook. Some of this can be tough, so be compassionate. This is a journey and a process, not a destination, a process of keeping at it and moving.

When you're at a point that you have a good sense about this bar, and have thought of possibilities to view it with a new perspective and attitude, have perhaps even envisioned how to use it to your advantage, I want you to remember a dream or goal that this bar is keeping you from.

Now, only in regards to this one bar, this one dream, I want you to ask yourself one question.

"What do I want?"

And again, because I'm serious about getting real with this.

"What do I really want?"

Keep in mind that "what you want" may embed other questions such as "Where do I want to go?" or "Who do I want to be?"

Also know that there is no right answer but *your* answer.

When you think of the question "What do I want?" what is your truth? Which do you prefer to keep or pursue—the bar or the dream?

Answering a simple question like "What do you want?" is the basis for forming your original intent. This will be a baseline to which you can return for clarity in setting priorities and direction for your Moments of Movement.

Perhaps this whetstone has revealed big shifts for you, or perhaps small ones. But no matter how big or small, even in asking the question you have moved in this moment. Remember, you don't have to move much in order to move far. Just keep moving.

The great dreamer Dr. Martin Luther King Jr. counseled movement with these words: "Take the first step in faith. You don't have to see the whole staircase. Just take the first step."

So take hold of your dreams and courage, and step outside the establishment of your cage.

Step into change and evolution.

Step into possibility.

Move with hope, because when you take a step toward your dreams, they take a step toward you.

STRIDE 3
Fighting & Surviving

The feeling: "I'm tired of being beaten down. I'm mad. I'm hurt. And I'm afraid. But I'm going to show up for myself even if no one else will. I'm going to fight for myself."

BAM! I saw the Milky Way, rockets and stars!! It was the summer of my tenth year and that left-handed punch came straight at me without hesitation and landed squarely on my right eye.

My best friend that summer and two years before was Sean Blakemore. We both loved to draw, explore the woods like Indiana Jones for ancient relics, and while the summers away at the pool in our apartment complex.

In the neighborhood there was a cast of ruffians known as the O'Malleys, an Irish family with ten kids, whose bad attitude had rode roughshod over the vicinity for years with their bullying and nasty mouths. Their reputation and cruel exploits were well known near and far, and every kid knew to watch their back on the way to and from school, or while out and about at the park or local convenience store. Kids everywhere were tired of feeling the oppression that hung everywhere like an ominous thundercloud threatening

lunch money and physical safety, but rarely did someone dare to
tangle with the O'Malleys. They ruled the neighborhood roost with
a heavy hand, and man, they were trouble with a capital T.

One day that summer the swimming pool was playing full bore
with a cacophony of neighborhood kids blaring away with screams
of glee and blasting boom boxes. Sean and I were playing underwater games like Marco Polo and Man from Atlantis, having the time
of our lives like we did every day in the haze of long summer days.
In the middle of one of our classic make-believe 007 James Bond
underwater knife fights, Elliott O'Malley, the youngest O'Malley
kid who was still a few years older than me and my buddy, appeared out of nowhere snatched up Sean and held him in a tight
neck cradle thrashing him about in the water without a chance to
breathe. This was of course the infamous feared water torture game
of bullies—Dunking! The classic mismatched contest where a bigger kid forcibly deprives his victim of the breath of life and steals
his pride as his own.

And this is what Elliott was doing to my best friend, dunking
the hell out of him with nothing to breathe but chlorinated H_2O,
heaving him up and down with no mercy in his eyes or heart until
Sean caught enough oxygen to cry out for him to stop. "Shut your
mouth, little baby," Elliott growled. "If you don't shut up I'll drown
you for real!"

Elliott had big pounds and inches on us both, but despite that
and the water being up to my chest, without a second thought I
started crawl stroking to my friend's side with iron in my eyes
and yelled, "Elliott, leave him alone!! You are a big meany and a big
A-hole!!"

Elliott turned toward me and dropped Sean in gasping convul-
sions with arms akimbo. "Hey little chump! What are you gonna do
about it?" he challenged.

"I will freakin' kick your butt, you bastard!" My words spat out like fire in hopes of scaring the big bully with my bluster and toughness. Instead, and without a moment's notice, his left fist came slamming in fast and hard directly to my right eye, and I fell back seeing rockets and stars as the water splashed in around me!

In such a moment of violence and oppression many courses of action are possible, but as for me at ten years of age, on that day I came up out of the water with my fists of fury a-swinging. I buried my head into my enemy's chest and just started throwing hooks and uppercuts to the body, a full-on onslaught of punches to the liver, belly, and ribs.

As I banged away I literally felt my blasted eye swelling shut, but I paid no mind, I was in the slipstream of the eternal fight for right. In the background the sounds of Sean screaming, "Get him, Rudy! You can take him!" rang through, further fueling the fire in my belly and the pressure of my assault.

"Get him, Rudy! Get him! You can do it!"

Then somehow, to my surprise, another sound began to filter in. It was Elliott's voice. Big bad Elliott, who until this moment I had only seen as someone to fear and acquiesce my pride and pennies to, was crying, "Rudy, stop! Stop! Pleeeease stop!"

Hearing these words from an O'Malley gangster didn't seem possible, so I kept right on pounding, but Elliott cried again, "I give up! Please stop, Rudy. I don't want to fight anymore! I'm sorry . . . I give up!!"

There's a similar scene in the popular holiday film *A Christmas Story* in which the neighborhood hooligan, Scut Farkus, has been repeatedly razzing Ralph and his friends on their way to and from school, leaving the boys in a constant state of run or get beat up. Then something happens. It seems like any other day of getting bullied by Scut, except that Ralph's now under the pressure of getting a C+ grade on his homework and losing his hopes of ever getting a Red Ryder BB gun for Christmas. So when the usual snowball and tormenting are lobbed his way as he walks home from school, this time something snaps; instead of running away, Ralph rushes forward and knocks Scut to the ground, impaling him with a barrage of punches and foul language. And he continues throwing fists until the bully cries out for mercy, and Ralph is finally wrested from attack mode by his mother. And for Ralph, things were different after that.

Courtesy of Reyes family

With my brothers at the swimming pool.

A similar thing happened in the swimming pool as I assailed Elliott with unabashed abandon and a barrage of punches for tormenting my friend with Dunking. As I realized the tide had turned, other realizations flooded over me. And so I stopped.

And things were different after that.

In the moments that followed I felt myself a champion and a hero. A hero to myself, to my friend, and to others looking on who feared the O'Malleys just like we did. I stood up for my friend and myself that day, and in doing so I knew something more about myself that I liked.

I liked knowing there was a seat of courage inside of me available to be tapped at any moment.

I liked knowing I can show up for myself.

I liked knowing that I am willing to fight for myself, no matter the odds.

I liked the thought I had done my heroes proud.

I liked feeling that on that day, the phrase "You are a hero" meant me.

The Time to Fight

In the Dunking incident with the bully at the pool, the life-giving supply of air was cut off to my friend Sean when his ability to breathe was suppressed. Without air, life continues on for only a few minutes, making fight and survive feel immediately paramount when we cannot catch a breath. In Latin, *spiritus* is the word for "breath," as well as "spirit" and "energy." So in a sense you could even say that his spirit and energy were imperiled.

In traditional Chinese culture, chi is taken to be the active forming part of any living thing, or the flow of energy that sustains living beings, the term literally translating as "air" or "breath." Chi is produced by the universe issuing forth to manifest as an ongoing cosmic balance of yin and yang, a continual process between seemingly opposing forces that actively give rise to each other in an interconnected interdependent relationship.

For thousands of years Asian cultures have given great attention to maintaining the balance and flow of chi in all things. For instance, feng shui is based on calculating the balance of chi as it relates to the placement of furniture or other elements in a living space because this directly affects the energy level of the occupants. In Chinese medicine, chi in the body is thought to circulate in channels called meridians, and when the flow through the meridians is disrupted, blocked, or unbalanced, it may result in illness. Thus treatments such as acupuncture are performed to clear those blockages and restore the flow of chi for optimum health.

In Dunking it is well understood that Elliott O'Malley had no intention of actually drowning my friend Sean. So if real mortal danger was not the intent, what instead was going on? Perhaps a number of things, but to me it seems that Elliott was primarily engaged in an act of theft rather than murder. By physically overwhelming and intimidating someone, by producing fear and angst in his victim, the bully created a scenario for taking. And by picking on someone younger and smaller, being willing to hurt and cause harm to another, he increased his odds to near certainty of being able to take. Much as a mythological vampire sucks the life giving blood of their victims in order to live, Elliott felt his own life energy stores swell when taking the energy and spirit of others, leaving the victim feeling drained and violated, distressed, anxious, or uncomfortable at the exercise of unjust authority. In other words, his tool in this robbery was oppression.

Oppression.

The Latin root of the word means "to press" or "to crush." And isn't that the way it can feel when the yoke of a tyrant weighs heavily down? From a childhood Dunking game to an unfair boss to a smothering relationship or anyone keeping another person or people under subservience and hardship.

In such moments as these is held an invitation to muster your courage and stand in resolution for yourself, for others, or "what's right," a seed of opportunity intoned as the loud quiet voice of the hero's call. The courage to stand up for yourself is an ever-present thread in the fabric of us all. Even when it doesn't seem so, seems out of sight, out of reach, feels missing or dormant, or even unwanted.

My grandmother on my mother's side was forged on the hard anvil of the 1930s Depression working the fields up and down the Midwest from Mexico to Canada. She had a strong jaw and the look of a fair-skinned Spaniard who had crossed many oceans. One of six children, she grew up hard tack and hard scrabble attending school in the small south Texas town of Pharr where deep-rooted racism and sexism were alive and in full force.

During WWII the man who would later become her husband was serving in the Army. He was handsome with his old world Latino style melding machismo and bravado with charismatic suave, and he cut a striking figure in uniform with his brown skin and dark eyes. In the jubilance of a postwar world where people instantly wed at the drop of a kiss, my grandfather wooed her with the style of a triumphant troubadour and they married.

Soon after saying "I do" they had their first child when she was still eighteen years old, and in their first eight years of marriage they produced four children, the youngest being my mother. Like most women of her generation, my grandmother stayed home raising her children, cooking and cleaning, and fending for her growing family.

Like most men of his generation, my grandfather was the breadwinner of the home. To support his young family, he worked as an auto mechanic and the boss man of migrant field workers. Like too many men of too many generations, whether it was his upbringing as a child, or the time at war in his youth, whatever it was, as many before and after him, the man was violent. And with a malevolent mean streak to boot.

By the time I knew him much later in life, he had dark stained teeth and eyes yellowed from so much coffee and whiskey poured down his throat. Whenever I heard him talk, or felt him beating the life out of me, I could smell cheap bourbon blowing on his breath. Back as a young man he was still handsome, but just as unsavory, demanding absolute dominion over his household, and the need for prescient awareness from his wife to foresee when the other shoe would drop raining down bitter tyranny on all those in his path. All would feel the ruthless smack of his hand and belt, and the sting of his furious words. Sometimes you could see it coming for miles like a storm brooding on the horizon, while others might strike like lightning out of a clear sky at an unbeknownst provocation.

As the days and months and years passed in this chaotic atmosphere of familial feuding, amidst working to raise kids and protect against a ruthless dictator, my grandmother would find the time to read. She loved books by Louis L'amour and others about the Old West, where heroes loomed large against the bad guys, and characters like L'amour's fictional Sackett family would inspire and keep her company with their cattle drives and frontier lessons learned cowboy-style of friendship, love, and the value of education.

As the heavy hand of her husband smacked away at her self-image bringing it low to the ground, she filled her heart and mind with images of the Western hero. While the social mores and constructs of the country around her said to "stand by your man," the hope of "the good guys always win" kept a pioneering light aglow in her life's landscape that was otherwise dark and desolate of loving-kindness. On the days when it seemed there was nothing left to hope for, I believe that somewhere inside a still small voice must have kept crying out like the little boy at the end of the movie *Shane*, "And mother wants you—I know she does!"

It was in this household of booming babies that my grandmother carried all the burdens of a battered woman. Perhaps it would really never happen again. This time he'll stop. Or perhaps she deserved it. It was her fault the house was a mess. Or maybe she could learn to walk more carefully on eggshells, or this time they could work it out, or . . . just somehow it would be okay, somehow, only if. She was stuck in the cycle, doubting herself and hoping for little more.

The problem with all that in this kind of situation is even though the storm may sometimes subside with a patch of sun shining through, the problem never really resolves and goes away. Like a twister, it threatens from they sky above, kicking up dust, then recedes back into the clouds, only to return and touch down with greater ferocity when least expected, carelessly rearranging fences and homes and lives wherever it goes without a regret. The oppression on such dark thundercloud days can be stifling.

It was on such a day as this that my grandmother received her Enlightenment. Like a lightning bolt, it hit her while she was in the tub.

After a long day of tending kids she drew a bath filled with warm water and bubbles to soothe away the tensions of the day and find a few minutes of quiet time for herself. But suddenly out of nowhere, like a loud blustering version of the shower scene in the movie *Psycho*, into the bathroom rushed her wild-eyed husband screaming with broomstick in hand. With no warning he tore into the shower curtain and began beating down on her naked body again and again until the broomstick finally broke across her back.

Like so many times before, she never really knew the reason for the attack.

But this time that was it.

Like in the western movies of old, where the bad and the ugly go "too far" or "crosses the line," the reluctant hero within my grandmother finally found its voice and shouted an inner resolution: "Enough! I'm tired of being beat down! I'm going to fight for myself!"

She didn't say anything out loud at the time, but within a week she was gone.

She moved from Texas to Kansas City and in the midst of Americana 1950s Donna Reed expectations of dutiful wife at home, as mother of four and at the ripe age of thirty; she filed for divorce and enrolled in college to become a nurse.

She laid stake and struck out on her own hero's journey to save her life, and in her case, the saving was perhaps even quite literal.

Whether or not this story of my grandmother's fighting and surviving is like your own situation, I imagine there may be some aspect of your life that at sometime or another, or now, may feel similarly entrapping or oppressive. Because no matter how extreme or pedestrian your experience seems to be, that is not the point. As a human family, we've experienced everything along this continuum, but in general I suspect many of life's events and circumstances typically fall somewhere in between.

For instance, take my buddy Jake. He has worked at the same law firm for years, watching as others less qualified are promoted around him to receive accolades and significantly more money than he earns. "I feel like I've not only hit a glass ceiling, but that the powers that be are pressing it down on me. I keep telling myself they must have their reasons, and I can guess at what they are, but it doesn't matter. I'm tired of the unfairness and feeling like I'm being held back. I know I do excellent work and I want more than this."

Another friend, Marie, revealed, "I think sometimes I'm my own worst enemy. Over the years I feel like I've given everything I've got to my family and kids. And while I have no regrets about that, so many times I feel taken for granted, or worse yet, feel taken advantage of by my adult children. They seem to think nothing of asking me for big chunks of money as a loan and then never paying it back, as if it has no effect on me. But it does, not only financially, but emotionally as well. So even though I've been the one saying 'yes' in this unhealthy scenario of give and take, I need it to stop."

In another case an acquaintance Kelly shared, "As a kid no matter what I did it was never good enough for my dad. Straight A report card, gold medals won, college scholarship, it didn't matter. For most of my life I haven't even been aware of the constant loop in my head of dad's voice repeating over and over, 'you were just lucky', 'you don't deserve this', or 'why do you even try'. Now it's been a whole decade since he passed away, but the voice is still there dragging me down into an utter lack of confidence. I hear my boss telling me good job, and I say thank you, but deep down I never really believe it or that I deserve the praise. But every time that happens, it feels like a piece of me somewhere inside is dying."

Whether oppression comes from without or within, the effects are the same and can feel like a death of hope and dreams, or a loss of self. We may have something taken from us, physically or emotionally, freedom or rights, in an instant or slowly over time, in plain sight or via sleight of hand so you don't really notice it's missing until it's gone. We may feel we are the doormat, the abused, the unworthy, undeserving, unloved, and that it just won't ever stop. But perhaps there's another possibility to consider.

If there are times you feel like this, but then ignore, resist, or otherwise put away or stuff down your anger or pain and do nothing, consider the words of an early American statesman Henry Clay, "an oppressed people are authorized whenever they can to rise and break their fetters."

An oppressed people are *authorized* whenever they can to rise and break their fetters.

In the case of national or societal oppression, perhaps a group or governing body will give approval for an uprising, much as the United States of America proclaimed its independence as its own country against Britain. But in the case of our individual lives, from where does this authority come?

Sometimes another person or groups or governing bodies may

still give approval for certain matters in life, and these may be real considerations. But I'd like to raise another possibility for why certain bars remain in your cage, why you continue to remain in particular oppressive situations. I raise the consideration because I've done this myself and have felt the power of such shackles. And if I've done it, I suspect it's possible that you may have too.

I realize there have been times in my life that the only real reason I was still under the weight of an oppressive situation is because I hadn't authorized myself to rise and break free. I had to *give myself permission* to fight!

Is it possible you are still caged in certain ways because you haven't given yourself permission to fight?

Have you not authorized yourself to feel angry?

Have you withheld approval to acknowledge your pain? To feel deserving, or worth it?

If so, if you can relate to this somehow, I can understand.

Emotions of anger and rage can in themselves be scary.

Pain can feel overwhelming.

Fear can paralyze.

Thoughts of can't or shouldn't, or feelings of guilt, of not being worthy, deserving, or lovable can keep us whirling as if moored in an eddy of the ebb and flow of life.

But whether you think you can or should or could, consider the possibility that each time you recognize the yoke of tyranny pressing down; this is an opportunity for freedom. Each moment you feel a little piece of you may slip away if you acquiesce, that is an opportunity to step into more of your life. All such moments are simply the hero's call sounding an invitation for you to stand up, sit down, draw a line in the sand, put a stake in the ground, or whatever it takes to tackle your enemies and fight the good fight.

The author of my favorite pirate book *Treasure Island*, Robert

Louis Stevenson once said, "You cannot run away from a weakness; you must some time fight it out or perish; and if that be so, why not now, and where you stand?"

Whether a cage, a weakness, or other oppressor, now and then in life there comes a time to submit or fight.

In such a time, the hero fights.

THE HERO'S WHETSTONE: BREATHE YOUR FLOW OF POWER

Hi-yah!

If you've ever seen a kung fu movie, you've heard the fighters shout "Hi-yah" when they're throwing a punch. In martial arts hi-yah is not so much a battle cry as it is the release of the fighter's concentrated energy in a single explosive focus of will.

In Japanese martial arts this is referred to as kiai. The term describes both the coordination of breath with activity and the audible sound. Kiai can also be silent, a relaxed and powerful exhalation that adds power to movement. Martial arts students endlessly practice various techniques for breathing, body alignment, and focusing intent, to use kiai while performing martial arts.

Some martial artists become so skilled with their mastery of the use of kiai or similar techniques, they may amaze onlookers by breaking through bricks or layers of boards. Bruce Lee was famous for his one-inch-punch demonstrations where holding his fist motionless just one inch away from an opponent's chest, he would then punch forward and literally knock them off their feet. Wow!! That's no joke.

You may never smash through a pile of boards with your bare hands, and that's okay. But for this whetstone we're going to invoke the power of kiai by focusing on a breathing exercise. So as with other whetstones we've already done, let's go ahead and start this one by taking three deep breaths in and out. As you breathe, close your eyes and feel strength flowing in and stress flowing out with each breath. Allow yourself to relax and feel settled.

As is comfortable for you, sit or stand with your back in an erect position, and place your hands on your belly. Breathe in slowly pulling the air from down deep in your abdomen fully expanding the lungs and belly, and hold your breath for a moment. Now breathe out through your mouth forcibly zpushing air from your abdomen. Feel your abdominal muscles contract while you exhale, and do not engage your chest to move your breath. Repeat this while concentrating on specifically using your abdominal muscles to blow air out, until you can clearly feel like your belly is breathing and not your chest.

Now using this same kind of abdominal breathing, I want you to focus on your *exhale only* and quickly blow out ten breaths. Concentrate on forcefully exhaling. Don't think about whether you're going to inhale, just blow and blow. And blow. And blow . . .

Feel how even though you're only concentrating on the exhalation that somehow there's always air available for your next exhale, the inhale happening naturally and automatically to fuel the next forceful blow of air. It's not something to worry about or spend time over thinking. Just exhale a powerful breath.

Now I want you to throw a punch. Yes, that's right, a punch. Whether you've thrown a zillion punches or not one in your life, I don't care.

If you're worried about "looking funny" or doing it "right," just tell yourself that for now it doesn't matter.

Stop thinking about it, and just throw your fist out there with gusto. POW!

Yes!

Now throw one more punch and forcefully exhale at the same time. If you feel the urge, even yell Hi-yah!

If you feel inner resistance, that's fine, just notice it, but still punch.

Go ahead, try it!

If you still feel any resistance from inside, I want you to keep punching with your powerful exhale, with one hand, or using both hands one after the other, until it feels okay to do so.

So go ahead and punch away. *Hi-yah!*

Courtesy of Allen Carrasco

Throwing my powerful Hi-ya punch!

Okay, now we're going to put it all together, and add a twist. Whether you're a seasoned boxer that's accustomed to throwing physical punches, or a first-time "fighter," as you do this I want you to pay particular attention to what's going on inside emotionally and mentally. Your body, mind, and spirit working together are the key.

First, think of a time, circumstance, or person, something in your life when you've felt beaten down, caged, or oppressed, where you didn't or haven't stood up and fought as you wish. It could be something going on in your life now, or from your childhood, adolescence, or last month. It could be an outside abuser, an internal enemy, a bar from your cage, or a difficult situation. It doesn't matter what you choose, but focus on something that's meaningful to you.

In your mind's eye imagine what this "enemy" looks like, and take mental note of your emotions.

Now just imagine punching at this enemy. Don't move your hands; just imagine doing it in your mind.

As you throw this imaginary punch, I want you to consider the following questions and do so without judgment or editing. Let the answers be whatever they are. Be gentle and compassionate with yourself, but be honest.

- What emotions are you feeling?
- What are your feelings about? Your enemy? The punch? Yourself? Some or all or none of these?

If this seems too challenging, try selecting another difficulty in your life to focus on, but try again until you can build a clear picture of your feelings and what they're about.

You may find that most of your emotions are directed at your enemy. Maybe you have anger or rage that comes to the front.

Or perhaps your imaginary punch brings up feelings of fear or guilt at the very thought of standing up for yourself.

Whatever it is, even if it's uncomfortable, it's okay.

Your emotions can feel powerful and even overwhelming, but

they provide information about your journey and can even serve as a compass for your journey. So for now, simply see it and feel it without judgment or editing. Whatever it is, these are the elements that oppress, that keep you caged, stuck and mired.

This is your truth.

Take your truth in hand, your emotions about your enemy, yourself, your ability to fight, whatever is there, and own it by saying it out loud.

There is power in the sound of words and hearing the truth in your ear, so say it aloud and clear.

Now with the truth in your mind and heart, take your truth in hand and punch.

Punch with your powerful exhale. Hi-yah!

Punch *at* or *with* or *for* your truth.

Hi-yah!

Punch with emotion.

Punch with abandon.

Punch for yourself, for your revolution.

Hi-yah!

When you are all punched out, settle everything down and mentally note any shifts in how you feel—in your emotions, in your body, mind and spirit. Just sit with this for a few moments, and feel what it's like. For I oftentimes feel as if in a revolution or even a festival when I fight for myself or against an oppression.

The past few years a lot of women have been coming to my boxing classes, more women than men. These ladies range from stay-at-home moms to busy professionals, many are middle-aged or even retired. Most have never thrown a punch in their lives and have zero interest in entering the boxing ring. The first time they put on boxing gloves they feel nervous and shy about throwing their fist to hit anything. They're outside their comfort zone, but they go ahead and manage to get out a few wobbly thumps.

What's amazing to me is to see the transformation that comes over these women as they drive on in the classes and become comfortable with throwing a punch. There's just something about the experience of a physical visceral punch that changes them inside and out. Not only do their bodies become stronger, but their mind and spirits alight. Suddenly they are powerful! Taking swings at me, and hard, they're seeing with the eye of the tiger and are having the time of their lives. It's wonderful!

And this is the same transformation that happens to any hero that answers the call to fight for his or her self.

Even if you're afraid, or don't think you can, I promise that you'll quickly learn you can do more than you thought. With the forward momentum of a punch, you will breathe and live the natural pulsating flow of your power.

You will discover your old limits weren't real.

You will realize that life is full of possibility.

Freedom is possible.

Consider Your Fighting Style

The author of Les Misérables, Victor Hugo, once wrote, "Those who live are those who fight."

Few things in life will make you feel more alive than combat experience. Combat is one of the most friction filled experiences in the universe, and to me one of the most creative. Whether on a real battlefield of war or as a metaphor in your life, if you can get through and survive, the learning that is achieved is lifelong and amazing.

Survival, Evasion, Resistance, and Escape, otherwise known as SERE school to Recon Marines, is an intense two-week course in learning how to survive if lost or downed behind enemy lines and resisting interrogation if captured and tortured. A few days of academic studying in a classroom and then you're dropped, quite literally, into the middle of nowhere in the desert with nothing but your wits about you. No firearm, no food, no water—just your clothes, a knife, a compass, a map, and some parachute nylon and cord. Your mission is to survive off the land and evade being captured by the enemy while enroute to an objective destination.

I had been on the run for about six days with only grasshoppers, ants, deermoss, and a little bit of rabbit to eat, the equivalent of one single meal for six days. By the third day of oppressive heat with no sleep and traveling long distances while foraging for food and evading enemy detection, the real truth of character starts to come out. Fatigue, hunger, pain—these things can easily degrade what you think of as your humanity, or completely lay naked your true courage and lightness of being.

One day in captivity is worse than a hundred days on the run, a

As a young Marine.

thought I took very seriously and used all my skills and creativity to avoid enemy capture. However, in SERE school there's no such thing as not being captured because part of the training is for resisting interrogation and surviving as a prisoner of war. But I made it until the sirens signaled anyone not already caught to show themselves, and I was one of the last taken in.

Although I had heard all the rumors about how brutally realistic SERE was, I still wasn't prepared for what I saw when I came into the detention area. People being corralled and pushed around like cattle. Female pilots being degraded and struck and put face down in the dirt. Servicemen and women in bonds and being abused. It's one thing to see it in a movie; it's quite another to watch it happen in the flesh. Even if it isn't "real," the feel of a fist in your face is the same.

The "enemy" guards spoke with a Soviet accent, and one of them pulled me out of the truck, called me *spetznatz,* and punched me in the stomach. My blood immediately hit boiling and I was ready to lay him flat, but he had his AK-47 pointed at my head and told me to lie down in the dirt. In my cargo pocket was a knife, but it was taken from me as I was searched while one of the guards had his boot on my neck. I could take no more. When the guard released his boot from my throat, I jumped up with my hands now ziptied behind me, and I shoulder checked and swept my oppressor landing him with a thud on the ground. I then steadied myself for the fight to come. One guard came from behind with his rifle and two others wrestled with me from the front until I noticed a gun across my neck and the guard was steadily squeezing. I thought I was going to die fighting.

"So, *spetznatz*, you think you are Rambo? Me think I know how make you listen and behave," the senior guard said in a thick Russian accent.

I was expecting to next get bloodied in a bad beating. Instead the guard very nonchalantly brought out a very small, very weak air crewman. His eyes were like a frantic sheep about to be slaughtered. Three guards commenced kicking this serviceman in the stomach and legs until he fell to the ground. Then they picked him up and smashed him repeatedly in the face with thunderous blows from their hands. Next they took turns judo tossing and throwing this already defeated man, his eyes tearing as he screamed for them to stop, but the guards only laughed at him. And the beating went on.

My shame and anger at having started this fight because of my pride sickened me. I began to plead with them to stop. "Please stop hurting him, I beg you! I won't step out of line again I promise, just please stop."

In the sixth century BC, Sun-Tzu wrote *The Art of War*, one of the world's oldest books on military strategy. From millennia long ago, Sun-Tzu's words still ring true: "If you know the enemy and know yourself, you need not fear the result of a hundred battles. If you know yourself but not the enemy, for every victory gained you will also suffer a defeat. If you know neither the enemy nor yourself, you will succumb in every battle."

That day I succumbed in battle and my enemy prevailed. They knew me better than I did myself; they understood my flaws and motivations. They saw my weakness in my willingness to engage in the fight with violence, not with a balanced mindfulness. My passion to protect and defend was exploited as well. And when I could not protect that young serviceman, my self-esteem and pride were shamed. I was so easily defeated by my enemy, not by their guns, but by their psychology.

I'll never forget that little American flyer that was beaten because of my pride. But I am so grateful for the lessons I learned that day. For the rest of my SERE school training I was successful because I chose a new fighting style, one of brains and not brawn. I kept my head in the game and my willingness to keep on no matter what.

1st Recon Battalion sticker I illustrated.

Created and illustrated by Rudy Reyes

As a Marine, a martial artist, a boxer, and a kid who had to fight to survive on the street, I've thrown a lot of punches in my lifetime, but this stride of Fighting & Surviving isn't about hitting with your fist or getting physical. The hero's power and courage is not about violent aggression.

In fact, one of my greatest and most inspiring warrior heroes never threw a strike during his battles. He innately understood the wisdom in *The Art of War* when Sun-Tzu wrote, "To fight and conquer in all your battles is not supreme excellence; supreme excellence consists in breaking the enemy's resistance without fighting."

This warrior grew up cradled in the arms of his culture, even marrying at the age of thirteen in an arranged child marriage. He went to school and started a family in the traditions of his home, and only traveled abroad for his higher education and training as a barrister. Although he wasn't particularly religious growing up, as a young man he began studying the various religions and philosophies of the world, expanding his mental and spiritual horizons, and became a vegetarian. His life was relatively sheltered and safe, but all that changed when his law practice proved difficult to establish in his homeland of India, and he ventured to accept a position in a foreign country.

Upon traveling to his new job, Mohandas Gandhi was welcomed to South Africa with the harsh realities of the social and legal discrimination directed at Indians there in 1893. For the first time in his life, he witnessed and experienced firsthand the oppression of racism, prejudice, and injustice. Can't sit in first class, must give up your seat, must sanction yourself as less because someone else deems so, legislates so, says so, and says so with force or else.

From the depths of who he was as a human being, his natural instinct was to resist the oppression. His action was to fight for himself. While still en route to his new employment, he resisted and fought by simply refusing the oppressive actions of others, for which he was thrown from a train, beaten on a stagecoach, barred from hotels, and other hardships that Indians endured in South Africa at that time.

But he didn't stop and he never gave up. For the remainder of his life Mahatma Gandhi was a warrior that fought for others living under the yoke of tyranny and oppression, whether in South Africa or later in his home country of India. He became the Great Soul and practitioner of nonviolence and truth. His practice and advocacy of nonviolent civil disobedience eventually led an entire nation to courageously stand and fight with their hearts and truth to be counted as its own sovereign self. On numerous occasions he was imprisoned for many years for his actions, but he understood that even these were weapons in his arsenal of truth, and eventually India was emancipated from the British Empire to rule itself.

So to anyone that may feel a resistance to fighting for yourself because it feels violent or somehow bad, I gently respond with find and live your hero truth. Fighting in the sense of this Stride is not about aggression to harm and take from others, it is about having a warrior mindset of strength and power for standing in the aspirations you hold for yourself and others.

To someone that may always feel at the ready to physically fight for what they want, I respond with vigor to find and live your hero truth. Physicality can appear and feel very powerful, and there are cheers when a hero like Superman uses his tremendous strength to protect. But perhaps even because of such bodily prowess, a true hero must be vigilantly mindful to not be seduced by his or her own strength and the ease with which they could wield it as a weapon to violate and take from others, or to exact revenge. Remember, with great power comes great responsibility.

Do not worry that you may make mistakes in fighting for yourself. I've made and still make mistakes, and I promise you will too. And when you do, these will be valuable lessons to take forward to the next adventure. If you find and live the hero truth of who you are, the true path will open before you.

In popular culture the term "martial arts" is often thought of as the fighting systems from the Far East, such as kung fu, judo, or tae kwon do, but the term actually applies more broadly and refers to any combat system from around the world. Martial arts are literally the arts of war, with codified practices and traditions of training for combat. From sword fencing in Europe to the wrestling of Native Americans, martial arts is comprised of more fighting systems, techniques, and styles than one person could ever hope to even study in a lifetime. The beauty and fun of this is knowing there is an endless source of fighting forms to explore and draw from that will always be at the ready for your journey. And the same is true for fighting for yourself or against oppression in a non-military sense.

So stand up and fight for yourself, yes!

Stand up knowing you are forever the student of your life, learning new strategies and tactics in following the guidance of Gandhi to "be the change you wish to see."

And if a shadow of doubt comes, remember these words also from the Great Soul: "Men often become what they believe them-selves to be. If I believe I cannot do something, it makes me inca-pable of doing it. But when I believe I can, then I acquire the ability to do it even if I didn't have it in the beginning."

Breathe this in and feel it in your heart.

Believe in yourself.

Believe in your hero truth.

Stand up believing you are and will be the skilled fighter needed for your life, capable of protecting and defending, reaching and dreaming. Whether you've experienced life so far as a seasoned bat-tlefield warrior or someone who would never hurt a fly, the lessons of the hero's journey apply to us all as a process of finding and living our hero truth.

Stand up knowing that by fighting the good fight you will truly live.

Fighting on the Other Side

Similar to the medieval knights of Europe and their concept of chivalry, the Samurai were a class of warriors in feudal Japan who lived by a moral code called Bushido, or "Way of the Warrior." Bushido puts an emphasis on loyalty, self-sacrifice, justice, benevolence, love, frugality, martial arts mastery, and honor until death. Buddhism and Confucianism influenced Bushido in philosophy, and specific etiquettes were practiced in everyday life as well as in war to temper the violent warrior existence.

Courtesy of Reyes family

Practicing tai chi in Kansas City.

Among these the discipline of the Sword was balanced with the arts of the Tea Ceremony, Brush, Poetry, and Flower Arrangement. The Tea Ceremony demanded meticulous attention to detail and adherence to strict protocols of dress, equipment, venue, and style, all intended for creating a sublime aesthetic experience. The sensitivity of preparing the hot drink for royalty and peasants alike was an immersion in the action of serving and being gracious in that service role. In doing so, the feminine nature of this act helps to balance the masculine warrior energy and berserker violence of a man who also serves in battle.

I write this in a place of realization about my own warrior journeys. For most every inch of my life I had been on the Sword side of life, from surviving the rough and tumble craziness of my childhood to fighting for years as a Recon Marine in three war zones. I had no real concept of softness especially when it came to my self-concept and internal dialogue. I had no compassion at all for myself, and often others unless I was in a "service" role to them.

Sword and shield, grappling and striking, guns and gravestones, that was the world that I was always in. I was in a constant mode of survival trying to protect myself and armoring my heart. By the time I was done on the battlefields of the Middle East, I lost some of my love for myself. Maybe a lot of it.

The philosopher Friedrich Nietzsche scribed, "Whoever fights monsters should see to it that in the process he does not become a monster. And if you gaze long enough into an abyss, the abyss will gaze back into you."

As I was thrown home from the abyss of war, I felt its gaze upon me and it was terrifying. Of all places, the abyss found me in the parking lot of an ice cream parlor. My wife and I were headed there for some cool refreshment on a warm summer day, just a few short months after leaving the overamped hot zone of war in Ramadi, Iraq. Ramadi had been a nonstop vigilance of kill or be killed, of dangerous raids and go numb and watch your back.

Although home for awhile the effects of Ramadi and my two previous tours, for which there is no decompression chamber afforded our warriors reentering "nice" society, plus my marriage shakily on the rocks, and . . . well, I still felt on edge. Or more accurately I was hypervigilant, walking around in civilian clothes but really just a plainclothes weapon at the ready at anytime and anyplace to fight.

I pulled into the parking lot scanning the area for an open spot when I came upon a car parked right in front of me blocking my way. I thought, "This SOB is out of his mind! What is he doing blocking *my* way?! He is messing with the wrong man! Today's the day he learns a lesson!" My wife sitting next to me saw my crazy eyes and veins popping all over my arms and neck, and before she could stop me I was out the door and running to the car that had stopped my passage.

From the car ahead a father and son stepped out in complete shock at the Terminator rushing them. I was screaming that I am here to kill them, and inside I actually felt elation because with two of them maybe they would have some slim chance of surviving. Like I wanted still to be the "Good Guy" and fight an honorable fight . . . or maybe I was hoping that together they could destroy me and stop my madness. In retrospect I think it was probably a mixture of both.

I remember feeling my blood rage at the perceived insult along with a simultaneous self-loathing for stepping into the insane killer pace I was walking in that parking lot in Oceanside, California. The father and son were stepping away from their car and then running, but I wanted them to stay and fight so I could somehow feel it again. The fear and liberation of fighting or dying bathed in blood and adrenaline, complete fury and violence, but somehow with a strange calm because I felt I was master of the moment, master of the chaos.

But they would not fight!

My wife may as well have been a thousand miles away, because even though she had been screaming and begging me to stop— "Please, baby, don't hurt them! They didn't do anything! Please, you have to stop! PLLEAASE STOP!"—I didn't hear anything. I had target fixation and was in the zone of the fight because they had dared to block me in. The reality was in fact they hadn't blocked me in, but in my insanity I couldn't see that either.

Courtesy of Rudy Reyes

Badass.

When I finally gave up on the father and son returning to fight, I sat back inside my car feeling completely ashamed that I did not get to fight and hurt those people because they ran away. I was so angry and ashamed for not finishing my enemies, and I apologized to my wife for my failure.

Then I saw her face. The fear she had of me. The fear and uncertainty in her face because I was nothing at all like the man she fell in love with and married. Now I was a monster. And for the very first time I realized that I had left something out there on the battlefield. Years before I had wanted to protect my brothers, defend my friend Sean, and rescue little birds that fell from a nest. And now, after years of warrior adrenaline, my answer to fear and rage was to kill. I had gained so much power and knowledge through all of those firefights and missions, but I had lost something so important and precious. And now I was completely mad sitting in the parking lot of the ice cream parlor with my wife witnessing my descent into insanity.

She saw emptiness where my kind soul used to be. I now saw the emptiness in the reflection of her cream soda colored eyes. The abyss was gazing at me through those same eyes that years ago had promised me to stay by my side and love me forever. The same eyes I would never get back to.

"When valor preys on reason, it eats the sword it fights with," penned William Shakespeare.

My "valor" had puffed so large there was no room for reason to exist, and not only was it eating my sword it was swallowing me whole as well. All my life I was a warrior to protect and honor, but staring back at me now from the mirror was an image of all the enemies and oppressors that had so often beat and crushed and dehumanized me. I had become my darkest fears; I was now my own enemy.

I am thankful for the truth shown back to me in those eyes, even though it hurt and felt ugly. But it's what I needed to see to even have a chance at beginning to regain my balance.

As the weeks and months passed I went in search of my own versions of the Samurai's Tea Ceremony, Brush, Poetry, and Flower Arrangement practices, the feminine caring aspects of myself, and began my work in fighting my way back to a more balanced self.

"The ultimate tragedy is not the oppression and cruelty by the bad people but the silence over that by the good people." Martin Luther King Jr. said these words when talking about the civil rights movement and issues in society, but I think they apply just as well to the individual.

When you see yourself out of line in an act of oppression and cruelty, no matter how extreme or small, it becomes the responsibility of your hero self to speak up and stand for the right.

If you are fighting for revenge, find your hero.

If you are acting out of malevolence, avarice or greed, ask where is your hero.

If fighting for what you want feels more like the antics of a spoiled petulant child, as in Veruca Salt saying, "I want it now," in *Willy Wonka and the Chocolate Factory*, find your hero before you find yourself declared a bad egg.

Or if you're fighting simply to fight, or out of spite, to make yourself look tough, or even out of laziness. Go find your hero.

When you see yourself in such a situation, have your hero show up with compassion and kindness, generosity and love. Be fair and truthful as a friend would be.

Then take responsibility and move on to bring yourself back into your balanced hero self. Because that's what heroes do.

THE HERO'S WHETSTONE:
A BALANCED FIGHTER BE

The ability to balance is something people do every day as a regular part of life. In keeping your balance to stand or walk, you are continually processing inputs coming in from multiple senses, such as vision, perception of pressure, and the muscle system, all of this done automatically behind the scenes without even thinking about it. But add on a heavy backpack and step onto a balance beam or on rocks to cross a rushing stream, and suddenly you're fully engaged in an attentive way to keep your balance and not fall off.

If you were to imagine a man that only worked out and trained one arm and not the other for a boxing match, you would expect his abilities to perform in the ring to be severely compromised. In life, just as in the ring, it's important to pay mindful attention to maintaining a balance in many ways as a fighter.

As we begin this whetstone, I want to remind you to engage that part of yourself that is your friendly nonjudgmental self to act as a third-party observer. Also, keep in mind there are no right or wrong answers here; it's just your truth to use as information for your journey. Not to be used to harangue yourself or others. This is such a powerful tactic, I want to be sure it's remembered here.

Sit in a relaxed comfortable posture and take three deep centering breaths to begin this whetstone, inhaling deep through the nose into the belly, exhaling slowly through the mouth.

As you sit in this relaxed energy, remember your work in the previous whetstone, Breathe Your Flow of Power, where I asked you to think of a time, circumstance, or person, something in your life when you've felt beaten down, caged, or oppressed, and then did a breathing and punching exercise. Hi-yah!

Spend a moment to consider your reactions to moving through the exercise of that whetstone, as well as other situations in your life similar to the one you used in Breathe Your Flow of Power, where you have been faced with a submit or fight scenario. Hold these in mind while you consider the following questions with gentle truth and honesty.

- What pattern do you see in how you typically respond to moments when you feel oppressed, whether internal or from outside? Are you more likely to submit or fight? Is there a difference in your response to internal or external oppression?
- When you stand up for yourself, what is your style of

fighting? Are you aggressive? Passive? Angry? Logical? Silent? Loving? Compassionate? Argumentative? Quiet? Loud? Overbearing? Have a tantrum? Get physical?

As you consider the questions above, you may find obvious patterns that jump out at you, or that your responses may be different for various scenarios or times in your life. Whatever the answers are, see and feel them for what they are.

In Chinese philosophy, yin and yang are interconnected interdependent seemingly opposing natural forces in the world that are in a relationship of continual process of balance. Yin translates as "shady place" and yang means "sunny place," describing the play of sunlight over a mountain and in the valley. As the sun crosses the sky, yin and yang trade places with each other over the course of the day, revealing what was hidden and hiding what was revealed. The mountain always contains some of both aspects to varying degrees, with each side in perfect concert and unison with the other, information available to the whole about the balance between the two and the value of each.

In thinking of his inner balance between the aggressive nature of Sword and the softer characteristics of the Tea Ceremony, a samurai warrior may choose to devote more time to studying the craft of the discipline where he needs improvement or more experience. For instance, if he find himself more aggressive in his daily life, he may choose to immerse himself in the service of the Tea Ceremony, or vice versa if his martial spirit is low.

As you think of your style of fighting in responding to oppressive situations, would you be well served to become softer or harder in your approach? Or to change your approach completely? Would it be valuable to look more to the feminine or masculine side of yourself for more skills and tools in dealing with the challenges in your life? I invite you to consider writing your thoughts down or speaking them aloud as there is power in giving them a concrete voice.

Take this information and explore the myriad possibilities of alternative forms to utilize in fighting for yourself and others. Perhaps even take a boxing class if that puts you more in touch with your own power. Or study dance or volunteer to read to children if tapping into your softer side feels right. Discover new ways of communicating your needs and wants with others. I invite you to get creative and have fun with it.

Another important aspect to maintaining balance as a fighter is balancing your resources and assets when a heavy burden is added to your load, or when you realize there is a fight to be had in order to survive.

- In moments when you decide to fight, do you give yourself enough room and energy to pay mindful attention to what needs to be done?
- Do you typically feel overwhelmed? Or that you are too thinly stretched and everything suffers?

To be an effective fighter, to survive the trials of the day, we need to engage our hero wisdom to keep us well balanced and attuned for the journey. If you find yourself without the resources you need or feel overwhelmed, find and live your hero truth for taking care to lighten your load, or find more support, even talk with a friend, something that will improve your ability to stand up for yourself as needed.

I want to take a moment to recognize and honor the work you've done with the whetstones in this stride of Fighting & Surviving. No matter what has been revealed in this stride by looking at your hero truth, it is such wonderful information to inform you on your journey. Always treasure and use it as such.

No matter your circumstance, the hero's path is always and ever, eternally here to call upon.

We all have the seed of hero inside as part of our cosmic makeup, always available to fight for the right.

The opportunity is always available right here right now to start where you are and make a difference.

As always you are a hero.

Fight to be the hero you wish to see.

STRIDE 4
Tools & Skills

The feeling: "Instead of fighting and resisting my obstacles, perhaps I should treat them as new sources of information for me. Maybe there's a way to use my mind, body, and emotional life to create new possibilities."

Knowing what's needed for your journey is a first requisite for determining where to focus your time and resources and what to pack in your toolkit. You must have wisdom for knowing what to do next, skill to know how to do it, and virtue to do it.

The ability to learn and do something well, with expertise, may come easily as a natural talent or take years of study to master, but I say that in your knowing what to do next, you should not deter you from giving it all you've got, no matter the course of time or outcome.

As a young man always fighting to protect myself and my brothers, I was in awe of the warrior ethos and studied my martial arts with committed reverence and abandoned passion. I was always at the discipline of pushing my body and skills, open to all comers as a test to find the warrior truth of my capabilities, and in most instances I found myself victorious in a match.

Courtesy of Reyes family

Practicing Shaolin kung fu.

While in my early twenties, I was invited to train with a Shorin Ryu karate master, Joe Roberts. His raspy New York baritone voice led the cadence with passion and vigor in "Make Punch!" and "Make Kick!" We would train outside in the bitter cold of a Kansas City November, and the guttural kiais rang out across the expanse as we did our calisthenics and practiced bunkai, a body-hardening technique from Japan that the Okinawans engaged in to prepare themselves for battle against the technologically superior samurai.

With his deep-set eyes and a developed and defined torso, at the age of thirty-seven, Joe was still the physical epitome of a fighting warrior. Trading front kicks to the solar plexus and smashing shins and fists with this "Iron Man" brought my mind into focus beyond pain, beyond the weather, the bunkai ritual was a pedestal on which to put my toughness, pride and perseverance for all to see. For Joe to see, and feel, and absorb, as he vigorously but compassionately returned the favor threefold.

As sweat poured and steamed away, we began to strike in a more organic and purposeful way, and I danced and hit him to the head and body. He remained composed, but seemed half asleep. Ha! I was winning! The old steel warrior could not escape my blows. Another punch and I overreached. And then paid for it.

Joe who was composed and patient then seized the moment and exploded a back kick that knocked me down and literally took my breath away. All of those strikes and punches I threw and not one sealed victory. While Joe with the act of one mind, one action manifested a mule kick to my abdomen that was as astonishing as it was effective. I lay on the concrete in pain and prideful silence.

Who was this man? What was his secret? Joe Roberts, the man of living steel, had a magic, a power that was beyond technique. Was it fearlessness? Was it intelligence? Over the next year I befriended and dutifully listened to Joe tell tales of cold black oceans and impossible cliff assaults, paratrooping with over two hundred pounds of equipment out of a helicopter into the dead of night. I could smell the brine of the sea as I listened to his stories of the brave and the bold.

Joe was a warrior of the highest class. He was something called Recon. He had been in the military's special operations forces of the United States Marines, but during peacetime in the mid-1990s he was a Zen fighting machine with nothing to do but train young martial artists. So I trained and listened and dreamed. I dreamed of whether I had what it takes to be like him, a special operations warrior with unlimited power and possibility. I was spellbound to the mystery and mystique of his world, and I knew that I wanted to make his world mine. My path was set.

Soon I was talking with my wife about joining the U.S. Marine Corp. The proving ground of the few, the proud, and for me, the ultimate test of warrior mettle. I told her about my dreams of joining Amphibious Reconnaissance like my hero Steve, but she kissed me and laughed. "Baby, you can't swim and you don't like cold water!" she said.

She had been a competitive swimmer her whole life and would sometimes go to the pool with me in Kansas City, where, being the competitive stubborn young man that I was, I would challenge her to a swimming contest. At which she skunked me, every time. Whether it was freestyle or backstroke or butterfly swim, it seemed I was almost swimming backward compared to her. Because I was a bigmouth and couldn't handle being beaten by a girl, I would even try a test of just treading water in order to win. But no, she held her hands out of the water and I almost drowned because I couldn't outlast her.

So needless to say her confidence in my aquatic abilities was absolutely nil . . . but for good reason!

We were at her parents' home in Nebraska and it was in the cold of October. My wife jokingly said, "Okay, if you were really serious about the Marines, you would go jump in the lake behind the house right now and swim across."

A challenge . . . I see! Well, I ran outside, stripped down to my underwear, and jumped in! It was so cold it took my breath away and my mind was just panicking, but I knew if I showed weakness to my wife she would never believe me about how serious I was— and I was serious. So I started pulling my arms and kicking my feet, and somehow I was moving to the other side of that freezing lake. I would not be stopped, and that was that.

Next thing you know, I had joined the Marine Corps and was soon on my way to boot camp.

I had no intention of immediately trying out to be a Recon Marine because as you may imagine I did not feel confident in my swimming abilities. My plan was to stay in a year or two before trying so I could have a better shot at making it with the benefit of improving my swimming skills over time. But after distinguishing myself and being meritoriously promoted in Marine Corps boot camp and the School of Infantry, I was given the opportunity to try out. My newfound buddies were shouting, "Reyes can do it!" so I felt compelled against my own self-doubts to give it my best and not turn away.

While I was often the strongest and fastest participant when it came to running and pull-ups and sit-ups and more, my lack of swimming skills was weighing heavy on my chances. I could make it across a pool, but I had no idea if I could make it through the water tests of Recon. Swimming, and swimming expertly, was a skill I needed for my journey. Without it, I wouldn't be able to continue on successfully. So I started spending all my off time at the pool training as hard as I could, all the while scared because it seemed the harder I trained, the slower and more exhausted I got. But I kept on driving.

The day of the physical fitness test, after miles and miles of running, sit-ups, pull-ups, and bunny hops through obstacle courses of walls and bars, I was the first initiate to arrive at the pool and was twenty minutes ahead of the others with time to rest—and time to mull over the next phase. There, all geared up in cammies and with my rifle in hand, I made the jump into the pool below from the top of a thirty-foot tower.

Perhaps it was my sheer will or general physical conditioning, but I think somehow the hours I had spent training on my own over the past month must have garnered me just enough swimming skills to in the end be one of only a handful of men out of an original fifty Marines to make it into Recon that day. I survived the underwater attacks from divers and passed other arduous water tests, and then ran the next seven miles in pure elation at the thought of crossing that finish line to be welcomed into the fold of Recon. As I crossed over I felt I was born anew with tears of joy inside to be part of a family I had never had or known, because I had shown them, myself, and everyone in creation that I was trainable and courageous.

I wasn't the fastest swimmer; in fact, I was often dead last on my times. But from then on I didn't worry about it and just kept right on training and learning more, and within two years I excelled as an expert swimmer who often was even the fastest and strongest.

Knowing what you want to do next, and then acquiring the skills and tools required for the journey keeps life an ever-expanding adventure. Even though it may seem impossible or overwhelming to think of learning new skills, or that it will take a lot of effort and time, it doesn't matter.

Assuming you have realistic expectations and a willingness to remove limits and push beyond, you will find the success of an adventurous quest. For instance, I will never be a heavyweight boxer, a horse jockey, a sumo wrestler, or a mother, because I simply don't have the physique for those things. My friend has always wanted to be a rock star, but he is completely tone deaf and sixty-three years old, so it is probably unreasonable to expect he will be the next Prince. No matter how much I want to have feathers and fly, wishing I were a bird won't make me one.

Being real with your circumstances and who you are while holding onto your dreams and aspirations in a balanced equilibrium will provide the natural compass point for the direction of what to do next. And once you know what you are doing, determining the skills and tools needed for your quest is the next evolution on the hero's path.

Lay Down Your Arms

Searing pain wrested me from falling asleep. As I lay in bed next to my wife and put my hands behind my head to doze off, a hot-blooded fury started to chew away at the fibers of my front and medial deltoid muscles. They felt like strained steel cables aching away as if frayed and rusted.

It was the same shoulder that had been torn during wrestling practice while I was a freshman in high school. A senior heavy-weight wrestler had taken me down on the mat and I tried to turn onto my belly but only my right arm made it around. Next thing I knew fire and pain were shooting through my right arm and neck, but I kept wrestling, and as the match went on the fire in my arm got so bad I almost expected to see flames.

In bed and under darkness as I brought my arm alongside my body it felt as though bruised and the purple ache was excruciating. Had I injured it while power lifting and swimming earlier that afternoon? I hadn't noticed anything at the time, and I couldn't think of another incident during the day that could have caused such an injury.

Pooled in the tenderness of my right limb, my mind racing to diagnose the reason, my thoughts turned to the last few years. It was only two weeks since returning home from my last tour of duty in Iraq, mere days since putting down my rucksack and gun of war. During my Recon schooling, I had trained as a scout sniper so in the field would spend hours upon hours upon days and weeks and years with a heavy gun almost surgically attached to my right arm. Endless carrying and hoisting and trigger pulling, firing and battling on and on, and I was left wondering if my Gun Arm was rebelling against its retirement from serving as a fighting machine.

Out of my wonderment I thought of all the fighting and punching and struggling I had been doing my whole life. In that moment a realization washed over me that my shoulders had always hurt. A lifetime of lifting thousands of pounds like a demon possessed. Years of navigating arduous obstacles on the battlefield, in school, and at home, no matter the pain, I just kept driving on.

Now lying awake aching next to my wife to whom I was completely numb, I suddenly felt alone and lost in my injury. I felt abruptly transported to images of that man touching me inside my underwear at eleven, my grandfather beating me with his skinny belt, and all my feelings of shame for being discarded as a child, along with feeling abandoned and a failure in my marriage. Those shames made me hide away deeper into my hero visions of strength and power.

As all came crashing into the abyss, I began to see that I was a very adept ignorer. I ignore and survive. Fight and survive. Fight with brute brawn and strength and incredible fury to drive on. Just keep lifting those weights, just keep punching and kicking that bag, just keep shooting that sniper system and erasing those targets from humanity. The slave master of my workouts and actions and mission to just fight and struggle and make myself fearsome, and it would be okay. The vigilant guard with my Gun Arm at the ready, my weapon engaged to dominate any firefight and destroy any who opposed me. Just pack on more muscle and I would not be hurt anymore, but all the while the purple hate rotating inside that shoulder joint just stayed inside.

All of the fear of being abused and controlled and discarded had compelled me to strengthen and discipline my mind and body into an outward appearance of the strong and invincible. But at the root were my fear and vulnerability paling inside. Had I been in a

Courtesy of Rudy Reyes

Deployed at war with my assault gun.

foreign land with weapons and destruction and killing energy because as a warrior I felt safe and not like the eleven-year-old boy in
south Texas? Is that what I became on the outside to protect that
little boy on this inside? I would go as far as to arm and armor myself to destroy other enemies and sometimes their families?

I don't believe those were the only reasons I became a fighter
and a Marine, but that's what my mind laid before me that night as
a possibility to consider. A clear vision of destroying in order to
protect myself in an endless loop of hurting others so no one can
hurt me, all along guarding my pain like a little wolf holding a paw
up after being injured in a trap. But in reality I had never healed;
instead I just made my other limbs super strong. But that little paw

stayed bloody and wounded. I was just so ashamed and scared of being the weak and hurt boy that I focused on strength and toughness and even violence to protect me. All these years I had been protecting the little wolf's paw with my Gun Arm at the ready for fear of being attacked or perceived as vulnerable. All this time my arm and shoulders had been sending me physical pain and suffering so I could look at my emotional pain, but instead I just ignored it out of shame for why I was hurting.

Finally, at last, there in the stillness of night, I saw how the roots of my desperate and cold fears had eventually become twisted from being too long in the fight.

Away from the sounds of grenades blasting and bullets flying, I finally heard the loud quiet alarm from my arm ripe with emotional gangrene signaling that this cycle had run beyond its use into the negative space of ultimately destroying my light and love.

I was now asking, "Who is my enemy? What am I fighting?"

Friend or Foe?

Even in the midst and chaos of all out war, the line between enemy and friend can surprisingly blur and shift.

"We can hardly believe that we've been firing at them for the last week or two—it all seems so strange. At present it's freezing hard and everything is covered with ice . . . There are plenty of huge shell holes in front of our trenches, also pieces of shrapnel to be found. I never expected to shake hands with Germans between the firing lines on Christmas Day." An unknown British soldier wrote this in a letter home recounting the events in a war torn field near Ypres in Belgium during Christmas in 1914.

Early on in a war that would criss-cross a continent with miles upon miles of trenches and millions of soldiers dead, troops from German and British forces in WWI met on a quiet battlefield in Belgium as artillery in the region ceased fire and soldiers sang

"Silent Night," exchanged gifts, and drank together. The breathing spell of this unofficial truce also allowed both sides to bring back their fallen comrades who were then buried with respects paid by soldiers from both sides of the battle.

When down in the trenches of life or fighting the yoke of oppression, it can seem easy and natural to view the other side as enemy. Often the face of the opposition is filled with hate or they may seek to harm or cause trouble. It may perhaps feel impossible to see this enemy in any other way, and it may even be appropriate when artillery is still pounding or mustard gas is in the air.

To prevent more "Christmas truce" occurrences during World War I, the higher levels of the military ordered artillery bombardments on future Christmas Eves, and began to rotate troops through various sectors to prevent them from becoming familiar with the enemy. Despite such efforts, during the Christmas of 1915, as French and German troops were holding positions in a French mountain range, out of nowhere another truce spontaneously unfolded.

"When the Christmas bells sounded in the villages of the Vosges behind the lines . . . something fantastically unmilitary occurred. German and French troops spontaneously made peace and ceased hostilities; they visited each other through disused trench tunnels, and exchanged wine, cognac and cigarettes for Westphalian black bread, biscuits and ham. This suited them so well that they remained good friends even after Christmas was over."

This account was given by Richard Schirrmann, a German soldier who pondered the incident and wondered whether "thoughtful young people of all countries could be provided with suitable meeting places where they could get to know each other." In 1919, after the war was over, Schirrmann went on to found the nationwide German Youth Hostels Association in support of those inspired aspirations.

General Colin Powell said, "No battle plan survives contact with the enemy." When these words are taken in relation to an account such as the "Christmas truce," they can take on even deeper meaning than the original context, implying a myriad of possibilities for evolutions in both battle plans and enemies as they play out and inform their interrelated interconnected dance.

The same is true in each person's battles of life. As you fight your battles, it is important to stay open and flexible to the possibility for change and remain grounded in the reality of the moment. Such an ability becomes a powerful skill and tool for your journey. Are you just surviving as you throw punches? Is your enemy even there anymore? What is your mission? Are you there to destroy or defeat or defend against your enemy? Or do you have another purpose? If things cool off and settle into a moment of truce, do you sometimes have an internal battle commander that wants to keep the fight raging, ordering artillery assaults to fuel the fire? Is your enemy still the foe, or have they set down their arms and now come bearing gifts? Have you been too long in the fight?

No matter what the original plan or initial response in a fight, simply by engaging in the motion of battle any well laid plans or reactions will inevitably play themselves out with the passing of time, requiring that we pay mindful attention to "be here, be now," "be here, be now," in a constant vigilance to maintaining relevance to the present situation.

There are also times when the dynamics of a fight seem to have altered that we must consider whether it's the battle or enemy that has changed, or if instead we ourselves are the agent of transformation or shifted direction.

When I first met Logan he said he was a shell of the man he once was, and he appeared emaciated not only in body but also in mind and spirit. Long before our acquaintance, he had gone through a painful process of falling out of love during a bad breakup with a girlfriend, during which he had fallen in with the "wrong crowd" and was now several years into dependency on alcohol and some very bad street drugs, addicted to the numbing agents for his aching heart. Along the way he had lost his job, estranged his family, and the friends who had tried to pull him from the precipice as he jumped into the dark abyss while yelling for them to come along. They said no to his invitation and helplessly watched him sink away.

Now somehow one day he happened into one of my boxing classes. He was unsure about himself, but he seemed to be looking for something to hit. Perhaps somehow something inside was aching to get out through the fog of his drugged haze and gasp a breath of clarity. Whatever it was, he started training regularly, and as the months rolled by he gained new skills for the ring, his body put on muscle and showed some definition, and where there was once a weak and flabby punch a solid hammer of a hit began to land hard.

This focus on improving his physical skills somehow became a watershed of transformation into other areas of his life, and at one point he confided, "I don't know how or when it happened exactly, but one day I realized that it had been a week since I had a cocktail or popped a pill. Then a friend I regularly partied with stopped by with a new batch of 'fun' to try, but before I knew what was happening I was yelling at him to get out of my house. Suddenly I saw my 'friend' as an enemy to my newfound clarity. I started shaking, but right then and there I picked up the phone and dialed a guy I had been close to years earlier. He was an old friend that one day when I was drunk had dared to say something to me about drinking so much, so I had yelled at him to get out of my house and I dubbed him an enemy and hadn't spoken to him since. Now all at once I understood it wasn't either of them that had changed from friend to enemy to friend . . . it was me. My desires and perspective had changed and in a flash my reference for defining my enemies had altered as well."

In the comic books superheroes and their arch villains eternally do battle in a black and white world of good and evil as each maintains their fixed archetypal position. In "real" life people and circumstances are multi-faceted and dynamic with shades of gray everywhere. When you are clear about the foundation of who you are and your own hero's journey, how to discern who is friend or foe becomes naturally clear.

In both Latin and Greek the word "friend" is closely related to the term for "I love," so quite literally a friend is someone we relate to with love. We think of someone as friendly when we share love for a cause or feel supported, when we have mutual feelings of affection, or are allied together in a struggle, with each friendship being built on its own relational foundation.

When it seems that a friend isn't being friendly anymore, it may be time to find your hero truth for rooting out the cause of such change. Who or what is shifting in the foundation of that relationship? The friend? Or you? Are they being a "good friend" by telling you a hero truth you don't want to hear? Or have they truly crossed the line into enemy territory where they now want to cause harm or impede your own hero's journey?

If you find you are wavering outside of the hero's path as your own enemy, thank your friend for their reminder to return to your hero truth.

In the event your friend has shifted their journey in another direction, thank them for walking with you during your time together and wish them well on their travels as they go their own way.

To anyone that is hostile or intends you harm or trouble, consider the possibilities for how you stay in the fight via this question posed by Abraham Lincoln, "Am I not destroying my enemies when I make friends of them?"

Even when an enemy remains fixed in their villain position of hostility or harmful intentions, instead of continuing in your own rigid stance of bitter resistance, consider making a shift to find the value and gifts of the relationship, perhaps even a friendly relation.

Consider the value in doing so.

The ability to give space to any relationship and interaction is a powerful skill to craft and hone.

The hero uses the obstacles and challenges gifted by his enemies as tools in their journey of self-discovery and development. In doing so, the hero finds newfound skills and strengths. And for this the hero is in humble gratitude.

THE HERO'S WHETSTONE: HONORING YOUR ENEMY

In his study of martial arts, Bruce Lee learned that fighting and combat is a living thing that at its root is relationship not conflict. Just as there is an interconnected interdependent relationship between yin and yang that ebbs and flows over the course of time, there is a similar living breathing dynamic between a fighter and an enemy.

Lee once said, "To know oneself is to study oneself in action with another person." It is the gift of more self that is offered by interacting with others, be they friend or foe. In this regard, an enemy is a benefactor of opportunities for knowing yourself better and in ways that would not be possible otherwise.

With the sound of *Hi-yah,* the powerful exhale or kiai relates to the projection of your own energy, or ki. Similar to kiai, the concept of *aiki* relates to the coordination of your energy with the energy of your attacker. The two terms use the same kanji character simply transposed, and are thought of as the inner and outer aspect of the same principle.

Aikido is a Japanese martial art meaning "the Way of unifying with life energy" or "the Way of harmonious spirit." It focuses on the use of one's ki through kiai in defending oneself, while employing the principles of aiki to also protect the attacker from injury by blending the motion of the aggressor and redirecting the force of the attack.

As one of the martial art ancestral masters Takeda Tokimune, explained, "Aiki is to pull when you are pushed, and to push when you are pulled. It is the spirit of slowness and speed, of harmonizing your movement with your opponent's ki. Its opposite, kiai, is to push to the limit, while aiki never resists." The opposing forces are perpetually informing and affecting one another in a dance of movement while still in full power of motion.

At the beginning of a fight in a formal combat sport, it is common for the opponents to bow to each other, as well as to the space in which the match will take place. With a bow they signify respect to the other for entering into a contest of learning about oneself, recognizing there would be no opportunity for exploration or glory without an opponent there to provide resistance as they mutually participate in a dance of pushing personal limits in a chance for discovery and growth.

Another instance of bowing is in relation to being flexible in the moment. As my consummate hero and father figure Bruce Lee said, "Notice that the stiffest tree is most easily cracked, while the bamboo or willow survives by bending with the wind." The ability to bow with strong winds that gust and bluster during a storm, to be flexible in our approach to life's challenges and opponents, brings life and living to the hero's path.

By bowing a hero shows gratitude and respect for the opportunity gifted by their opponent.

With heads lowered there is reverence for the moment.

A hero is fully present in "be here, be now" engaging an opposing force with flexibility for both to cocreate a moment of possibility and discovery and learning without limits.

As with other whetstones we've done, let's again start with three deep breaths to relax and focus the mind and body. Breathe in slowly and deeply, pulling air in using your abdominal muscles, then exhale gently through the mouth. Take another inhalation with a focus on opening the mind, and breathe out any stress the mind is holding. Allow your body to let go of any tensions and slip into a relaxed state.

Also check in and find your friendly self, taking special care to maintain a space inside of third-party observer. That place where judgment is suspended.

Now take a few moments to think of a time, circumstance, or person, something in your past when you've felt beaten down, caged, or oppressed, and you faced the enemy and fought for yourself. It can be from any time in your life, long ago or last week, something big or small; simply choose something that's meaningful to you.

Whatever this fight was, from a physical altercation to a battle with addiction or an internal war with a looping voice beating you down, in your mind's eye imagine what your opponent looked like and revisit the nature of your fight. Allow yourself to settle into the experience of that fight without attaching to the emotions of those moments. Maintain a third-party observer position.

Now I want you to consider the following questions, and do so with creativity and a spirit of adventure. Even have fun exploring your answers. Whatever your answers, it's okay, no matter if they make you laugh or cry or just think.

- How did you feel about your opponent when you decided you would fight? How do you feel about them now? What are the differences?
- What has changed in you or the opponent since the beginning of the fighting engagement?
- Even if this opponent remains hostile to this day, imagine you are friends, and consider if there are characteristics they possess that you respect or admire.
- Can you see or imagine something about your opponent's situation that accounts for their position of hostility? If the hostility had not been directed at you, would you possibly understand or have compassion?
- Is there any humor to be found in the experience?
- Did you learn something about yourself through this experience? Did you gain or improve any skills?
- Even if it seems minor, what are you thankful for from this experience?

Often an enemy may be demonized as a static unchanging person with whom we primarily battle, like the Joker is to Batman. But in fact, people and our relationships with them are dynamic. It may even be our closest loved ones that present our greatest "enemy" moments, and in turn offer the most information and opportunities for knowing ourselves by watching how we interact, how we contend for space or what we want, how we care for the other person or ourselves or not in the course of the fight.

And that's okay. It's okay to show up with your truths and contend for them. Not in an action of violence and aggression, and knowing that the other person may not do or give or provide or accept, and if that's the case, we must accept and respect that. But it's okay to fight and contend; it's essential and elemental to life. It's learning how to contend with integrity and compassion that brings an honoring to your truth and for your enemies for revealing and gifting more to you.

Even if thinking of an adversary with a literal gun, or a voice inside your head that loops negativity, no matter the opponent or your original perceptions, as the fight wears on, alternative points of view and fresh assessments are always available. To the extent that we can view and honor our enemies as the bringers of gifts, we create a space of learning, an attitude of adventure and discovery, and opportunities for a possibility of more than we thought. Perhaps even a chance for discovering more of your self or moving your limits for being able to understand or feel compassion, even find forgiveness, or maybe even find a friend.

Even if this seems unobtainable, rash, or silly, or that you would be letting down your guard or letting them off the hook, or perhaps you have hurt feelings or still want them to pay. If you are still in a space where you want to get back at your enemy, consider these words from the author and poet Oscar Wilde: "Always forgive your enemies. Nothing annoys them more."

Wherever you are at is okay, simply sit for a few moments with your thoughts and emotions, and observe your observations with interest and curiosity.

Now take your observations, whatever they are, and find at least one thing from this experience for which you are grateful. If you find more, that's great, but find at least one, and see it as an object in your hand. It can look like anything, whatever you want, big or small, light or heavy, bright or dull; it's up to you.

In your mind's eye see your opponent again; see them in front of you. Now take your object of gratitude and place it between you and the opponent, or even offer it to them to take.

Feel the emotions that may come in doing so, and observe them.

Now speak aloud the words "thank you."

If you're comfortable, even physically bow with respect and honor, but say "thank you" aloud and hear it in your ear.

If you're so inclined you can even take this a step farther in a spirit of adventure and humility. Actually tell your opponent "thank you" for real, in person, on the phone, in a letter. Tell them and see what happens.

Even if nothing happens between you, even if there's no response, or a response you were not expecting or hoping for, it doesn't matter. What does matter is what happens inside of you.

No matter what, you know your self better.

No matter what, you are in discovery of newfound skills and tools.

You are in a place of honor.

Honoring your enemy for the gifts on your journey.

Honoring the hero's adventure.

Honoring your self.

The Toolkit of Skills and Tools

As a Recon Marine working in the field behind enemy lines I would carry my equipment that was best suited for the mission. There were the basic tools required for any expedition, such as protection and nourishment for my body, and then special weapons and gear needed dependent on whether the mission was a parachute insertion, long-range reconnaissance patrol, or a combatant diver operation from miles out in the cold ocean. I had to pack the right gear in order to assure the best chance for mission success.

Whether on the battlefield or in civilian life, learning to see one's enemies and obstacles as opportunities for discovery and growth is an important skill to have in your toolkit. It is one of many skills you may need for your journey.

In answering the call to adventure, it may at times feel that you have crossed the threshold only to be swallowed into an abyss of the unknown. In this new world it is important to continually assess and develop skills and acquire tools needed for the adventure, and not give up or settle back into the old habits of stagnation.

When we are skillful at something, we are knowledgeable and efficient at achieving predictable results. Our skills can be general in their nature, such as being a good leader or team player, or more specific, such as playing an instrument or baking bread or other tasks needed to perform a certain job. Some skills come easily, while others may seem beyond our reach of perceived limits.

The hero's toolkit contains skills as well as other devices needed to facilitate certain work. For instance, a dragon slayer may need a sword, or an author may require a pen, while everyone needs basic tools for acquiring food and shelter. Of all the skills and tools one can possess, I believe the most important and powerful are the ones that we all have at our disposal every moment of every day, every one of us. Those of Mind, Body, and Spirit.

Simply by existing here on planet Earth in the human form, you have in your possession an ultimate instrument for experience and exploration. Sometimes we may overlook them, but they are by definition, by default, always there. Right at this moment you are scanning this page with your senses and integrating this into your stream of consciousness, along with other information you are sensing from your environment right here, right now. Perhaps there are sounds or smells or other sights to behold in your purview. Are you aware of what they are?

It can sometimes be all too easy to tune out what we are feeling or sensing, especially when something seems unpleasant, but in doing so we are limiting our information and tools available to use along the path. Anytime this happens, we diminish our toolkit and may fall prey to our own devices—or as the father of humanistic psychology, Abraham Maslow, said, "It is tempting, if the only tool you have is a hammer, to treat everything as if it were a nail."

Although they may be discussed or even thought of as separate, the Mind, Body, and Spirit are never disconnected or independent from each other. We may feel or think we are out of touch with one facet of our self at times, but there really is no such thing as an experience or moment where any aspect is out of the loop. Mind, Body, and Spirit are always an integrated whole.

When we feel disconnected or out of relationship with any component of Mind, Body, or Spirit, those elements are not missing, we are simply out of balance or out of touch and are, in fact, affecting the whole system, often bringing it down.

A young woman, Nicole, started coming to my workout classes wanting to lose the extra weight she had put on during her first few years of marriage. Although they had been active growing up, as an adult she and her husband, Patrick, had both fallen into the routine and trap of "get up, go to work, come home, relax, go to bed," and then doing it all over again the next day, not making time or caring to move and nourish their bodies.

This very quickly spiraled down to manifest not only in the extra physical weight, but also the internal weight of an eroding self image and feeling unhappy. Nicole felt poorly about herself because she was out of shape and overweight, and Patrick would feel angry because there was nothing he could do to make her feel better, so they circled around each other in a mutually bound cage of samsara.

As Nicole described, "The losing battle of gaining control of my body and eating habits was bringing me down. I felt trapped by my negativity. I would sabotage myself each time I would start any sort of progress. Voices in my head were saying, 'I am not seeing any immediate results, so why even bother! It's over; I've lost what I was, so I am stuck with what I am now! I hate who I am inside and out.' I was afraid of failing, of not being good enough. I was afraid of embarrassment."

"But as I showed up for the class, showed up for myself, and kept going even when I felt like I couldn't go on, I learned not to make excuses for myself, which turned out to be the key to my prior self-sabotage. After the first week of intense training and nutritional way of eating, I knew this is what I had needed for so long and my body finally committed to permanent change."

The beauty and reality of giving a balanced focus to each aspect of Mind, Body, and Spirit is that all are naturally buoyed up or brought down by our focus and actions. Nicole answered the call to fight for herself and set her mind to show up for class, giving herself the gift of moving her body with purpose. As she took action with her body, the very act of doing so also fed back and informed her mind and spirit of her true potential. And in stepping into her true potential, living her hero truth, the weight lifted from her heart and melted from her body.

Nicole went on to say, "I was given the tools to become the best me I can be. One major benefit has been to have my husband who is my best friend and life partner, go through this journey with me. It has saved each of us as individuals and saved our marriage. I have learned how capable, smart, strong and sexy I am. I have learned how to love myself. I have learned how to overcome obstacles and never give up. I have become a Hero by saving myself from the self destructive course I was on!"

Buddha once said, "It is a man's own mind, not his enemy or foe, that lures him to evil ways."

In Nicole and Patrick's case, it was their laxity of mind that led the way to their eventual loss of bodily condition and strength, turning the entire system into something that felt like an enemy entrapping them from happiness. But just as we can shift our perception of an enemy from one of fear and hostility to one of honor and appreciation, we can be mindful of our mind and use it as a tool by nourishing it with the positive and short-circuiting those negative loops that lure us down into self-destructive thoughts and behavior.

I, Rudy Reyes, have been fully engaged with my physicality every day of my whole life. Beyond muscle and sinew, I rely on my senses and emotional life to be in the here and now with awareness and a feeling of power and control in my circumstances.

Sometimes people look at me and figure I'm just a big muscle head who spends all his time in the gym lifting weights. What they're missing is the real story and essence, the real "secret" of my performance and success. They see a body of flesh and blood and bone, but that is just one way of looking at it.

When I work out and train, I am actually training more than my body. I may lift some weights, but more importantly I become fully immersed in the process and completely give myself over to being present in the moment of right here right now, and focus on breaking through limits and exploring possibility. For me, the experience is actually more spiritual than physical. I learn things about myself by doing. Those things inform my mind. And when my mind is right, my body follows and I feel and can do more. And when I fully engage in the experience of living in possibility, my spirit is free.

In fact, one of the best workouts I ever had in the gym was when my girlfriend broke up with me. I was crazy in love and she used to work out with me at the gym, boxing, swimming and lifting weights, and then kissing each other all sweaty and laughing. So after hearing the news that she was leaving town and me, I was devastated and hurting. I wanted to cry as all my energy just fell out of my body and my mind, and my stomach was a pit.

Instead I gathered myself together and went to the gym. I put on my favorite motivational song and got the drums and guitar blasting in my ears. I focused on really feeling the depression of sadness in my chest and heart, and then imagined all the bad flow-ing through my body into my arms and out of my hands.

I took hold of those big weights and started pressing and feel-ing the pressure of three hundred pounds. Using my pain as fuel I engaged and pressed the weight effortlessly. I kept pushing my arms like pistons and contracting my chest hard and with power, and the weight moved off of me repeatedly. I was now in the zone. I was now competitive and the fuel of pain was turning into the beautiful possibility of ACTION!

I was making a shift. I became a u-joint for the bad that was coming in by turning it to good coming out. My heart and my guts were sad and hurting and I wanted to just curl up in bed and feel sorry for myself. But as the great Helen Keller said, "Self-pity is our worst enemy and if we yield to it, we can never do anything wise in this world."

So with one consideration, one suggestion, one stride, I flipped on my favorite weight-lifting song and got positive energy moving first inside, then I let it manifest outside. The energy that started as pain and limitation and "what if" turned into a power of positive action. I used the fuel with no judgment and instead just made a hot fire of possibility.

My brain was firing the neurons, my body was sweating and breathing, but my heart was beating with personal power. In so moving I was proud of my lift and happy that I was pulling myself up from my bootstraps to new heights that at one time seemed impossible.

In doing so, my body became a tool for me to use in managing my world and experiences and perceptions. It is the Mind, Body, and Spirit performing in concert together that is the essential in-gredient to being fit and balanced inside and out to make the very most of your life's journey.

Beyond the physical senses such as sight, hearing, and taste, I use my emotions as a gauge and barometer to inform a wide variety of feelings, thoughts, and behavior. Like the voices in your head that can seem to loop endlessly and without your bidding, it can sometimes feel as if emotions happen on their own or are beyond your control. But in fact, they too can be used as skills and tools in your toolkit as well.

I think of my variety of emotions as a big set of tuning forks. Each one resonates on a certain wavelength and corresponds to a particular emotion. From sadness to joy, fear to ecstasy, happiness, embarrassment, guilt, and everything in between and beyond, there is a tuning fork that sounds with the intoning of a particular mental and physiological state of each emotion.

When my girlfriend broke up with me, my emotional tuning fork of heavy sadness was resonating loud and filling my heart. I was disappointed she did not want to be in my life as my girlfriend any longer, but the action of breaking up resounded with something much deeper inside. It echoed back to long ago and I was informed of my lasting and still present fears and pain of abandonment, shame, and worthlessness from my experiences of feeling unwanted as a child. I was not only informed of my present circumstance with my now ex-girlfriend, but my unfinished emotional business of my past. In this sense, my tuning fork became a tool for invoking my awareness and providing information about my emotional life.

In another way, I took the energy from my tuning fork of heavy sadness and transmuted it for my own purposes by using it to plug into another wavelength. Instead of ignoring the resonation of heavy sadness, I moved into it with music and the exhausting movement of my body. I gave it focus and room to exist, then moved into it and used it for my own purposes.

I was still disappointed and sad at the loss of relationship with someone I loved, and my emotional baggage was still waiting for me, but I no longer felt like curling up in a ball of self-pity and crying.

Instead I felt empowered.

I had a sense of control about myself.

Instead of succumbing to my pain in negativity, I moved to a more positive position for handling my sorrow and baggage.

I felt master of my destiny.

THE HERO'S WHETSTONE: PACKING YOUR TOOLKIT

What I love about my toolkit is I get to decide what goes in it. As I acquire new skills and tools I can add them in, or I can change it all up at a moment's notice if my mission alters. I can pack it however I want, by color or feel or name, or arrange it so that the tools I need most for my journey are easily accessible. Everything about it is up to me.

Packing your toolkit is similar to how you would pack for any trip. You may take comparable items on a vacation versus a business trip, but there would likely be differences in your selection of clothing, such as jeans and a t-shirt versus a business suit. If you are simply heading out to buy groceries at the market, perhaps all you need is your shopping list and wallet. But wherever you go or whatever you are doing, you get to decide what it contains and how it is used.

If you have not packed a bag for a while, no need to worry, this is your bag so you get to decide everything about it without concern for right or wrong. A toolkit doesn't care what goes inside, you do. You can load it up or keep it light. Spend a little or a lot of time in packing. You can share information about your toolkit with others or keep it to yourself. It's up to you.

What I do ask is that you give this whetstone about your toolkit your honest attention and bring your imagination and dreams to the process. And I invite you to have fun with it.

So to begin let's start with three deep breaths, inhaling deep into the abdomen and exhaling slowly through the nose. With each inhalation breathe in the positive, and let go of the negative with each exhale. Breathe in possibility and breathe out limits, and relax into your Mind, Body, and Spirit.

Now take a few moments and see in your mind's eye the most fantastic toolkit you can imagine. It can look like one you have seen or used before, or be completely made up. Whatever you imagine and see in your mind's eye, let it feel visceral and be something that you like, find useful, and aesthetically pleasing.

What is this fantastic toolkit like? What material is it made of? What are its size and proportions? Does it have pockets, drawers, snaps, zippers, buckles, or secret compartments? How does it feel to the touch? Does it have smell or make any sounds?

If you like you can even give it special properties like being waterproof, or able to fly, or automatically rearranging your tools as needed by reading your mind.

As it comes into focus, continue to give it shape and form and see it clearly.

This is your toolkit for your hero's journey.

To begin packing your toolkit, it will be helpful to return to the work already done in previous Hero's Whetstones. In particular, refer back to Using Your Inner Eye from Stride 1—Stagnancy & Paralysis, on page 35, as well as both whetstones in Stride 2—Moment of Movement, Be the Dreamer of Dreams and Reading Your Map, on pages 50 and 58, respectively.

If you made any written notes from these whetstone exercises previously, pull them out for reference, or at least flip back to re-mind yourself of any mental notes and images that come up.

With these in mind, I would like to invite you to consider a mission of your choosing. Do not concern yourself with whether or not you are going to accept and go on this mission; that can be decided later if you choose. For now this is simply a sample mission of "what to do next."

Take a moment and think of a mission that would be personal and meaningful to you. It can be something related to one of your dreams, or a bar in your cage that you want to address, from get-ting in shape for a marathon to changing a destructive negative loop in your mind. It doesn't matter if it's lighthearted or serious, big or small, simple or complicated—just choose something that you feel would make a difference in your life or that you just like. And make it realistic, no missions to a galaxy far, far away for this whetstone.

When you have thought of a mission to your liking, consider the following questions with some detail. I recommend writing your answers down.

- What is the goal of this mission? Why is it important to you?
- How long do you think it will take to complete? Can it be completed? How will you know when it is done?
- Can you do this mission on your own, or do you need help from others? If you need help, what type of support do you need?
- Does this mission require any special equipment, tools or skills?
- Are there particular aspects of Mind, Body, and Spirit that are important for this mission?

When you feel comfortable that your mission is well outlined and understood, set your notes aside for a moment and mentally reach for your toolkit. With your mission in mind, look the toolkit over again and see if there are any modifications you would like to implement in it. Feel free to make a few minor changes, leave it as is, or completely start over again from scratch. It's up to you.

Okay! Toolkit ready to go?

If so, then let's start the packing.

Take up the notes for your mission and consider the following.

- Of the skills and tools required for this mission, which do you already possess? Do any need to be refined, improved, updated, or refreshed?
- What new skills or tools must you acquire to be successful?
- If you need help from others, are you comfortable in asking for it? If not, add that to the list of skills you need for success, the ability to ask for help.
- Do you have the time and energy available for this mission? Do you need to rearrange your schedule or reprioritize something in your life in order to make this happen?
- Is your Mind, Body, and Spirit fit and prepared for this mission? Would improved physical fitness, mental clarity, or a lifted spirit better your chances for success?

Now take your answers and put them into two columns or buckets. Make one for what you are already equipped with, and the other for that which you need to acquire for the mission.

Got it? Great!

Whether it seems you are ready to go, or need a lot of preparations, it's okay. If you happen to feel overwhelmed, I suggest you consider the possibility of somehow turning the energy of that feeling into something you would need for your mission. Wherever you are, that's perfect! Just start where you are.

Now take the two lists, those items you have, and those you need to acquire, and see them clearly in your mind. For the things you need to obtain, consider what it will take to acquire them and attach those thoughts and notes to each of those items. For instance, if you need a college degree to become a nurse, think about how much time, resources, and skills are needed for that and make a note next to that item on your list. Or if you need better communication skills to improve your marriage, you could consider writing down counseling, books to read, classes to take, etc., as what is needed to acquire that skill.

Now take each skill and tool, whether in your possession now or later, and see each one as a single implement. It can look like an actual tool, like the item itself, or as anything you see fit to represent it.

Now grab your toolkit.

In whatever way it makes sense to you, mentally take the items from your list of skills and tools for this mission and see yourself placing them in the toolkit you see in your mind. Whether you have a little or a lot to pack, it doesn't matter, you can do it all at once or a little at a time. If it feels overwhelming, like there's a lot to do or that it seems heavy, simply note those feelings but keep your attention focused on the adventure ahead, and continue packing. You can magically place your items in simultaneously, or arrange each one on its own. They can be adjacent to each other or in separate areas, how they are arranged is up to you.

Next I want you to sprinkle in the essence of your dreams and spirit, those elements of positive thoughts and energy that help fuel a hero as they travel along their path.

As I said earlier in this whetstone, you may choose to accept this particular mission or not. Whether or not you do, remember this whetstone as one you can return to as you prepare to take on new directions, or have new aspirations for "what to do next" along your life's journey.

With your toolkit packed you are prepared and with a plan for your journey.

You have the tools, you have your direction, so pick up the tool of your choice and get started.

STRIDE 5
Practicing & Honing

The feeling: "I am ready to seek out challenges and missions that test my skills, refine my training, and integrate my life force. I am now driven by movement, not by a destination."

After three years of study with my first martial arts teacher practicing swords and staffs in a secret warehouse, which seemed very ninja, I found myself looking for something more.

There was quite a blossoming tai chi community at the time, and I came across a man originally from China who was known as a bona fide teacher of real Chinese martial arts. In meeting him for the first time, I imagined he would look like a wise old Sifu with a long wispy beard or perhaps someone like Mr. Miyagi in *The Karate Kid*. Instead he kind of looked like a little Mexican Chinese man with a mustache and a new age attitude, and was really into jazz and reggae, loved to dance, and *really* loved to cook and eat. What's more, I was surprised to learn that his favorite fighter was not Jet Li, but Muhammad Ali!

As it turned out this wasn't the only assumption that proved to be wrong, but I was still in my early twenties and prone to those

snap "know-it-all" judgments of my youth. Chun Man Sit was revolutionary and forward thinking, and in many ways not so very Chinese. His Six Elbows kung fu was a very no nonsense and direct
approach to close quarter fighting, so I was excited about learning
from such a teacher.

"Rudy, if you want to be a good fighter, you will practice three
to four things and *always* train these techniques," Sit instructed.

What was he talking about? Just three or four things . . . What
about all the awesome forms and techniques in the kung fu movies?
Man, I thought at the time that Sit was almost blasphemous. But
even though I was bigger and much younger, he could easily defeat
me with his striking and wrestling, so I really listened to him and
executed all his training instruction with vigor and intensity.

If Sit told me to do five hundred kicks a day, I would do a thousand! Tens of thousands of repetitions of those three to four things,
along with simple plyometrics and other power training techniques
comprised the training regimen. Sit was there to guide, mentor,
and critique through my journey. He made me feel like I had po-

With Sifu Chun Man Sit at practice in Kansas City.

Courtesy of Reyes family

tential even though compliments did not exist for the first two years. And that for sure was very Chinese.

I and my brother had been training with Sit for sometime, and decided we would take our kung fu skills and see how they stacked up against the best in the world at the Chin Woo competition held in Plano, Texas. The Chin Woo is a martial arts association founded in China by the legendary Master Huo Yuanjia in 1910 that today has over 150 branches and schools around the world. It is the Chinese school that was made famous in the West by Bruce Lee in the film *The Chinese Connection*, or *Fist of Fury*.

Although the premier Chinese martial art and culture organization, this was my first big competition and I really didn't understand what a huge deal it was going to be. I was simple but determined, and somehow because of my confidence in Sit's training, I was calmly confident in myself as we drove the eight hours to Plano talking about kung fu legends and fighters the whole way there.

Before the competition began, a technique demonstration was put on with a famous fighting monk from the Shaolin Temple, the Iron Leg of China, Xian Lieu. I was in the audience watching, and I imagine because I was Western and looked big and muscular, the monk somehow keyed in on me and asked me to demonstrate with him. And of course I accepted.

Did I ever mention that I was not always the smartest or the wisest guy?

Next thing I knew I was out there as a crash test dummy for kicks, punches, sweeps and throws. I landed hard on my hip, my leg got smashed on the knee by what felt like a baseball bat, and I was thrown on my head hard enough to lose consciousness. The mad monk just kept coming, and my competition had not even started yet!

The demonstration ended and I was hurting.

My brother was getting some ice for my knee and head, and Sit was talking to an acupuncturist, but I wasn't going to back down.

Limping on I began my events of Fencing, Two Man Fighting Set, Shaolin Long Fist, and Shaolin Staff, and after a whole day of competing I prepared myself for the fighting competitions. However, there were no middleweight competitors, so I had to fight three heavy weight contenders. Man, just my luck.

The first fight was fairly easy. He was out of shape and by the third round he could barely keep his hands up, and I hit and kicked him with impunity. My brother was in my corner cheering and jumping up and down, while Sit looked me in the eye and said nothing.

Next came a Russian Chin Woo fighter and champion with a blocky square head and blocky square attitude. "You pretty good kid for American. I hit like truck so you be careful," he taunted, and I took note of that.

The fight began and ended with me striking, sweeping, and throwing the big Russian all over the place. I just used footwork to make him overcommit and then side-kicked and counterpunched him in the belly and head. When the fight was over, my hand was in the air while my little brother was rubbing my shoulders, and the crowd was going crazy because their guy had lost.

Then screams of electric excitement burst out as the throng glimpsed my next opponent. He was a big karate fighter about four inches taller and fifty pounds heavier than me, with a very forward, brutal, and aggressive style, who only competed in fighting. No staffs, swords, forms, or meditation competitions—just fighting. He had a mustache that reminded me of "Tom Selleck", and in his blue fighting uniform I knew he meant business.

He had just won his fight and devastated his opponent, so the crowd was cheering for him to make me pay retribution.

Sit looked on, but said nothing and just watched.

The first round banged away with kicks and punches traded with no quarter asked or given. I made it through the first round, but although I didn't show it, I was feeling smoked.

"Brother, how am I doing? Man, I am tired, and he banged me hard. What should I do? How do I win?" I implored while catching my breath in the corner.

My brother, always to the point, short and sweet, said, "Rudes, just do what you do! You're doing it!"

Round two and my footwork was slowing while getting blasted in the head and body, but I was stinging him with jabs and front kicks to the body and legs.

By the third round, "Tom Selleck" from the Cobra Kai was fired up. He was used to winning, and no little nobody from Kansas City with a strange unknown fighting style was going to beat him. I thought for a moment that I wished I could just be kicked in the head and put out of my fatigued misery, but I caught myself with an internal "Shut up with that talk!" and refocused my efforts.

Bruce Lee once said, "I fear not the man who has practiced ten thousand kicks once, but I fear the man who has practiced one kick ten thousand times."

I had thrown my three or four things so many thousands of times it seemed infinite, and the result was razor sharp strikes and footwork. I persisted with my mobility and stick and move strategy, and suddenly I was whooping "Tom Selleck"! Even though the crowd was going through the roof, I heard nothing. I saw nothing but my opponent. I felt my breathing and my gravity, moving in slow motion as if in a dance, but with razor precision when the big karate man stepped in with a huge left-right combo and was flat on his feet. I ducked out and fired a sidekick to his vulnerable ribs and my knife foot cut him so deep he fell to the floor.

I saw Sit's eyebrows jump while the referee was counting and counting with "Tom Selleck's" face twisting and gasping . . . nine, then ten . . . You're out!

The place erupted full blast with the crowd yelling and screaming like crazy!

My brother ran in and picked me up, and I was so happy and so fulfilled I felt I was going to boil over with pride.

"Where is Sit? Where is Sifu?" I asked looking for my teacher while I tore off my headgear and gloves. I vaguely heard the tournament sponsors tell me I was the grand champion of the competition because of the five gold medals I had won. All of these things were going on, and then Sit appeared in front of me.

"Rudy, you did not do too bad," Sit said with directness. "You won because the best guy did not show up."

Boom! My wind dropped out of my sails.

There I was giving everything I had for all those years to make myself a champion, and in my moment of glory Sit told me it didn't really matter. Even though I had fifty people all around me touching me and hugging me, I was ashamed and looked to the floor.

"Don't be sad, Rudy," Sit explained. "You have the most important skill in kung fu. You have the skill of dedication. You have the talent of a perfect student."

With water in my eyes, I asked, "What is that talent, Sifu? What talent do I have?"

"Rudy, you are obedient."

In his ultimate wisdom, Sifu Chun Man Sit offered me something so much richer than gold medals. He fulfilled his role as mentor and father figure with a gift of insight I hadn't considered before, and I was humbled. Not humiliated. Humbled.

I have long been a fan of the power and precision of great dancers as in many ways it reminds me of the same skills in martial arts, so I appreciate the words of the eminent Russian ballet dancer Mikhail Baryshnikov when he said, "It doesn't matter if every ballet is a success or not. The new experience gives me a lot."

And that's what Sit gave me on that and so many other days. So much more than punching and throwing techniques, not just kick drills and dim sum ventures. My teacher guided and invited me to be a humble student of my journey. Focus on the practice and the process and everything works itself out like a beautiful blossom of life.

The destination was not medals from strangers placed around my neck; the real gold was found through the experience and practice and process of the path.

The gold was inside the Student and the Warriors and the Sages and the Mothers out there on the hero's path.

That is the hero's gold.

That is what it means to stay golden.

THE HERO'S WHETSTONE:
YOUR PRACTICE

It doesn't matter whether you are a master practitioner or craftsman of every skill and tool needed for your mission. Simply by practicing what you already know, you will in time discover new and hidden skills and treasures.

A hero starts where they are with what they've got.

A hero practices and refines their skills and tools.

To learn and rehearse skills, people often do so in places designated particularly for that purpose, such as dancers in a studio, martial artists in a dojo, a chef in the kitchen, or a surfer on a wave in the ocean, while doctors and lawyers run their practices in spaces specifically designed for their professions.

In such places of formal practice, the space is designed and equipped with the elements needed to test and rehearse particular techniques and skills, and may often have a prescribed method or way of training, or have official teachers and leaders for that practice. Everything in the space is about the practice, or practicing for a mission, and does not contain things that will distract or detract from the purpose. A dance studio has a lot of space to move around with mirrors for watching your technique, and bars along the walls to hold onto for support while rehearsing and engraining certain moves. It doesn't have much else.

But for many practices in life, a traditional space or formal instruction may not be commonplace. For instance, parenting is practiced whether or not the kids are at home, or practicing patience or good listening skills can happen anywhere with anyone, even with your own self. Finding a mentor to help guide and instruct with such things may be a challenge or not seem readily available.

But the hero still finds a way.

This whetstone is great because you can use a lot of imagination and creativity and have fun with it. As we get started, it may be useful to revisit the work you did in the whetstone Packing Your Toolkit in Stride 4—Tools and Skills, and recall the mission from that exercise.

So let's begin with three breaths in and out, and as you inhale feel yourself filling with all the air and oxygen your body needs, and exhale out all that which is not needed. Slowly draw air all the way into your belly, and push the air out with gentle force through your mouth. Breathe and relax, relax and breathe.

What I'd like you to think of is a mission of your choosing, for which there is not typically a formal place to practice the skills needed for that mission, and also does not have a standardized method of training or official instructors. If the mission from the Packing Your Toolkit whetstone is appropriate, feel free to use it here too. If not, think of another mission, or if you'd like to think of a new one anyway, feel free to do so.

This mission can relate to one of your dreams, or a bar in your cage that you want to address, but it should be something for which you can readily think of the skills and tools you will need for this adventure. Or if helpful, use the Packing Your Toolkit whetstone to identify those skills and tools.

Once you have your mission in mind and have assembled your toolkit for it, then move on.

Now take a few moments and use your imagination to create a place of practice for this mission in your mind's eye. It can look like a place you know, or be imaginary, realistic or fanciful, it doesn't matter, that's up to you. Simply create a space that makes sense to you for this mission. Indoors, outdoors, anything your mind can think of is great. Go ahead and dream it in rich detail.

What does this space look like? Is it bright or dimly lit? In a building or outdoors? Spacious or small? Are there any aromas in the air? Sounds to hear? What is the temperature? Is it humid or arid? Noisy or silent? See and feel it in all its living color aspects as if you were there in this space.

When you have this clearly in your mind, think of your toolkit and the skills and tools you need to practice and hone for this mission.

Now pretend for a moment that you are the teacher and mentor of this training space and class. As teacher of this class, you are now responsible for developing the training and practice regimen for your student. You are now in charge. So as you think of what training methods might be effective for developing your student's skills, consider the following.

- What repeatable actions can be practiced over and over that would be a basis for acquiring and refining certain skills? Are there movements to make? Words to say? Sounds to make? Thoughts to think or not think? Rhythms to follow? People to engage? Quizzes or tests to take?
- Are there any special tools or equipment needed to practice certain techniques or methods?
- Are there specific items or elements that should *not* be

present during practice in order to achieve the best result or be successful?

- Are there other skills the student may already have that can be used or built upon in order to acquire new skills or improve techniques?
- How will you know when the student is prepared for their mission?
- Do you understand the student's goals and motivations in this mission?
- What or who can you turn to, or where can you go, for ideas and inspiration in developing this training method?

I recommend writing down your answers as you contemplate the above, or get really creative and even make up a formal class syllabus or instructions.

Do you have a good idea of what this looks like? Great!

This is your training program.

Next keep this in mind while turning your attention to the mission, your own mission that you chose earlier. Now think of your own life and real circumstances, along with your contemplative mission and training space and program, and consider this.

- Are there any incongruences between your real life and those of your contemplative training space and program that would compromise your mission success? If so, what are they?
- If you choose to carry out this mission, what adjustments might you need to make in your real life in order to be most successful in practicing for your mission?

Perhaps your life is already consistent with the goals of this mission. If so, great!

If not, that's great too, this is good information. Now you can look at it objectively and decide what adjustments need to be made for success in your mission and life.

For instance, if you're on a mission to improve your body by eating healthier, you may need to get rid of all the unhealthy food in your pantry and fridge, and replace it with only healthy items. Or perhaps your mission is to kick a drug or alcohol addiction, it may be that you need to rethink who you call "friend" and allow in your space. Or if your mission is to stop a negative loop in your head, perhaps arming yourself and filling your space with positive messages is needed.

Whatever your mission, in your role as the leader and teacher, it is your responsibility to determine your course and hold yourself accountable for staying on the path.

As the student in search of more, it is your responsibility to exercise discipline with yourself in practicing and honing your skills and tools. To humbly follow the path, and remain focused on the process and in gratitude for the real prize of the journey.

If you falter, don't worry about it, simply remind yourself of your original determination. What do you want? What's important? What's your priority? And steer yourself back on course.

This is your practice.

The practice of a hero.

Practice Makes Perfect

"They say that nobody is perfect. Then they tell you practice makes perfect. I wish they'd make up their minds." Winston Churchill spoke these words, and I like them as a gentle reminder to not get too fixated and axle-wrapped around the mythical notion of "perfection." Perfection is something of our desire and imagination, that which we pursue and invite and practice for, and in so doing we are perfectly perfect in the doing.

Martha Graham was one of the foremost pioneers of modern dance who gave her whole life in devotion to her craft. I admire such great dance artists because I find a lot of parallels between the world of dance and martial arts where in both arenas the artist is engaged in a lifelong practice of learning and honing skills. Endless repetitions and hours of practice, over and over training the movements of the body in preparation for those few moments on the stage or in the ring spent in a pursuit of excellence. Graham once said, "Practice means to perform, over and over again in the face of all obstacles, some act of vision, of faith, of desire. Practice is a means of inviting the perfection desired."

Sometimes in practicing a skill over and over again, the obstacles become the practice itself. The boredom. The fatigue. Sometimes even the pain of it, or the distractions that inevitably pop up along the path. And if you've ever been in a practice of an art or sport or job or other pursuit that requires endless repetitions, you know what I'm talking about. Because no matter how much passion you have for your passion, there will be a time when you are bored or tired or distracted.

When I first went to Sifu Chun Man Sit, I was pretty cocky having been in training for sometime before with another martial arts master who had a focus different than Sit's simple and gentle style. I was sure I could take him in a match, but he quickly handed me my hat. Not once, but twice. I felt humbled, and for me, my humility made me hungry to learn everything I could from this great master.

For months on end, Sit would have me train in a standing meditation. For one full hour every day I would stand in a stance with knees bent, feet over shoulder-width apart, rooting into the heels and holding balance as if riding a horse, with arms outstretched as if grabbing a large barrel, hands held at shoulder height and counting breaths while focusing on the air as it goes down into the lungs and back out into the atmosphere. You count one, and two, and three, and . . . and after a few counts you forget what you were doing and your mind drifts. Anytime this happens, the assignment is to return to one and start counting over again. In all the times I've done this, I've never made it to ten. My mind drifts all the time—to my burning thighs . . . my heavy arms . . . my dripping sweat . . . I lose count of my breaths and have to start over.

In the beginning it's difficult for the mind to quiet, to understand why you're just standing there for minute after hour after week after month on and on . . . endlessly counting breaths and feeling the burn with sweat pouring down. Then something happened for me after three to four months. I started to go into a vision. A vision where I was simply observing myself. I became the space around the observation. I was the vacuum outside of the space, and all dualities dissolved into a singular oneness of being. And there's no way to really know what that's like without doing it. You can intellectualize about it, but doing it is another experience.

Sit would tell me "You know you're really making progress when you're losing passion for what you're doing." When you feel your practice is becoming mundane or you are losing the passion, that is the moment of truth, the crux of your mental and spiritual evolution. Sure it's boring, sometimes it sucks, but it is revealing. And that's the most important part, revealing to yourself and to your art, your true character. Because there's nowhere to pretend on that thousandth repetition, there's nowhere to pretend as all preconceived notions or images of self evaporate into the creation of a new reality. If you navigate the crux where the climb is hardest, you will venture into unknown territory in an exploration of moving past limits to summit a whole new vista.

When fatigue or boredom or giving in sets in, that is the time to remember your original determination. Sometimes even keeping a physical reminder around is helpful. For instance, my tattoos are constant reminders to me of family and brotherhood and, of

Courtesy of Reyes family

In standing meditation practice with master Yang Yang.

course, my Recon family and the determination to drive on no matter what. You don't have to get a tattoo though. Just find a simple way to make it real. Draw a picture. Find a photo. Write it down in big letters with a magic marker. Put it on your fridge or the dashboard of your car or keep it in your pocket. Create something that will give you the reminder daily or hourly or at any moment of your original determination. Doing so could at some point even be the thing that breaks you through on those days of temptation and struggle.

Another point to keep in mind is that everything changes. Little did I know when I started martial arts training that my attitude and reasons for pursuing the initial goal could change. But as I continued in my practice, I learned new things about the process, about boredom and triumphs, and about myself with new epiphanies informing me about my journey and real character.

Sometimes it seems that when people are stuck or bored and not going all the way, there is a general lack of power and energy. Whether emotional, physical or mental—they're all related. Without that power and energy it just seems so hard to move or to stay in practice. If you find yourself feeling this way, if you're tired of feeling tired, it's time to set some new things into motion.

Even the practice of a practice has to be cultivated. What do you put in your body? How do you move your body? What do you feed you mind and spirit? This is your vehicle, so paying attention to supplying the body, mind and spirit with proper rest, stimulation and nourishment is ultimately important.

Out of this attention to making caring choices about what you take in, you will find that the strength to fuel your practice even in times of boredom and fatigue will naturally come from within.

Out of this practice will come the means of inviting the perfection desired.

As a Recon Marine, practicing skills for carrying out missions is a constant and endless exercise where the "perfection desired" concerns life or death situations. My first year in Recon, I attended school upon school at Camp Pendleton in Oceanside, California, to learn new skills as a military practitioner capable of combat on land, sea, and air, fighting and surviving under extreme conditions as an individual and team member.

Every hour of every day for weeks and months on end was spent repeating drills to train the mind and body for mission success. The first few weeks of Combatant Diver school consisted of

Created and illustrated by Rudy Reyes

Amphibious Recon sticker I illustrated.

punishing four-to-six-mile runs at the six-minute-mile pace under the cloak of darkness every morning, followed by open ocean swims in the late morning all geared up in boots, cammies, combat load vest, carrying an M16 and full-sized rucksack, and swimming up to ten kilometers every day.

In the afternoon the mind was immersed in a breakneck pace of academics with study and memorization of dive physics and procedures, including maintenance of our rebreather and other equipment. Rote exercises again and again that must be followed to the letter without exception as a measure and method to insure safety, so that when the chips were down for real we could reliably and without thinking fall back to our best automatic level of competency.

With the grueling physical conditioning and so much subsurface ocean work, the attrition rate of the class was about sixty percent, so by the time we hit the pool for "Shark Week" there were only about twenty students left.

All through my training my instructor, Hull Technician First Class Loveland, used to say, "It's a thinking man's game, gents. It's all in your Brain Housing Group." He always used to call me "Just Happy to Be Here" because of my enthusiasm and relative naiveté, as I really had no experience outside of the schoolhouse yet.

So far my time inside the schoolhouse had been okay, except that I had failed miserably the first time I got in the pool with the "Sharks," a.k.a. instructors. Copeland attacked me with a vengeance pulling my straps, smacking my head off the side of the pool and tearing away my mask. My fins were gone, my head was spinning, and after fighting for my tanks for what felt like a lifetime, I desperately moved my hand across my throat like a knife signaling for emergency buddy breathing!

Feeling like an infant with all my gear splayed everywhere, I felt Loveland smash his regulator into my mouth. I could breathe and was alive, but as I gave the hand signal to ascend and we headed to the surface, my fear took over. I was not properly exhaling. I was in combat, but with myself.

I had become my own enemy.

In scuba diving, strict adherence to protocols and procedures can make the difference between life and death. Dive injuries such as pulmonary overinflation syndrome or arterial gas embolism, otherwise known as the bends, can cause the lungs to burst or tear, or the brain to hemorrhage. It's no joke.

Caught up in fear I was not exhaling correctly and the ornery Tiger Shark instructor Loveland could see this. Not exhaling could injure or kill me, so BAM! The Shark punched me in the mouth as a reminder that the lesson was to *exhale when ascending no matter what!* I was pissed, I was angry, and I was defeated. Blood was in my mouth and I could taste the iron in the back of my throat.

For round number two I found myself back at the twenty-foot-deep training pool, with scuba tanks, regulator, mask, snorkel, weight belt, and fins, where students were instructed to swim around subsurface in long circles only looking down at the bottom of the pool. All the while, the instructor Sharks stayed patrolling with their eyes peeled and fixed on the "sea bass" below—me! I was going to be dinner.

This was sink-or-swim time, salvation or obliteration. If I failed this round, failed to control my fear, I would be on a one-way plane ride to Palookaville as the embarrassment of 1st Recon. Circling and circling nearly blind at the bottom of the pool, I just took full deep breaths in and out and tried to calm my mind of the fear and terror of failing and being sent back to the unit shamed. My head was just going over all the scenarios . . . the lonely plane ride home with my head held low . . . all of the pressure of failure.

Then I remembered the Tiger Shark's words: "Hey, 'Happy to Be Here,' it's a thinking man's game. Your biceps and your kickboxing aren't going to help you here. It's a thinking man's game."

So I thought to myself, "Shoot, Rudy! The human brain can go without oxygen for six minutes, right? You only have to hold your breath for three minutes, which is easy day! If you just keep your cool and don't waste energy tightening up and resisting . . . Just be cool. You got this." And suddenly I was in the fight!

And just in time two Sharks pulled off my fins and weight belt, and another one tore off my mask and applied a strong rear choke, but I tucked in my chin as another pulled at my tanks and kicked me in the body over and over.

Through it all I focused on one thing. My lifeline to air and life. I kept my eyes open and a vise grip on my left shoulder strap. No matter what they did, if I had positive control of my air source, I would live. Kind of laid it all on the line there, so that's what I did. And did and did until an eternal minute later I heard the sound of a dive watch buzzing.

BEEP. BEEP. BEEP. BEEP.

The choke on my neck went slack, my scuba tanks suspended in the water column. I was no longer under attack, but it wasn't over yet.

Time to get to my mental checklist!

Look left, look right, up and down, and use the universal head and arm signal for ditching and donning tanks.

Swing the tanks over your head in a controlled fashion and secure the tanks with your legs and feet.

Next, purge your regulator so you can untie it, then turn on your air and cycle your reserve. And once you're breathing, be cool.

Now I knew the hardest stuff was over!

I finished putting on and adjusting my gear, then tapped my knees to let the instructors know I was staying down on the training tank floor, and *not* shooting for the surface! The Sharks would blast and tackle and keep you down there if you didn't tap your knees before getting off your butt. They must first come down and check out all of your gear and check off your procedures to make sure you accomplished every task by the numbers. Then and only then did you don and clear your mask and use proper ascent procedures to complete the mission.

To be fit for action as a Recon Marine, extreme training develops the body and mind as skilled tools for enduring long, arduous, and potentially dangerous conditions in completing missions in the field. I have swum and run in full gear for thousands of miles, fallen through the air from the highest stratospheres, punched and kicked countless times, learning standard procedures and repeating actions over and over again until the Mind, Body, and Spirit begin working together in concert of desired perfection and on instinct.

As Martha Graham put it, "We learn by practice. Whether it means to learn to dance by practicing dancing or to learn to live by practicing living, the principles are the same."

While you may attend a dance recital and appreciate the skill and beauty of it, if you want to dance then you must practice dancing. If there is a skill you want to learn or hone or polish for your mission and journey, the skill to *do* comes by *doing*. You cannot sit on the edge of the pool and wish you could learn to swim. You must get in the water and stroke. You must stroke and stroke again and again with purpose to refine your technique.

Graham became the iconic dancer "Martha Graham" because of her lifetime practice of *doing* to be so.

Similarly, I was a Recon Marine and martial artist because I made it my practice of *doing* to be so.

With aspiration and a mission plan in hand and heart, the hero is forever in the process, a humble student of doing.

Whether engaged in formal training such as for dance or martial arts, or the informal repetitions of life, no matter what you do, you are in the constant action of practicing a practice. An occupational practice, a practice of marriage or relationship, practices of community, of solitude, even destructive practices of depression and addiction, oppressor and oppressed.

In the habits and motions of every moment of every day of every year, whether conscious of it or not, you are practicing and honing *something*. You are acting and forming habits.

You are creating your character.

Creating your destiny.

A hero acts with purpose in those actions and habits.

A hero acts as the master and creator of their destiny.

THE HERO'S WHETSTONE:
PRACTICING YOUR DESTINY

More than two thousand years ago, the Greek philosopher Socrates said, "The soul, like the body, accepts by practice whatever habit one wishes it to contact."

"Whatever habit *one wishes.*"

Wow! That's powerful.

For millennia untold members of the human family have understood about a person's ability to make choices about their character of Mind, Body, and Spirit. People throughout time have mentored the way, individuals who know we are not simply at the mercy or the whim of the winds that blow. We can hoist our sails of dreams and aspirations and pilot our way ahead. We may not control the gale of a storm, but we can turn our bow into the face of the wind and use the forces as *one wishes* in our journey, like so many that have gone before.

I believe this is true of both external and internal forces. For instance, there are times in my life that my emotions have gotten the best of me, like being overwhelmed by fear and panic in the pool during Combatant Diver school. Moments I've felt swamped by anger and hate, self-pity and sorrow, and have given way to the weight of those forces. Emotions are full of energy, so they can naturally feel overwhelming and powerful, as if they wash in and over like big waves beyond and out of our control.

Body, mind, and emotions are built-in tools, divining rods for Hero Living. When tapped and used intentionally, they can provide crucial information and rich guidance for the hero inside. I believe there is a powerhouse of energy at your disposal when you begin to practice the art of purpose driven awareness and attentive discipline of the Mind, Body, and Spirit. Simply by practicing your skills of integrating the Mind, Body, and Spirit, you plug into your own energy plant and experience a harmony that yields a life force of synergistic vibrance.

No matter what your mission, take up your toolkit and make a habit of practicing those skills that bring a positive force to your life. Make a practice of taking control of the helm as the captain of your ship.

For this whetstone, as with others, we're going to start with three deep breaths in and out. As you breathe in notice the feel of air moving through your nose down your throat and into your lungs. Is the air warm or cold? Are there any aromas? Exhale through the mouth and feel the breath moving out of your lungs through your throat and passing over your lips. Notice how it feels to take air in and breathe it out, and sit in the energy of this movement for a few moments. Plug into all your senses as you breathe and notice the information they are providing, right here right now.

Now I'd like you to consider for a moment . . . Have you ever watched an advertisement on television that within a few moments has you laughing or crying? What about heard a song that puts you in a certain mood? Are there foods or kitchen smells that right away remind you of your childhood?

I think of my variety of emotions as a big set of tuning forks. Each one resonates on a certain wavelength and corresponds to a particular emotion. When I consider how easy it is for my tuning forks to be pinged by simply watching a movie, listening to a song, or smelling a cup of coffee, I start to think of how I can use this as a tool for managing my Mind, Body, Spirit connection and emotions.

Not to suggest my tuning forks couldn't shouldn't wouldn't continue to resonate with external forces, but perhaps it's possible for me to be in a more conscious and creative position for how long, or if, or when they resonate according to those forces. Or how they resound with my own internal dialogue or moods.

I mean if other things can hit these forks, why can't I learn to play them as I like?

Instead of sitting in the audience to this performance, I'm going to learn to be a virtuoso musician and bandleader in the concert of my Mind, Body, Spirit connection and emotional life. Much as a musician sits in on a jam session playing off the other musicians, while simultaneously orchestrating the whole with conductor cues for major directional shifts, all playing in concert as they explore the tonal and rhythmic possibilities.

So take a moment and visualize your own set of tuning forks. They can look however you like. What color or colors are they? What is their size? Are they light or heavy? Are there a few or a lot? Where are they in your toolkit? Simply get a clear image of them in your mind, and then consider the following questions.

- Does it feel like your tuning forks are easily pinged with your emotions running on a rollercoaster all the time? Or do you generally feel more even keeled and steady?
- Does it seem there are particular emotions that resonate more often, or most of the time in your life? If so, what are they? Do you often feel angry, sad, happy, worried, ashamed, confident, numb, loving, compassionate, etc?
- If you had to choose one tuning fork or emotion that you feel resonating often and strong, one that feels more negative in its nature or that somehow impedes your path, what would it be?
- What are the events or other things that easily cause this tuning fork to resonate? Is it constant or intermittent?

There are no right or wrong answers here; there is just information and your truth. So whatever your responses, for now just hold them in your mind, or write them down, and we'll move on.

Martha Graham's father was a doctor specializing in nervous disorders with a keen interest in diagnosis through attention to physical movement. This belief in the body's ability to express its inner sense was pivotal in Graham's desire to dance, and her choreography was at times designed to evoke emotion through bodily movement versus feeling the emotion in order to move. She said, "The movement gives you back, very often, meaning. You don't start 'I will express anger', or 'I will express grief'. You move in such a way that it gives you back anger or grief. So that you have your roots very far in fundamentals."

I find this very analogous to my own experience with the many physical disciplines I've practiced during my life. That physical movement, engaging the body, can also have a visceral effect on my mind and emotions. Perhaps it's the hormones or other chemicals released while the body works, or something else, but whatever it is I feel it.

As a fitness coach, I have worked with many people struggling with their weight, who feel they are at the mercy of their food cravings and other bad habits. In the beginning they talk about their body issues, but in most cases the more powerful underlying issues are those of emotion and mind.

They feel bad, so they don't move.

They feel uninspired, so they don't move.

They are stuck in a misconception, a pattern of waiting for an emotional cue to get started. So they don't move.

What they haven't understood is that if they move their body even when they don't feel like it, that very soon they will start to feel like moving their body. And as they continue this practice over time, the opposite starts to kick in, and they not only feel like moving, but indeed they even crave it or can't imagine not doing so. They have essentially retuned themselves to resonate on a different wavelength of being.

The mind body connection is just that, an inextricable connection, an interrelated dance of thought and feeling, stimuli and chemistry, that moves and experiences itself in perpetual motion. While not possible to control the external elements that may storm around us, we can learn to maneuver and navigate our emotions in a never-ending expedition and process of exploratory adventure. The secret for those people that succeed in addressing their body issues not only do the motions of the physical training, but also practice the related skills and techniques of plugging into and tending their mind and emotions, to harmoniously move their bodies with purpose and intent.

Graham said, "Your work, you do what you know, you experiment with movement. Until you find some little secret language which speaks for your body and your heart."

With whatever emotions or thoughts or physical sensations you experience, there is the opportunity to experiment and find the language of how your Mind, Body, Spirit connection and emotional life operates and by so doing open the door to move into more possibility.

As you consider that, also consider this: Have you ever noticed how being around certain people can bring you up or drag you down? Or been at a musical concert where everyone seems in the same emotional space according to the song being played? Or seen a hostile situation averted by the laughter of some comic relief?

In physics, waves that cross paths have an effect on each other depending on the points at which they intersect. If you've ever seen a wave graph it charts the low and high points of the wave through space and time, reminiscent of the up and down graph on a heart monitor. Waves can *cancel each other out* if the high point of one meets the low point of another. Or they can *amplify* each other if two high points or two low points happen to meet. In some scientific disciplines the phenomenon is known as the ripple effect.

Is it possible that we can experience some similar sort of quantum ripple effect on our emotions? On our whole Mind, Body, Spirit connection and system? If you're feeling angry and put on some pounding acid rock music, would it amplify those feelings of anger? Or if you instead play something easy listening and soothing, would it soften or otherwise transmute the anger into something else? I do not intend to suggest an exact science here, but I think it's a concept worth considering as a possible skill or tool for your toolkit.

So now take a moment and reflect on the one tuning fork you identified earlier as one that you feel resonating often and strong with a more negative impact on you, and think of the events or other things that easily cause this tuning fork to resonate.

For a moment pretend this is simply a tuning fork and not your emotion, and you are a musical conductor or perhaps a physicist conducting wave experiments, and consider the following.

- For this tuning fork, can you think of something that could potentially amplify this wavelength? Or cancel it out? Would it be certain music, physical movements, artwork, people, places, memories, smells, etc? Really explore the possibilities for what could either amplify or cancel the effect.
- What could you possibly do to either cancel or transmute the energy from this negative wavelength into something more positive? Would it be possible to take the energy of anger or pain and focus it into your work-

outs, your work, your art, cooking, caring for a child with extra care, etc?

If you don't know what makes you happy or brings you joy or peace or a feeling of being hopeful and positive, experiment doing things outside your usual behaviors and habits until you find a glimmer from inside. Switch it up and move your body, tell a joke, laugh for no reason, sing in the car, dance in the shower, make an anonymous gift, volunteer your time, give to charity, do a somersault, slide on a slide, swing on a swing, explore and entertain and appreciate.

Find a way to hold yourself responsible and accountable, to accept responsibility and accountability for your Mind, Body, and Spirit connection and emotional life.

Experiment and treat it as a skill to hone. Or even be a parent to yourself by only allowing so much time for self-pity, shame, guilt, or anything that has the long-term inappropriate effect of bringing you down, or paralyzes you in stagnation.

"Find a place inside where there's joy, and the joy will burn out the pain," wrote Joseph Campbell, the legendary philosopher and expert on world mythologies, who not only understood the power of myth, but the power of practicing the management of your emotional life as a way of affecting your Mind, Body, and Spirit and hero's journey.

Remember that nothing lasts. Every moment is precious and holds a gift of possibility. No matter what's happening it is a window of possibility into more understanding, more learning, more of your self, more life. Remember that the way to get through a bad time is to acknowledge "this too will pass," and the way to cherish a good time is to know "this too will pass."

So move with the wisdom of Mahatma Gandhi, who said, "You may never know what results come of your action, but if you do

Courtesy of Reyes family

**With my brother Michael, practicing our martial
arts in the park in Kansas City.**

nothing there will be no result." So even if it feels silly, do it. Move
with awareness of your choices and own them, for even when you
do nothing you've made a choice.

In the martial art of aikido, practitioners blend with the motion of their attacker to redirect the force of the attack rather than
opposing it head-on. This strategy requires very little physical energy as the practitioner leads the attacker's momentum with various movements and techniques. The goal is to defend themselves
while also protecting their attacker from injury. An aikido practitioner doesn't view an attacker as positive or negative, but simply
as energy to be danced with and managed as desired.

We can take a cue from aikido with our set of tuning forks or
emotions, to honor your feelings, refrain from judging them. Feelings are just feelings. They provide information much like a barometer or compass. You may choose to act on them or not, focus on
them or not, that is a choice. If you simply let them come at you then
you are at their mercy, but if you can find ways to harmoniously work
with them, you are now the conductor of your symphony.

As you get the hang of how your emotional world operates, and begin to exercise your abilities to work with the energy instead of against it, a shift will begin to resonate throughout your life.

You will practice and hone and find "some little secret language which speaks for your body and your heart."

And you will remember.

You are a hero.

No matter where you are, you are in a place of practice.

Whatever you are doing, you are a practitioner.

No matter what life throws your way, you are an adventurer driven by movement into more possibility.

You are a hero of possibility.

STRIDE 6
Pure Unedited, Uninhibited Potential

The feeling: "My life is literally coming to life because I know who I am. I am free, I am pure possibility, and I am here for something bigger than myself."

After practicing and honing my skills for years as a Recon Marine, I found myself on my third tour in Iraq. In zone for three or four months going between Ramadi and Fallujah, my team was doing the most dangerous and bloody missions that the Battalion passed down. By then I was one of the saltiest team leaders. I had been through heavy ambushes, single-handedly demolitioned a bridge under cover of darkness, raided and kidnapped enemy bomb makers, led over fifty missions behind enemy lines, and been bait for insurgents to then turn the tables and kill them in the dirt.

There is no way around it. The business of war is a hard, harsh and terribly brutal job. It unequivocally demands that a person who lives as a warrior hammer of the war machine be incontestably rough to survive. Or as John Rambo put it in the movie *Rambo: First Blood Part II*, "To survive a war, you gotta become war."

The grinding of a man into roughness is so extreme, it almost seems strange to comprehend he still retains compassion and love and laughter.

But that is the ironical mixed up truth of it. For in the same breath of bullets and terror, I felt very much a father to my younger and less experienced teammates. I kept my heart beating with a sliver of humanity. I was still here alive, while some of my brothers were gone. Some maimed. Still I remained. My heart and mind and body washed in blood and the stimulation of violence, but there was my heart still beating for my teammates, the Iraqi children, and the war torn families caught in between.

Into our hard base the enemy had been blasting rockets and mortars killing and injuring dozens. A number had exploded in our medical triage and killed some of the surgeons as well as previously wounded Marine patients. The task fell to my unit to find and kill the insurgents responsible.

I used every skill and insert method possible, from clandestine helicopter insertions to Trojan Horse plain clothes operations, sniper missions, night patrols, anything we could do to find these guys. After a few months I knew the area well, so while updating my map I noticed that just south of our hard base near Amiriyah, known as Tower Town, there was a five-story water tower that gave a fantastic bird's-eye view of a well traveled road alongside the major canal in zone.

From such a crow's nest I could easily cover a kilometer in every direction with my sniper rifle, plus raise airpower on our communications to drop ordnance on the enemy and their vehicles. My platoon commander and I talked it out, and my team was tasked with occupying the water tower while the rest of the platoon did snap vehicle checkpoints in zone.

On the day I approached the water tower I was pleasantly surprised to meet a kind older man with white hair and a damaged eye smiling as he said, *"Marhabaa"* ("welcome"). He lived in the little farmhouse at the base of the tower with his family who tilled the land and tended their livestock.

I smiled even though my M4 rifle was still high on my shoulder. I smiled because the demeanor of this man was kind. He was a benevolent soul. He reminded me of my own benevolent self.

As my team took up their security positions, the Iraqi man was joined by his wife and three children. The woman was dark skinned with tattoos on her chin, and she smiled at me warmly. Her head was wrapped, but she was not wearing a burka. I must say that of all the Iraqi women I met in two tours of duty, none was ever so kind and heartfelt as this man's smiling wife.

The kids were curious about these men in camouflage, so I took a knee and let the little ones get closer to me. I pointed to the tower and in broken Arabic and with my eyes told the Iraqi farmer that we wanted to go up there. Soon my team and I were invited inside their home to enjoy some hot cha, or ginger tea with sugar, but I expressed that it was too dangerous to stay here very long and that we would be back that night under the cover of darkness.

Before leaving I offered the smallest boy, who was intrigued

Courtesy of Rudy Reyes

With the children in my Iraqi "family."

with my camo paint, some chocolate from my MRE (meals ready-to-eat) field rations. Seeing this, the father motioned to me to follow him to the side of the farmhouse, where upon turning the corner I saw the family store full of candy and soda and some Muslim prayer items. He then offered me some of their highest-quality candy, and I accepted a German chocolate bar.

There living in the desolation of a war zone, this family was an oasis of human kindness. In the midst of so much ferocious hostility I saw them as the embodiment of Bruce Lee when he said, "To hell with circumstances; I create opportunities." And their opportunity for true freedom was to choose to simply live in the space of possibility for creating love and kindness no matter what was exploding around them.

When I returned that night, I came bearing a case of bottled water, medical supplies and a soccer ball for the boys, along with my rockets, sniper systems, grenades for my launcher and three teammates who were armed to the teeth. The father quietly greeted us and unlocked the gate to the tower, and my team began the long hard climb laden with a hundred pounds each of ammunition, weapons, optics and thermals, water, communications and rappel rope. Sweat and cammie paint dripped onto my body armor and the straps of my assault pack gripped my shoulders burning into the neck muscles as we climbed.

Three stories into the ascent it fully dawned on me how vulnerable my team was. We continued climbing and when I made it safely to the top I looked down and said a silent thanks to the beautiful family that was giving my team safe passage. Our lives were literally in their hands. Understandably most Iraqis lived in fear of all sides of the warring factions around them, afraid to do anything that could appear to be taking sides. Even giving the impression of taking a side could spell disaster or death. Even so, this beautiful

Iraqi family without question or hesitation warmly and cheerfully lent us their protected assistance.

For months on end we conducted operations from the tower and interdicted insurgents, killing and capturing the enemy in zone, and after a time the area had gotten more stable and secure. During the day my platoon would drive by the water tower and my Iraqi family would come out to wave at us, while all the neighboring children would be over at the farm playing soccer. Just a look and a wave and suddenly the weight of my mission lifted and I wouldn't feel a single ounce of heaviness. They made me smile and laugh and helped keep my humanity alive.

I felt I was actually a good guy in Iraq for those moments. All the rest of the time I was fighting for my team's survival and following orders to complete missions, but in seeing the children playing with the soccer ball that I brought them on that very first day we met, I felt like a hero, more like my true self.

In those months I came to feel close with the family of the water tower. The mother was so warm and loving, her kind eyes gave me

In my Humvee during my second tour in Iraq.

Courtesy of Rudy Reyes

hope and trust that maybe we could make a difference for these people. The father wanted a life for his sons and his family. He wanted safety and security. What any father wants. His family to be provided for and protected from perils and assailants who would do them harm.

So in my own heart, I was now there not only to protect my brothers in arms, but felt on a mission to protect my Iraqi family as well. Making a positive difference to someone, helping them realize their own dreams, that was the essence of me under the hard exterior of war paint and gear.

At the time my seven months' deployment was coming to an end, 2nd Recon from Camp Lejeune was en route to do a battlefield turnover and take over the zone. My 1st Recon platoon would soon be heading back home to Camp Pendleton in California, so I was spending time on ride along missions with the 2nd Recon teams showing them the tricks of the trade and the lay of the land.

On my last day outside the wire for my final ride along, I got a call over communications that some large bombs were exploding near the water tower east of our position.

My stomach iced over and my mouth was dry.

I gave the coordinate to the point man and we were on the move to the farmhouse. While burning up the dirt roads at sixty kilometers per hour, we could see a large plume of smoke billowing up in the distance.

BOOM! Two seconds later another explosion was shaking my teeth.

"Push! Push faster damn it!!" I screamed to the driver.

As we approached the canal we were met by the sight of smoke and dead cattle and water streaming everywhere like a flash flood. The father with blood on his face and hands was walking but despondent, and the mother appeared from behind the half destroyed farmhouse, praying or crying or cursing or all three with tears in her once joyful eyes.

No! No! No!

As the smoke cleared I saw the tower was toppled. All the water had flooded the wadi, or valley, that was the farmland for these people, and the generator that gave electricity to the whole village was destroyed by the fallen water tower.

Everything destroyed.

NO! NO! NO!

And where are the children?

I assessed and then sent Recon Marines to cover sectors as I called headquarters, or HQ, to report what had happened.

Then the noise of children sounded as they came out of hiding. The smallest one ran to me and pointed toward the house. I picked him up and ran him to his mother and father, and they pointed inside where there was still another bomb in the farmhouse!

I got on the radio to report back and put out the order to get all the Recon Marines back over.

"Sir, these Iraqis have been helping us and are now targets of the mujahideen. We must help them," I stated. "Interrogative, are we going to help them?"

The radio was silent for what seemed like an eternity.

I urged, "I say again, these Iraqis risked their lives for me and my team. We need to help them . . . we need . . ."

"Roger, Echo Five Romeo. Return to base," headquarters sent back, cutting me off.

I was in disbelief, and the Iraqi mother was now weeping and looking right into my eyes. I took off my goggles and looked into hers.

"Interrogative, HQ, if we leave these sympathetic Iraqis here, they will be killed by mujahideen death squads. We must get them out of here!" I begged.

I was a Recon team leader, and I was begging that we give safety to these human beings who trusted and protected me. This family could have easily told the insurgents of our position and we would have been killed. Instead, they helped us because they trusted us. They trusted me.

I waited as the Iraqi mother held my hand and my eyes got hot and wet and I waited. I waited. Then finally it came.

"Roger, Sergeant Reyes. Return to base."

The order stunned.

Although moving my body, I felt frozen in the destruction for what felt like a hundred years of slow motion hell in a mad rush.

The bomb squad arrived and I watched in guilty fury and horror as they detonated the explosive and blasted what remained of this family's home because the device couldn't be disabled or safely moved.

This family, this village of people, and their way of life was now a detail of "collateral damage," with no livestock and livelihood left, and the wolves waiting in the bushes to rush in once we left.

At the core of who I was, I knew that for me this was it. But I was helpless to change it, I didn't know what else to do. I knew I wasn't Rambo that could single-handedly rush in and save the day.

Yet at the same time, I knew I was just like him.

In the bright fully saturated colors of real life, I knew I was just like the Rambo of moving shadows and sound when he said, "I'm expendable."

These civilian people were expendable despite the nature of a friendly and supportive relationship.

What I thought of as the honorable "warrior" in me, the defender and protector of those in need, was expendable. My kind of warrior wasn't required, what was wanted was a universal soldier and team leader that simply followed orders and accomplished missions.

With all of the "surviving of war" that I'd done, this realization had been resonating in me for sometime, but in this surreal moment of militarily brushing away breadcrumbs I knew that it didn't matter to the war machine how this warrior hammer was going to have to live with himself. How the humanity of all was going to live.

As in every war, both sides are wrought with the irony of such conflict, so my story, this family's story, is not unique. We are all connected in the nature of war. Our wars.

I stood there for a few moments longer in that battle zone as Recon Marines piled into the gun trucks, and I was the last soldier to load up. The trucks pulled out and drove away while I looked back at the blood and smoke, the tears and loss. And that was the last time I saw my beautiful Iraqi family that had given me so much.

There was no way for me to go back. No recourse going forward.

Five days later I was stateside. And I will never forget.

I was being courted by another special operations program at the time that offered more money and prestige and I was very close to doing it. But as I felt all the artifices and charades coming down, I asked myself, "Am I a warrior or am I a soldier?" And there was simply too much dissonance and discord with the notes being played around me for *who I am* to accept that course of direction.

So I left and took my own "warrior" path.

Into my toolkit I packed up all the skills and tools I had practiced and honed and appreciatively acquired in the Marines, and repurposed them to retune the instrument of my life in a way that resonated more closely with *who I am*.

I didn't know exactly how or what I was going to do for work or money, but I knew I was going to turn this knowledge and experience into something of my choosing. Something more than a weapon, that which could give back to humanity a portion of the humanity my Iraqi family had given to me.

My heart ached for my lost brothers and sisters.

But living in possibility does not mean that everything in life will always be easy or free of trials and pain. It may even be that when the forces of negativity are pushing hardest, is when a door of opportunity will push open for you to choose and define or offer new insights for knowing *who I am*. You stay in pure possibility and keep yourself open to positive potentials despite the stress and pressure.

Who could have guessed what doors would have opened to me in taking this path?

A phone call asking that I take the director and producers of HBO's *Generation Kill* onto Camp Pendleton to see how real Recon Marines are trained. And from that first meeting to being hired as a military adviser to the show, a trainer for the cast, and eventually even the opportunity to act as myself in the series.

What an unforeseen chance to be part of something bigger that could honor my fallen buddies and lost war torn families through story telling and sharing. An opportunity and tremendous blessing to somehow redeem and heal my soul by looking at the story of my platoon and myself through the lens of others.

On the set filming HBO's *Generation Kill.*

So instead of wielding a soldier's sword of combat, I can choose an artist's sword of truth and brush of compassion. I can use my warrior skills to somehow make things right and fight for what I believe to be right.

To honor the heroes of my lost Iraqi family, I will follow in their hero footsteps of love and compassion.

Because they have given me that gift of seeing.

Because that's who I am.

I know who I am.

The Selfless Self

Bruce Lee once said, "When there is freedom from mechanical conditioning, there is simplicity. The classical man is just a bundle of routine, ideas and tradition. If you follow the classical pattern, you are understanding the routine, the tradition, the shadow—you are not understanding yourself."

You practice and practice to learn and become proficient at a technique or skill, to know a concept, or master a discipline or domain, and may even become proficiently expert in what you are practicing. As a young boy Lee was a diligent student learning martial arts skills from his father and other teachers, and over the years he became exposed to and expert in many different fighting styles including traditional Asian martial arts as well as Western boxing.

One of the things I love about Bruce Lee was his openness to exploring ideas and ways of being and expression. Although best known as a martial artist and actor, Lee was also a champion cha-cha dancer as a teenager and also majored in philosophy in college. Martial arts was his chosen method of self-expression, and even in this he kept himself open to exploring different styles and using that which he found to be useful.

In his continual pursuit of self-knowledge and expression through martial arts excellence, Lee identified a key element to freedom for and from self when he said, "A martial artist who drills exclusively to a set pattern of combat is losing his freedom. He is actually becoming a slave to a choice pattern and feels the pattern is the real thing. It leads to stagnation." Further, "Do not deny the classical approach, simply as a reaction, or you will have created another pattern and trapped yourself there."

While Lee was referencing the study of martial arts in his comments, his fighting philosophy also applies outside of martial arts. Different than what you may already recognize as bars in your cage or those negative things which keep you trapped, in a sense a person may also become trapped by the routine, ideas and traditions of a particular pursuit. That by simply going through the mechanical motions or adhering closely to one school of thought, you may become walled off from other possibilities for more of yourself or better or more comprehensive solutions to a challenge, to which Lee admonished, "All kind of knowledge, eventually becomes self-knowledge. . . . Use only that which works, and take it from any place you can find it."

The ability to be open to seeing yourself outside of your conventions, as different or more or doing something new, to push your own boundaries and move past limits opens the door as a key to pure possibility.

In 1985 the U.S. Army funded a classified military experiment, the Trojan Warrior Project, to teach Eastern awareness disciplines ranging from aikido to meditation to a group of twenty-five Green Berets. Leading the project was Richard Strozzi-Heckler, Ph.D., a psychologist and consultant on leadership and mastery, and a martial artist with a sixth-degree black belt in aikido, who chronicled the story in his book *In Search of the Warrior Spirit*.

To many the project seemed a strange nonsensical paradox to even consider teaching meditation to "trained killers." And the martial art of aikido seemed counterintuitive to battlefield concepts of war and destruction, as the very idea of aikido is the release of power through harmonizing with, or perhaps even loving, an attacker, in a modality of "giving in" or "noncontention for space."

At first many of the commandos thought Strozzi-Heckler a complete fool for thinking that the "not doing" of meditation was an action useful for high-level, high-stress military work. "What the hell is this Zen s@#$ gonna do for me in a firefight? Why do I need to relax in order to be more effective in hand-to-hand combat? Shouldn't I just work on speed and power strikes?"

In neuroscience terms, a program objective was to train the soldiers to learn how to consciously induce the alpha wave brain, a relaxed but alert mind-and-body high-energy state that is conducive to accelerated learning and creative problem solving. Being uptight and making too much of an effort can move people out of the multidimensional alpha state into the less open, more linear beta state. For most soldiers, especially combat war veterans, the capacity for alpha can be debilitated in order to cope with the stress of battle, and being open and relaxed even while off the battlefield can feel unmanageable and vulnerable.

Further, the whole idea of "giving in" or the "noncontention for space" as part of a "martial art" in order to be more effective at being tough commandos was at first completely foreign both in physical training and in mental framework. But in the ancient practices of the Way of the Warrior, such as the Japanese samurai, a focus on meditative practices, arts, and service were part and parcel to being a warrior. A warrior without compassion, fairness, justice, and politeness would not be considered a warrior. A true warrior defends and protects, and will defend that honor to the death. For the warrior death is not to be feared. Death is a natural part of life and inevitable to all, so what is important is living in the moment for good and as the best possible you. Or as Seneca, the first-century Roman Stoic philosopher, said, "As it is with a play, so it is with life—what matters is not how long the acting lasts, but how good it is."

For the project, the Green Berets learned and practiced various aikido and meditation techniques, as well as utilized clinical biofeedback to learn how to consciously move into an alpha state.

Over time as they became more in tune with meditation and biofeedback, quieting their mind and listening to their body, some began to notice an improvement in their aikido as well as their overall energy and attitude. At the same time they were baffled by it. Their newfound fluidity and power in movement while practicing aikido was tangible, but it came with less effort, which didn't make sense to their rational mind.

Additionally, the work they were doing began to have the effect of these tough men actually feeling and moving into their emotions. Men who were raised to endure, be strong, and not be carried away by emotions, who were fearful of not being masculine enough, found themselves in tears while at the same time saying, "I'm not supposed to cry." All of which didn't fit with their definition of *who I am* as a strong Special Forces warrior.

However, as the Tibetan meditation master Chögyam Trungpa Rinpoche put it, "The key to warriorship . . . is not being afraid of who you are. Ultimately, that is the definition of bravery: not being afraid of yourself." And as Strozzi-Heckler went on to say, "When we no longer are afraid of who we are we act from integrity and authenticity." Knowing who we are, whoever we are, even the newfound versions brought about by exploring new territory of the self, enables a mode of living in the space of the possible. For we are no longer bound by conventions that don't serve us. We are born anew from moment to moment.

As the Green Berets bravely came to experience and view themselves with new eyes, they could see certain of their previous constructs as transparent and fragile, and the new modes of being became a framework to live in for bringing more life to life. Constructs of ideas, routine and tradition can sometimes turn out to be very thin windowpanes in a self-constructed glass house held in shadowy suspension between you and the full experience of the electric phenomenon called life. But you can open your eyes to see and then make a choice, perhaps throw a stone to crash down the glass limits that you live in, or merely open the window and breathe new air and then step through the doorway to a possibility of more self.

In aikido the martial artist becomes passive and accepting as a method to totally observe a relationship without judgment, fear or tension. They are not fixated or bound by the notion of enemy, but stay in detached openness to what is and what may transform. This is truly "Jedi" training, a Mind, Body, Spirit evolution in which a Soldier moves into Warrior. From the unthinking universal "Clone" soldier who follows orders and accomplishes missions, to the "Jedi" warrior who uses violence as a last resort and instead seeks relationship to an enemy or obstacle in order to better understand the point of friction. And in better ascertaining the friction point, the solution whether tactical, strategic or diplomatic, can be found and used effectively. To not contend for space is not just a technique to better defend oneself from a knife, punch or kick, it is a philosophical place of third-party objectiveness that one can use to dismantle resistance. Seeing an enemy as part of the whole system of life, not as a target to simply destroy, creates opportunities for a more harmonious and responsible way of being.

As the Trojan Warrior Project progressed over time these once doubtful students became some of the best with many going on to Delta Force, the Army's highest-level commandos. Two Delta snipers in particular went on to be awarded the Medal of Honor for their courageous actions that were recounted in the movie *Black Hawk Down*, when they knowingly and bravely requested to be put in the line of fire in defense of another and faced certain death with a heart of purity and love.

In the end this experimental project demonstrated how integrated Mind, Body, and Spirit techniques can work to yield significant and impressive increases in physical fitness, mental focus, values enhancement, and team cohesion. As a result of the project, Strozzi-Heckler went on to become instrumental in the development of today's Marine Corps Martial Arts Program, which combines combat with morale and team-building functions, and uses an advancement system of colored belts similar to that of most martial arts, as Marines train in pursuit of the "Warrior Ethos."

Even as a quiet hero in day-to-day life we can learn from this alpha state and the relaxed but alert holistic ability to create and respond with attention and skill to any problem that arises. With so many stresses that come with hectic modern life, I wonder whether many of us are living primarily in a beta state and would greatly benefit from mindfully cultivating alpha capabilities, just as the Green Berets did.

A hero takes useful knowledge from anywhere he or she can find it and applies it as needed in the here and now and now.

The hero continually acts bravely to cultivate a sense of pure self that is "no longer afraid of who you are" and opens his or her mind and spirit as doors to explore new paths and modalities of being.

In this sense, a hero's courage and compassion can fluidly take the form of anything. Any space or action or stillness can reflect the power and wisdom of the hero.

As my hero Bruce Lee counseled, "Empty your mind, be formless, shapeless—like water. Now you put water into a cup, it becomes the cup, you put water into a bottle, it becomes the bottle, you put it in a teapot, it becomes the teapot. Now water can flow or it can crash. Be water, my friend."

The Real Me

"Know thyself."

Inscribed on walls and over doors of ancient temples, written in sacred texts, related in stories and myths, prescribed by sages and gurus and philosophers around the globe for thousands of years, this phrase resounds as a fundamental compass point, a true magnetic north for the human path of being.

I can ask, "Who am I?" and very quickly rattle off a long list of this and that.

I am an author, a brother, a son, a fitness trainer, a speaker, a triathlon athlete, a martial artist, an ex-husband, a former Recon Marine . . . I love my family and friends, comics, reading, movies, traveling, peanut butter, boxing, mixed martial arts . . . I have this much money; I own a house, a car, clothes, a suitcase . . . I have this . . . I've accomplished that . . . I'm this tall . . . I have brown hair . . . I was unwanted . . . abused . . . I was a champion . . . a hero . . . I did this . . . I will do that . . .

While I may think of myself in these terms, this biographical inventory of roles and responsibilities, successes, failures, physical traits, haves and have-nots and happenstances, only goes so far toward answering the question. Or in some ways this description may not answer the question at all, or may even be a way to avoid actually digging deeper into the matter.

Because, in fact, I am not my house or my money.

Whether I like smooth or chunky peanut butter isn't very revealing or consequential.

I am not my job.

I am not my social position.

I am not my circumstance.

These may be aspects of my life experience or elements of a self-portrait I show myself and others, but they are not my essential self. They may be a means of expressing or sharing or learning more about myself, but they are not my essential self.

My house may burn down, I could lose my job or suffer a debilitating injury, but I, my *self*, my true essence, would remain.

To *know* thyself is not a guess. It is not in the future.

To *know* thyself is to perceive or understand the truth. It is not a distortion or avoidance of what is.

I may be wrong or even deceived about something I *know*, but evolving what I *know* is an ongoing active process of "know thyself" squarely planted in the here and now and now . . .

To "know thyself" I must plug into the river of my experience as a sentient captain of my ship, to exercise my authority as the only person with a viewpoint to see the vessel of *who I am*, to discern and accept and take responsibility for myself as I am.

This takes courage and hope and trust.

I must have the courage to be radically honest.

I must trust myself to be compassionate and forgive.

I must rely on myself to be strong with integrity, to take action wisely and when needed and learn from my missteps.

This is why "know thyself" is part of a hero's journey—it takes a hero's bravery to "not be afraid of who I am."

In the movie *Superman III*, Superman turns to evil ways when he unknowingly becomes exposed to a synthetic version of kryptonite. An internal battle ensues and is waged between alter egos Clark Kent and "Evil Superman" to settle the character and direction of his life on the whole. Mild-mannered Clark makes a stand against the aggression of his sickened egoistic self not only to resolve the conflict, but to see himself wholly as he is, and forgive and not linger too long in shame or guilt for his misgivings. Superman makes right his wrongs against others and gets back to the business of living in the essence of his true hero self.

In real life, Christopher Reeve, the actor who played Superman, was later paralyzed as a quadriplegic in a horse-riding accident. In a depressed state after the injury, he once considered suicide because of his severe disabilities. His wife encouraged him to pull out of the depression by saying, "I still love you, no matter what. You are still you."

Reeve pulled himself together on the inside after that; he freed himself from his cage of depression and got back to living in the essence of his true hero self. Although he was paralyzed, his true essence flowed like water as he continued to work as an actor, as well as labored diligently to raise awareness of the issues and possible solutions for others with spinal cord injuries. Reeve once said, "What makes Superman a hero is not that he has power, but that he has the wisdom and maturity to use the power wisely." Even though there may be times of faltering, the hero wisely finds the way back to center.

To "know thyself," no one else can fulfill the responsibility or substitute for me. There may be support or encouragement from others, or not. Either way, it is up to me.

I can decide to not be the hero. I could alternatively choose the path of villain or victim or bystander or just not care, but that's not what this book is about. Because I simply believe that true happiness and a life free from suffering are found along the hero's path. A path of love, compassion, joy, and equanimity, where compassion and love are not mere luxuries, but a fundamental source of inner and external peace. Along this path a person is super whether or not there are super villains to battle. We may need villains for interest and morals in our stories; we don't need them as a necessity for heroism in real life. A child can be a hero simply by sharing a toy.

We can rescue an animal, a friend, or a stranger, and in so doing rescue ourselves. We can all be heroes in peace.

But no matter my direction if I truly want to "know thyself," I must be willing to choose and cast off the lines, hoist anchor and set sail into the unknown waters of *self*, and push my limits in a great adventure to explore and "know thyself." As Reeve said, "Either you decide to stay in the shallow end of the pool, or you go out in the ocean."

Or as the pioneering psychologist and philosopher William James wrote, "Seek out that particular mental attribute which makes you feel most deeply and vitally alive, along with which comes the inner voice which says, 'This is the real me,' and when you have found that attitude, follow it."

When I follow this attitude of "the real me," I am following my bliss in a wondrous act of creation. I am not on an adventure to "find" myself, I am venturing forward in an act of cocreation between "me" and the "knower" of me in a practice of "know thyself" right here right now.

In something as simple as my everyday fitness training sessions, I could simply go through the motions of a routine—this much weight, this many reps, run this far—or I can take a deep breath and dive into my *self*, my Mind, Body, and Spirit with an attitude of "the real me" and explore past perceived limits of weight and reps and distance, right here right now and now . . .

So I begin with my mind. I dive in as "me" and "knower" and set my mind into my pure zone of breath, rooting to the earth with a balanced stance and courage for the unknown. Only then do I begin to move my body, rolling my shoulders like I have fifty thousand times before, my trapezius and neck relax and my skull is stretched tall through my spine as my heels become one with the ground. Deep inhalations and power exhales create a cadence that onlookers can feel and touch.

I am in creation, creating my reality.

Now, now, now driving energy from my core and pistoning my fist forward in free flow punches. I inhale while throwing three punches, and exhale while throwing three more, so that there is always action with breath. No separation. I am punching fists flying forward on the outside but on the inside it is the firing of the back and the twisting of the waist and the pressing on the toes that is responsible for the power.

It is all relationship. It is all in and out. Pulleys and levers and u-joints that take energy flowing in from one direction and channel it into another.

I feel the heat and the metal taste in my mouth from the exertion and fast paced movements, but I don't call it pain. It's just stimulus. It's just an experience. I may get fatigued but I never get tired. Tired is a state of being, and my state of being is anything but. So fatigue does not have a negative connotation either, because soon the dualism of "good" and "bad" is gone and I am breathing my body into pure possibility and powerful self-realization.

Run in place and breathe and sweat and believe and dream and see yourself in the ocean, in the Colosseum, see yourself in the Olympics. See yourself. Be truly yourself and all that is possible in being you. Completely integrated Mind, Body, and Spirit. One is a component of the other and all are connected and manifested in action. When I lift weights I imagine myself as Hercules or Samson. I envision the weight of the heavy bench presses as a bar in my cage or something that feels oppressive, then engage my emotions as a power source and I just get more fired up as I press it up and up. I just won't let those things that trap and enslave me weigh heavy on my chest. I will push it up as *my choice of cocreation*. I choose to make these feelings into the event of my Body Olympics. My feelings become obstacles or weights to move or lift or leap over.

This is not about looks. I am not interested in looks as the primary. The primary is to create this "me" as a vehicle of *now*.

When I am able to show up and be fully present, with my Body vital, powerful and flexible, then Mind and Spirit synergistically engage and follow along on the path of truth. No dogma, just the truth brought about by discipline and sweat and the brain and nervous system connecting in a process of knowing.

People are sometimes surprised to learn that a key element of my physical fitness is to have no routine and never do a maintenance workout. Every training session is so much more than just spending an hour at the gym as I am now engaged in an adventure of exploring and exploding past limits. I am feeling my body, focusing my mind, and feeling my emotions.

I am fully engaged in a process of "know thyself."

I am fueling the power plant of my life force and awareness, realizing my potential and reaping the real prize . . . a channel open to myself as I am and the possibilities beyond.

To me it is a feeling of my Body is Mind is Spirit is *pure energy*. I feel completely connected and just me. Just me.

It doesn't matter whether you're in a gym or at the office, at home, on a mountaintop or sailing the seven seas, the invitation into more of yourself is always and forever extended with strength and warmth and loving-kindness. *You* are always there to *know* now and now and now . . . no matter where you are, no matter what you're doing!

In following "the real me" I am not bound by limits or obstacles, because I actively rework and use them for my purposes, for knowing more of myself. Even in a simple workout, each experience and circumstance and moment is a possibility for more freedom from and for myself.

My Body and Mind working honestly and pushing limits in a concert of truth to open up and let my Spirit free.

I am following in the footsteps of my hero Bruce Lee when he said, "Let the spirit out—discard all thoughts of reward, all hopes of praise and fears of blame, all awareness of one's bodily self. And, finally closing the avenues of sense perception, let the spirit out, as it will."

THE HERO'S WHETSTONE:
KNOW WHO I AM

As a kid I had a knack for drawing, and eventually I learned to become a skilled illustrator in school and also while making sketch surveillance drawings in the field as a Marine. Occasionally I have drawn a few pictures of myself, and I've had the honor of being painted and sculpted by others as well.

Artists have been representing themselves through various art forms since ancient times. In Europe there was a boom of self-portraiture that occurred during the Renaissance with the increased monetary wealth and interest in the individual as a subject, as well as the availability of better and cheaper mirrors.

An artist makes many choices in developing their own portrait, from the medium of expression, to colors, poses, alone or with others, the angles, wardrobe, facial expression, location, lighting and more, all of which combine to present a singular fixed image. In asking the question, "Who am I?" every person similarly engages in the making of their own self-portrait in choosing what to focus on and present to his or her self and the outside world.

I can describe my physical attributes, my behaviors, morals, temperament, and ideas, my place in society, my financial position, my home, my stuff, or where I've been, where I want to go, my dreams, my emotions and moods, or less or more, and paint it in a colorful portrait that catches the eye with a label "WHO I AM." I can examine this picture as the "knower" of "me." If there's something I don't like or doesn't seem right about the picture, I can change it. Or others can look at the picture and convey their opinions about the accuracy of the representation from their own perspective. I may feel very attached to these descriptions, or even emotional about them. I may have certain thoughts and beliefs about or because of them. Similarly, I can look at other people's portraits and have an opinion about them. There may be things I like or not; we may even have disagreements over them.

Every moment we are all presenting and sifting through the fluid multitude of living color images that surround us.

In a way this can be fun. Like in the funhouse I went through as a kid at a small carnival in town and loved the room with all the mirrors because they made you look funny and all distorted. And because it reminded me of the scene in the movie *Enter the Dragon* with Bruce Lee where he had to discern which images were real and useful for his fight with an enemy. He broke through the false images by cracking the glass on the mirrors until the only image that remained was the true self.

I think in many ways life is like that.

We project images, we see images, and we mirror them back to others and they to us. And we have to continually sift through and discern, engage and create our reality.

For this whetstone, it will be helpful to first review all the contemplative whetstones and your truths from the first five strides. From tuning into yourself and identifying your cage and your hopes and dreams, to packing tools and practicing skills for your mission, including to understand the ins and outs of your tuning forks.

Now find that aspect of yourself that is the wise "knower," your self that can see with a detached third-party view and compassion. Also tune in to your sense of adventure and attitude of fun.

Does that seem like a lot? If it does, don't worry about it, just let it go. You can do this in your own time and in your own way.

So let's start with three deep breaths. As you inhale breathe in an attitude of openness and pull the air deeply into your lungs using your abdominal muscles. And as you exhale let go of all thoughts and quiet the mind as you slowly breathe air out through your lips.

Breathe in openness.

Exhale all thought.

If your mind resists with memories of the day or things you need to do, simply make a note of it and let it go for now. You will attend to it later. This moment is for you in simple mindful awareness. If you need to take a few moments to settle yourself into it, go ahead and take as much time as you need. Sit in the quiet and the energy for a moment; then, when you're ready, move on.

Now I want you to think of a friend. It can be someone from your past or a person you know now, but choose someone where you both know each other well, and you like and respect them. As you think of this friend, think of how you see them. If you were to create a portrait of them, what would it look like? Or if it's simply a verbal description, think of that or even write it down. Consider your friend for a moment, and then consider the following questions.

- If you were to share your picture of this friend with them, do you imagine they would see the same things, or in the same way, or agree with all aspects of your depiction?
- What is it that you like about this friend or picture of them? Is it their humor, intelligence, their looks, money, job, home, social standing, compassion, honesty . . . ?
- Is there something about them that you don't care for or that bothers you? If so, what is it?
- What do you imagine their picture of you would be like? Would it be similar or different than how you see yourself?
- Do any particular emotions come up as you think of this? If so, what are they? Do you know what they're about?

I believe every person holds a mirror of possibility for us to look into ourselves in a deeper way. A potential for us to peel back another layer to reveal who we really are.

This is true of anyone, friend or foe. They all hold information for us to use and examine in understanding our true nature.

The noted psychologist Carl Jung once wrote, "Everything that irritates us about others can lead us to an understanding of ourselves."

Wow! That's quite a statement.

So let's try a little experiment and think of something about your friend or another person that irritates you. Now instead of simply focusing on the irritation, try this exercise for diving in deeper to knowing thyself. As you think of this irritation, consider this.

- What is the nature of this irritation? Is it minor or serious? Intentional or not? A common occurrence or occasional?
- What specifically about it bothers you? And why?
- How much does it irritate you? Does it seem to push any of your buttons? If so, is the irritation all about this person?
- How do you deal with it? Ignore, yell, confront, cajole, cry, beg, laugh, rationalize, or smile?
- Do you understand why this person does this?
- Do you carry a grudge about it? If so, what purpose does this serve?
- Can you forgive or have compassion for this?
- Can you imagine something that would help this person better handle what he or she may be struggling with in doing this?

It's been said that what you like and dislike in others is actually a reflection of what you like and dislike in yourself. I don't know if this is always true, but it seems like a good sounding board for seeing and examining those things, and asking whether or not they serve or are useful for your journey. In so doing you step into the aikido modality of "giving in" or "noncontention for space" to find a release of power through harmonizing with the irritation in an exploration for new insights into yourself and others. Even in the case of a serious irritation, as in causing physical harm or taking away your life, even this can serve to inform you about your feelings and attitudes, your approach to life and death. Do you shrink from the thought paralyzed in fear, or do you have another approach? How does this attitude ripple through the rest of your life?

The Dalai Lama has said, "Awareness of death is the very bedrock of the path. Until you have developed this awareness, all other practices are obstructed."

While it may be uncomfortable to look at or accept your own mortality, I suggest that staying in fear about it serves no one. Instead consider this approach. Take death as your adviser to living. In this way death becomes a challenge to not waste time. It tells us to love each other right here right now. It tells us to tell each other that we love each other. In the moment that we take on this attitude, this reminder of death becomes our ally in sifting through what is or is not important in our lives. It tells us right here right now to drop the petty differences within ourselves and with others and get on with the business of sailing in the deepest channels of our life.

On the popular social networking Web site Facebook, users can paint picture of themselves with photos and written descriptions as they interact with others who have done the same. Always at the top of their profile page a user can type in an answer to the question "What are you doing right now?"

When I click to type my response, the beginning of the answer always fills in automatically with "Rudy is" and leaves the rest for me to finish or leave simply as is.

"Rudy is." That I am.

To me, this is at the heart of "know thyself." Every moment of here and now, the loud quiet call of the hero invokes, "Who am I?" In each moment is intoned, "I am . . ."

If you have access to a mirror, please take a moment and look into it now. If there's no mirror available simply close your eyes. Know that you are breathing the answer to that question now. Starting now, take a moment and say out loud, "I am."

Say it again and add more words if you like to *who I am* and in creation of "know thyself." You choose the answer: "I am———."

For the next week, every day look in the mirror or close your eyes and thoughtfully say, "I am . . ." Continue for more days if you like, but do this for at least one week and notice the direction of your life and how you feel about it. Notice how your truth and "I am . . ." resonate through you.

The teacher, author, and philosopher Joseph Campbell once said, "The way to find out about happiness is to keep your mind on those moments when you feel most happy, when you are really happy—not excited, not just thrilled, but deeply happy. This requires a little bit of self-analysis. What is it that makes you happy? Stay with it, no matter what people tell you. This is what is called following your bliss."

As you check in with yourself and say, "I am . . ." every day, notice how close you are to resonating with and following your bliss. If you don't like the answer you are creating with your thoughts and actions, change it. Or as Thomas Jefferson once wrote, "Do you want to know who you are? Don't ask. Act! Action will delineate and define you." You have the power to act and steer the course of *who I am* and bring your life to life.

You have your authentic "this is the real me" self as your compass. You have the inspiration and company and footsteps of your fellow heroes.

You are a hero.

Be the hero you wish to see.

You are Hero Living now and now and now . . .

Living Life Out Loud

Living in possibility is an attitude available to anyone of any age, any gender, any nation. It's something to be cultivated at any point of life—young or old, in sickness and in health, good times and bad, in joy or in sorrow. A child or the elderly can all live in the mode of possible. While living in possibility is a cultivated outlook, it's not one to be acquired over time; it's one to be stepped into at any moment. For instance, one of my most fun experiences of such living was while I was a young adult.

It was the annual Spirit Festival, and on the lawn of Liberty Memorial in Kansas City ten thousand music fans at were screaming like mad in anticipation of the big acts—Stabbing Westward, Ugly Kid Joe, and Candlebox—to take their turn on stage. But there was one band left to play, the king of the local regional bands, and as the announcer shouted "Venus Auto" through the sound system the crowd revved up to a raucous roar as we hit the stage and I grabbed the microphone while my buddies struck drums and guitar chords. We felt on top of the world!

Five years earlier my life in Kansas City consisted of working full-time and a half waiting tables at Lucille's Restaurant and training full-time in kung fu. I was twenty years old enjoying the adventure of working and training and living with both of my brothers. We didn't have much "stuff," but at least we could get by and have a little extra spending cash to buy comics and training gear.

My life was very simple but full, and I loved working at the restaurant. There was movement and speed, and I really took pleasure in the interpersonal relationships and laughter of cooks, wait staff, management and customers. On the weekends we were open twenty-four hours so there was always a varied mix of people coming in late, on their way home from the theater or a romantic date, out late bar hopping, or just the local high school and college kids hanging out drinking coffee and having milkshakes.

On one such very busy and late Friday night, some rockers in their late twenties came in looking like Guns 'n Roses with their long hair, tattoos, headbands, and leather pants, and their girls all dressed up in heavy metal tight jeans, too much makeup and big hair. Although I was very straight edge with my kung fu—I was a vegetarian and didn't even drink alcohol—my hair was grown out long and cascaded way down my back in a counterculture gesture, so the rockers and I were "cool" with each other.

I got their order of biscuits and gravy, omelette, pancake stacks, milk shakes, and coffee, and noticed that the guy I thought must be the lead singer was looking kind of dour, so I made sure to keep the energy high and in a positive space. The other guys seemed a bit frustrated as well, but every time I came by and asked how the food was or if they needed more coffee, I lifted everyone's spirits a bit.

Next time I came back around, the lead guy said, "Hey, man, you've got such a great attitude. It's three in the morning and most everybody here is drunk, a jerk, or both. How do you do it?"

"My brother, I practice kung fu and chi kung—it's like a super-powerful moving meditation. Nothing gets you down when you live the Tao," I replied with zest. "It just turns every day into possibilities and dreams. You know what I mean?"

The leader was now smiling and so were the other guys, and the girls were looking at me like somehow I was now cool.

"Well, bro, my name is Greg, and this is my band, Channel Zero. We had the biggest show of our life tonight and our singer was horrible and blew it, so he got fired after the show. The band was just thinking of breaking up, but I think you just saved us."

"You mean you guys want to start practicing kung fu with me?"

I was ecstatic, feeling like I was making a difference by turning people on to a way of life that brought happiness and health. I started telling them about the classes, but was immediately interrupted by Greg.

"No, you're not getting it, Young Blood. I want *you* to be our new front man. Our new lead singer."

What?? Was this guy crazy?

"Greg, I've never been in a band before, I don't even know how to sing like a rocker!" I said completely surprised. I was a kickboxer and a weight-lifting comic book collector—what did I know about being in a band?

"Listen, little bro, I can teach anyone how to sing or play drums and guitar, but what you have already in presence and attitude, the ability to connect to strangers so that they become friends . . . That is amazing!" Greg said to me. "That's what this band needs. That is the kind of energy that is creative and fun to work with. That's why we want *you*!"

Man, what a crazy life!

My life was already full to the brim with work and kung fu. I didn't know if I could learn how to sing or be part of a rock band. I didn't even know these guys! But if they were willing to take a chance on a kid bringing coffee, the realm of possibility just might be possible if we tested the limits. So when Greg said, "So Young Blood, what do you say?" he was smiling because he already knew. I mean, what else would a kung fu waiter who loves Daredevil do but take a challenge to be the change you wish to see? He understood and so did I.

So with honor and pride I responded, "Greg, or should I say maestro, when do we practice?"

And that was the start of my rock-and-roll career.

Although I was beyond enthusiastic to learn to sing and be part of something bigger and more artistic than I ever imagined, I was at ground zero at that first practice in the warehouse space above the Venus Auto Body Repair shop. But I jumped in with gusto anyway and started training my voice and learning lyrics with the guys who were the Shaolin keepers of the rock-and-roll temple.

I was the young grasshopper of five guys banging away at two-hour sessions three nights a week. In the beginning I could only get out a couple songs without straining and blowing blood vessels in my eyes from having to sing every note with gale force lung power to even hope to register over the Peavey guitar amp turned "all the way to eleven" and Greg smashing his drum set with loud intensity.

I was not very good at first, but Greg was an excellent musician that could play every instrument and also sing, and he was incredibly patient with me and an exceptional teacher and mentor. Just like in fung fu where you must practice a skill or a technique ten thousand times to know it, music is the same where perfection comes in the practice.

So we rehearsed and worked and rehearsed some more and finally did a first trial run in front of our friends and family where I went almost completely hoarse by the end of our set of five songs. But we kept driving on in the spirit of possibility cultivating a space of true creativity where all kinds of ideas flowed easily during practice sessions because everyone was plugged into the inventive current. By the time we had our first "real" gig, after six months of practicing, Venus Auto was "playing out" and I could kick out at least four songs with mad power.

That first gig was at a small bar called Neiners, some joint I'd never heard of in a strip mall in the churchy trailer park part of town. I thought, "Awesome, an 'easy' bar to get started on and then maybe Madison Square Garden after a few times out." Ha! Not only was I dreaming about the Garden, but the "easy" bar wasn't so easy either!

Thirty or so people were scattered around Neiners as we did

a sound check while Lynyrd Skynyrd's "Freebird" played from the jukebox. Three days earlier I had cut off my little pinkie finger while practicing knife and sword fighting with my brother, so I had a big cast on my whole arm, but the show must go on! We started our first song and by the time we got to the end we were playing it so fast and loud I felt like I'd run a marathon. First gig jitters were taking over the tempo and volume controls and driving everyone so hard and fast I could hardly keep up or be heard over the drums. Between this and my not really having a clue about how to be an entertainer on stage, I was almost surprised to hear some applause from the mullet heads in the audience for our little five song set.

Over time we developed our skills and repertoire of hard lashing, guitar driven, thunderous sonic assault songs of drowning in the undertow of Rock! Two years later when we played at Neiners again, the place was packed with over two hundred people. Many big bar shows and festival gigs later our set was fifteen songs—and I could keep going if I had to!

Rocking the stage with the Venus Auto band.

Courtesy of Reyes family

All of our songs were completely original. In the beginning I just followed Greg's mentorship and gave him lyrics that I thought had merit, but a few years later I was writing and arranging songs too. I was totally in the flow of creative energy, and no matter what the size of the venue or our set, the skill of our songs and range of my voice improved. The deeper we dove and the longer we stroked in the stream of possibility, the more doors opened to extraordinary times of living and performing, and getting paid to do it! When you feel grounded in that space, the energy seems endless and ultimately powerful, and the lessons profound.

I love this other quote from Bruce Lee when he says, "If you always put limit on everything you do, physical or anything else. It will spread into your work and into your life. There are no limits.

Flying in pure possibility off of Dune 7 in Namibia.

Courtesy of Rudy Reyes

There are only plateaus, and you must not stay there, you must go beyond them."

It seemed that if I could manifest such a powerful means of living by exploring and expressing and pushing onward through art, simply by starting from where I was at, even as a comic book reading weight-lifting waiter with no rocker skills but a good 3:00 a.m. attitude, then there must be no limits but ones we place on ourselves!

What a revelation!

And to me it seemed clear.

A hero lets go all thoughts of limits.

The exploration of limits is left to the experience of now and now and now . . . no matter the outcome.

A hero lives in pure possibility and brings life to life.

The Hero's Boon

"The truth is, Rudy, I am unfulfilled."

Now here's a guy who has all the external appearances of success—he makes good money, has a beautiful girlfriend, a big house, drives an expensive car, and by all appearances he seems to "have it all"—yet inside he's unhappy.

My friend Benny and I had recently fallen into a discussion sharing details about each other's workday. I talked about how I had spent much of my week along the beaches in San Diego working while enjoying the fresh air, and I was feeling genuinely excited about training and motivating people with their physical fitness and just feeling the energy from some great workouts.

Benny worked out in the morning, then spent the day in an office cubicle making phone calls, writing proposals, and sending out e-mails. He'd also gotten a promotion and a bonus for closing a big deal he had been working on for several months, so was thinking about taking a trip with the windfall cash he'd soon be getting.

So with all this "success," I was surprised to hear his comment.

But at the same time maybe I wasn't. I mean I hear this all the time from a lot of people. Even from those who are financially wealthy or successful businessmen and women. They have their health, plenty of food, live in comfort or even luxury, but there are even people who are rich and famous that feel like my friend Benny. Unfulfilled and unhappy.

So I asked him, "What do you want?"

"I want more," he said. "I want to be at the top and tell other people to do the work. I just want more."

I saw my friend Benny was caught in a myth.

The myth of "more."

There's nothing wrong with "more" except that it's always in the ungraspable future. I'll be happy when . . . or if . . . or once this happens . . . So when happiness is defined as "more," life becomes an endless pursuit of the carrot in baubles and trinkets, power and prestige, the thrill and rush of fleeting moments of acquisition or instant gratification and entertainments that quickly fade with little else to stand on, except to go off in pursuit of "more" once again and again and again.

The philosopher John Locke once wrote, "The necessity of pursuing happiness is the foundation of liberty. As therefore the highest perfection of intellectual nature lies in a careful and constant pursuit of true and solid happiness; so the care of ourselves, that we mistake not imaginary for real happiness, is the necessary foundation of our liberty."

In other words you must exercise your Mind, Body, and Spirit to discern and carefully discriminate between imaginary and "true and solid" happiness.

"True and solid" is foundational bedrock.

In mining for precious jewels, finding that rare stone may be hit or miss or purely a matter of luck. A miner may spend his or her entire life looking for the mother lode, carting off tons and tons of rock and dirt in the process. If the miner loves the process of mining regardless of whether they find the prize of shiny rocks, they are foundationally happy. They are engaged in the process of following their bliss now and now . . .

Having a focus on a future prize or of simply going through the motions of mining a living, can leave a person open to feeling unfulfilled, perhaps even unhappy, in the moments of now and now. By chucking away the bedrock of dirt in search of momentary jewels and pleasures, we miss the very thing that can truly satisfy and fill us up.

The satisfaction of a job well done.

The pleasure of partnership and enjoying another's company.

The wake up call of the natural senses to the awe and wonder held in the beauty of sky and ocean and terrain. The beauty of the process in which one is engaged.

And in this focus on "true and solid" happiness we find Locke's "foundation of liberty" because we are freed from enslavement to those particular fleeting desires that distract us from *who I am* and the immediate joy of "know thyself."

You understand that happiness is a habit to be cultivated.

You live with purpose.

You may still enjoy the beauty of baubles and trinkets, the pleasures and entertainments, but they do not define *who I am* or are a prerequisite to happiness. And there's the wisdom of Joseph Campbell who said, "If you follow your bliss, you put yourself on a kind of track that has been there all the while, waiting for you, and the life that you ought to be living is the one you are living. Wherever you are—if you are following your bliss, you are enjoying that refreshment, that life within you, all the time."

To place yourself on the hero's track is a simple notion of immersing yourself in the present moment, now and now . . .

For my friend Benny, he doesn't have to immediately quit his job or find another girlfriend, he must simply dive into the hero treasures inside of what is joyful and purposeful and fulfilling for him in this moment right here right now and follow that bliss. He must let go of the fixed ideas that this particular "more" will make me happy, so as to accept the gifts of now and be open to the possibilities that are coming to him from living in the slipstream of following his bliss.

The truth in Hero Living is a practice to paint your self-portrait and tool a habit of living in the authenticity of your true character. Your character—not your house or money or job—but your true essence and actions. To bravely awaken to your dreams and breathe life into the continual process of engagement in Mind, Body, and Spirit.

The English mathematician and philosopher Alfred North Whitehead wrote, "Our minds are finite, and yet even in these circumstances of finitude we are surrounded by possibilities that are infinite, and the purpose of life is to grasp as much as we can out of that infinitude."

There are moments while drifting between dreamtime and wake time that I feel an awareness of my finite self connected with the infinite, like pinholes breaking through into superconsciousness.

Several years ago while I was in my early twenties, as I slowly awoke from sleep one morning, I became aware of my dreaming and consciously remained in my dream world as an observer. In my dream my body was growing very large very fast, so quickly the world soon became a tennis ball in my hand, then like a little peppercorn, and then Earth became invisible amongst galaxies of stars scattered everywhere. I looked down and saw I had a handful of stars all at my fingertips, and then my fingers and hands became the stars.

There in my dream, a never-ending fractal repeatedly duplicated on and on through endless magnifications of space, a microcosm of the macrocosm, a macrocosm of the microcosm, twisting its beautiful array in a unique DNA pattern of "me" and "not me." A drop of water in the ocean, the finite me in the infinite.

This dream of oneness felt powerful and resounding. I have since kept it in my mind as a visceral reminder and feeling of how we are all connected and part of that something bigger than me. In this state of bliss and connection with the eternal, I "know thyself" as fulfilled and free, living in the great spirit of possibility.

Although a dream of lucid sleep, it still somehow makes sense to my wakeful awareness—that we are all aspects and part of something bigger than our individual selves. We are connected as one.

So think of your dreams . . . of that which brings you real joy . . . that makes you feel most deeply and vitally alive.

Bravely see yourself, as you are, all the foibles and quirks and charms and delights and compassionately accept *who I am.*

Break through the myths of disillusionment and let go.

Listen for the inner voice which says, "This is the real me."

This is your bliss.

Now follow it . . . now and now and now . . .

In this you have the hero's boon.

The illumination of the hero's path as timeless and experienced in the here and now, with the bliss of the eternal journey as the prize.

More happiness and fulfillment from within, less needed from without.

You share the wisdom of the Chinese philosopher Lao-Tzu, who wrote, "When you realize there is nothing lacking, the whole world belongs to you."

You are on the hero's journey.

You are a hero.

STRIDE 7
Reciprocity of Sharing

The feeling:"Now that I've become my own truth, it mustn't be kept in the temple. I must share Hero Living in my unique way, because in sharing the light with others, we are all transformed."

The truth of my life at nineteen years old was actually pretty great. Not long before, I had legally emancipated my brothers Ceasar and Michael, and brought them to Kansas City from the Omaha Home for Boys so we were finally living together again and free at last. They were everything to me. It wasn't always easy being big brother and dad rolled into one, but protecting and caring for them gave my life purpose. We were the Three Musketeers and without them my life would have been very different, and I don't imagine better.

Our life was simple, but full. Ceasar was seventeen, Michael was sixteen, and we shared an apartment in midtown close to the action. They went to school and we all worked at Mama Stuffeati's, a packed and trendy restaurant at Westport and Main, where we earned enough money for food, shelter, and clothing and a little extra spending cash.

At school Michael had some problems with gang altercations, so he was looking at dropping out in order to avoid the trouble there.

"Rudy, I like making money," he'd say.

"Little man, I know the school isn't safe but work without higher learning will limit you. You gotta learn from my example and experience," I told him. He took my advice and enrolled in a GED program as well as continued with his moneymaking pastimes.

To my mind, my mission, our mission, was the cause of furthering our muscle, mind and movement capabilities, not only for protection purposes, but also as a healthy way of being. Looking back now I really discouraged bad habits and influences because times were really tight and I never saw the need to waste hard earned sweat and elbow grease on anything that did not further our cause. So I kept myself and my brothers away from drugs and alcohol and instead focused our free time into weight lifting, music, comics, role-playing games in which we used our imaginations, and indulging in the occasional Reese's Peanut Butter Cups. We had a membership at the YMCA, but the front room in our apartment was also a home gym with an Olympic bench, dumbbells, and barbells.

Maybe it was because he's the middle child, or maybe not, but whatever the reason Ceasar was always the rebel. I loved him dearly, but at the same time it would drive me nuts to find him smoking behind my back or being a general pain in the neck. I will tell you though; he's as funny as all get out and had those Richard Greico looks that could charm any girl around. He was always doing his own thing, but he was hip!

Lifting and bodybuilding was what I knew to be disciplined and successful, so it's what I knew and wanted to share with my brothers for their own success. I wanted them to make it! Plus it was something we could always do together, and a family that push-ups together stays together.

In the Omaha Home for Boys, Ceasar was a skilled gymnast and wrestler. He had also excelled in a lot of fistfights in the gladiator academy of a high school he attended, so he was nicknamed Julio Ceasar Reyes after the famous Mexican boxing champ Julio César Chávez. Of the three of us boys, I think he was probably the most naturally talented athlete of all, but still I would feel like I was almost babysitting him every time we went to the gym. I always tried so hard to get him involved with lifting weights and training, but he would resist, perhaps even simply because I wanted him to. I mean he would still come with Michael and me to the YMCA for a workout, but often he'd wander off to hang out or do his own thing. He wasn't really interested in it like me, so he was always wandering around and I would be constantly engaging him to keep him involved. I would feel like I wasn't doing enough or he was missing out and I'd end up feeling frustrated when he didn't embrace my way of doing things.

It was the same thing late one evening when we went to the YMCA and I headed upstairs with them both in tow and commenced getting our workout going. My little man Michael was always at my side and just amazing and to this day is my most dedicated training partner. So per usual about ten minutes into it Michael and I were doing forced reps on pull-ups, but Ceasar was wandering around elsewhere and after awhile he was out of sight.

After the end of another great workout adventure, Michael and I looked around for Ceasar. When we finally found him downstairs, I didn't know what to think because he was just glowing and grinning ear to ear!

"Ceasar, what are you so happy about?" I asked.

"Rudes! I just had my first Shaolin kung fu lesson and it's about fighting like animals . . . but you never fight, you only defend . . . and it's from ancient China and it was created by Buddhist monks and . . ." Ceasar was just pouring out information and passion like I had never, I mean *never*, seen before.

"Whoa, Ceasar. What are you talking about? You were learning martial arts?" I said.

I was amazed. Martial arts had always been my love and light, with Bruce Lee and ninja films inspiring me to train my techniques day and night. But never had I considered that I could afford to train formally or have my own Mr. Miyagi like in the *Karate Kid* movies. Twenty dollars a month for the YMCA dues was about all I could afford after taking care of the basic necessities of life. So I just couldn't believe there was a martial arts teacher right here in my YMCA, and one that would just take a student and teach him so much history and culture in one session.

But somehow it was so!

And somehow while I was so into my workout that I didn't notice a group of esoteric looking guys in black pajamas with swords and staffs move into the building and disappear into the bottom floor, my little brother had. And Ceasar, the Wanderer, from a few paces back had followed them down.

"Ceasar, show me what it looks like!" I pleaded.

He snapped some kicks and did some strange arm movements that he called the "Praying Mantis" or the "Soaring Crane" and he suddenly became Bruce Lee and Daniel-san and Spider-Man right in front of my eyes! And I thought, "In two hours my little brother Wanderer learned all of this?"

Meanwhile Michael took notice. He was always used to seeing me teaching and leading, but now it was Ceasar that held court and I was the humble observer.

"Push me," Ceasar commanded.

So I pushed and he split my arms and twisted me to the ground. It happened so fast I was in a daze! I thought, "All right, little Wanderer, I'm going to show you on the next try!"

"Rudy, now punch me," Ceasar said with a smile.

I hesitated. Not three months prior, we had gotten in a serious fight with each other and I had hurt him, so that recent event was not lost on either of us in the moment of our little sparring exchange.

"Are you sure, Ceasar? I mean do you really want me to try?" I looked him deep in the eye.

"Sure, big bro, just do your best!" he jovially replied.

Boom! I threw a corkscrew right hand to his chest—the rest was ballet.

Ceasar moved his arms and torso like a "Falling Bird" for which the technique was named and took me in the same direction I was going, except now twice as fast and off my feet! He had complete control of my arm and as I was about to crash on my head, he cradled me from the fall to protect me from injury.

Wow! What just happened?

In one moment I was the one with the power and the next I was completely handled!

"See, brother, the monks that created this don't fight, they defend. Your intention should always be to protect. Even you—my sometimes stuck-up older brother!" Ceasar beamed smiling with his eyes and his whole face.

I was completely humbled and also enthralled to take this journey. To have a sifu to teach and mentor me. To explore a new warrior relationship with my brothers that would carry us forward and protect us during our trials and struggles, where we were just brothers and I wasn't "dad." And to see Ceasar engaged and happy and with purpose, which was probably the greatest gift of this Shaolin kung fu. In this one evening Ceasar found and followed his bliss, then shared it with Michael and me and completely changed all our lives onto the track of the martial arts warrior path.

We all became involved and took to kung fu like fish to water.

My first thought when I saw Sifu Jon Reider was "Give that man respect." He looked like a cross between a grizzly bear with a lion's mane and beard and a white Barry White, with 220 pounds of muscle and square squat feet made of stone. In his forties with a mysterious and violent past, his eyes looked tired, but to me he seemed an old soul and wise.

Sifu was quite secretive about his past and the nature and roots of his kung fu teacher, a mysterious Chinese man named Bi Sang who had befriended him as a boy shortly after he lost his father. But I knew the two had been inseparable and Sifu Bi Sang instructed him in the arts and secrets of kung fu with very hard ways of training that had an almost inhumane approach to injuries and pain. In turn our training was similarly severe and Spartan with absolute loyalty demanded. Sifu was so thunderous with his palm strikes and mambalike snake techniques that anyone not completely committed would soon find the door. My nature was to be kind and gentle, so when I would instruct others under him I often sensed that he wanted me to teach with more pain, more hate, but also somewhere back behind the terror and fury of his past I believe he also saw a redemption with us.

Sifu Jon had no children of his own, but in meeting Ceasar, Michael, and me, it seemed that he somehow now had a family of three sons, and the possibility of fathering and experiencing family in a different way. He never charged us money for our training; he felt it even degraded the true spirit of the tradition to commercialize it. The only payment was humility, discipline, toughness and the ability to control fear. So in his own way Sifu took us under his wing and made us family and imparted his wisdom with each battle of swords, staves, and knives, all giving and receiving in a circuit of learning demanded and shared with every punch and kick we practiced with each other. The YMCA and then a warehouse downtown became our Shaolin temple where we immersed in the hallowed

Courtesy of Reyes family

In training in the warehouse in Kansas City.

halls of ancient tradition and became three warrior brothers and
"sons" humbly following the instruction of our "father" sifu together
as a family practicing and honing our Mind, Body, and Spirit skills
of martial art.

Even in the moments of Sifu's harshness, I understood we
were connected in the reciprocity of learning, a sharing of growth
and life.

Eventually we Reyes brothers went onto train with other great
masters in a continual pursuit of happiness and hunger for more
knowledge and skills, and in the following decade Michael became
a world champion in Chinese Wushu and kung fu, and a sought-
after martial arts teacher.

Courtesy of Reyes family

With my brother Michael, fighting with staffs.

Ceasar became a highly skilled martial artist, but life took him in another direction to be locked behind bars where despite the darkness, hatred, and melancholy stinking in the place, his kung fu kept him alive and disciplined while away for those long hard years. In fact, one of the most beautiful memories I have of Ceasar is years later while visiting him in prison. Inside penitentiary walls dark with rancor and hostility, even though separated by glass, for Ceasar and me it was the dojo again! We both practiced our forms and Ceasar taught me some of his style that he had been perfecting and testing while on the inside.

I was his humble student again.

I just watched and learned and was taken back to that first evening when my brother Ceasar changed my life. As we moved in our prison dojo the mentoring of sages before us flowed through in a full circuit from me to him to me.

By sharing his bliss Ceasar really gave me the gift of the special

Courtesy of Reyes family

With my brother Ceasar.

journey of martial arts in my life, of training with my sifu masters, and of having a place to be just a brother with my brothers.

These are gifts of relationship and the adventure of pushing to explore past limits in knowing ourselves and each other.

We are all in relationship. An interconnected web of relating every moment of our lives.

The life of relationships is dynamic, a never-ending mutual exchange of experiences and ideas and apportioning of resources. Sometimes as teacher, sometimes student, we influence and share with and engage each other in the varying roles and modalities of life.

By living authentically as yourself in following your truth, your light shines inside and brings light to another, and as their light beams your own light is fueled in return.

In the time since those early years I have gone onto coach and mentor many others in martial arts. One student in particular came to me as a teenager struggling with school and drugs and alcohol. He came from an affluent background, but when his father left the family, Andy felt lost and adrift without an anchor or a sail to hoist. He was smart and intelligent, but when I met him he was at a sixth-grade reading level in high school. He was quiet and introverted and just didn't feel engaged in life anymore. He was going to drop out of school.

We started training with martial arts, swimming, and running and gradually he began to make a shift. His physical fitness improved, his confidence improved, his school work improved, his attitude . . . And whereas in the beginning he was very much the "son" and I the "father," over time this too shifted into a relationship of discovery and joy in which I would learn from him just as he from me.

And therein lies a key to a true reciprocity of sharing.

Even in the role of teacher or the one with information or authority, the hero remains the humble student always in search of new information from any source, regardless of age, status, or rank. A hero will automatically be the ready student or humble teacher as needed in the reciprocal sharing of "when the student is ready, the teacher will appear."

If a person becomes attached to their role as teacher, mentor, boss, or authority in a fashion that they lose their flexibility to learn from and respect the value that others bring, the cycle of reciprocity, of back and forth, becomes short-circuited and the hero's light goes out. By retaining this flexible approach and not attaching to the image of being in charge, or the smartest, or at "the top," we're able to create a process of real sharing. Through my light Andy's own pilot light was sparked and he found his own way. He not only fueled my light by sharing his own knowledge and experiences back to me, but in so doing could see a reflection of himself as courageous and strong, a hero for himself and others.

The kid that was going to drop out of school a few short years later enrolled in college. He grew strong and in his first mixed martial arts competition he easily won hands down. His life came to life as he took one step at a time with the help of another to show the way in getting him started on his hero's journey, and at the same time he gave as much back in return.

And so goes the circuit of the reciprocity of sharing.

Teacher and student, mentor and mentee, parent and child, in the mutual exchange and sharing of ideas and experience, we all give and take, contribute and receive and take part in the ongoing cycle of Hero Living.

The course of the hero's path, like water downhill to the ocean, naturally opens to the symbiotic exchange of inner light and wisdom to manifest and shine in and between all things. A hero mentor reflects back to the student an image of the hero inside. Perhaps even believing in the student before they believe in themselves. And in so doing they can light the path before another with a hero's inspiration and hope.

My friend Allen lives in Oceanside, California, with his wife and kids and he coaches his son's little-league baseball team. He works hard to teach the basics of the game and practice good sportsmanship, and their team does great—win or lose. He also has a great love of the ocean, and surfs, fishes, shoots water sports photography, and owns a boat for the occasional fun adventures with friends and family. One weekend his love for his son, the ocean, and baseball all combined in an unsuspecting way of a hero's light and courage.

Allen's eleven-year-old son Landon had made the all-star baseball team and was starting pitcher for the tournament. It was one of those gorgeous California dreamin' days perfect for spending a few hours out on the ocean fishing with friends, so before the baseball game later in the afternoon they decided to go out for some fun in the morning. Allen with his son and daughter, another dad and two boys, all packed up their gear for the adventure and made their way down to the marina and launched the motorboat into the water and headed out.

The day passed with fun in the sun, but as the time came to head back home, the motor suddenly quit and despite repeated efforts to revive the engine, they were dead in the water almost a mile offshore. Although they were able to phone a buddy with a boat to come help out, there wasn't going to be enough time to get Landon to the game. So Allen made another phone call while he considered his options. In the cubby of the boat was stored one of his surfboards, so after getting off the phone Allen turned to his son and announced they were going to "go for it" by paddling to shore on the surfboard while the rest of the party waited for the other boat to arrive.

"What?" questioned Landon. "No way. It's too far, Dad. We won't make it! That's impossible!"

"Hang on, Landon, we can do this. Impossible? Let's go for it!" Allen answered, and he grabbed the surfboard and placed it on the water.

Landon resisted and shook his head. It was a long way in and who knows what they might encounter along the way. Not two months before there had been a great white shark attack a few miles down the coastline and it was fresh in his mind. Even brushing this aside, he thought, "Even if we do make it into shore, there's no way I'll make it to the game on time, and if I'm late I don't play." Nonetheless his dad insisted, and before he knew it Landon was on his dad's back, on the surfboard, chopping across waves as his father began captaining the cocreation of their reality on the long paddle in.

The waves and ocean currents pushed them this way and that, muscles ached and groaned, but along the way Allen would gently tell his son that everything was going to be fine and they'd make it in.

"Okay, Dad, we'll make it," Landon would repeat back.

And they kept driving on.

And somehow forty minutes later father and son found themselves nearing the wave break. A big wave crested on the outside and they caught it all the way into shore, skidding up onto the beach yelling and cheering, "We made it!"

The pair salty on the sand smiled at each other and Allen gently grabbed his son by the ears and pulled him close.

"Look, son, we did it. Just like we said. We could've sat out there on that boat and gone nowhere, but we didn't. We did the 'impossible,' so now you know that anything is possible," Allen said encouragingly to his son. He sincerely looked into the boy's eyes. "When you get to that mound today, I want you to remember this. You take it and put it forward into your game, that anything is possible."

Landon smiled back at his dad and nodded his head yes.

The other phone call made from the boat had been to his wife, and she was already there to greet them and rush her son to the game. So while Allen went about the business of retrieving his boatful of friends to make it back in time for the game, Landon hopped in the car with his mom and his dad's words in his heart and headed to the fields.

That afternoon the miracle of living in pure possibility shone through from father to son to the ball to the bat and beyond as Landon pitched a nearly perfect game. And when it was his turn at bat, the boy swung away and made a connection deep into inner space that drove the ball over the fence for two homeruns and the thrill of crossing home plate to cheering teammates and most valuable player of the game.

The crowd cheered and his father smiled.

The smile of a leader who understands the power of cycling a loop of positive possibilities.

Aware of the boon that comes in shifting fear and negativity into a positive gear of no limits and "know thyself."

The smile of one who shines and shares his light.

The smile of a hero.

THE HERO'S WHETSTONE:
LIVING THE HERO EFFECT

The *butterfly effect* is a phrase popularly used in the mathematics of chaos theory to describe large variations that can be produced in a dynamic system based on initial conditions. It's the notion that a little thing can make a big difference over time.

For instance, if you were to run a weather prediction model on a computer, the slightest variation in the initial condition would produce drastic differences in the forecast. And this is how the term was coined, when mathematician and meteorologist Edward Lorenz posed the question, "Does the flap of a butterfly's wings in Brazil set off a tornado in Texas?"

He answered that while the butterfly doesn't cause the tornado, the flap of its wings is an essential contributing factor to it. The tornado would not be the same or perhaps even exist without it. Everything in the system matters.

In the dynamics of human relations, what you think and do does in fact make a difference. Taking care to be aware and mindful of your interactions can make a world of difference to your experience within yourself and with others. A kind word can lift the spirits when you're feeling down, or a good mood can swing in another direction at a thoughtless utterance. And this effect ripples through you and out into the world.

You count.

Simply by being right here right now.

You make a difference.

Sharing the uniqueness that only you can bring has bearing.

As Martha Graham said, "We are all of us unique, each a unique pattern of creativity. And if we do not fulfill it, it is lost for all time."

The pattern of you is yours to create.

Every moment is an initial condition for the next, and it is yours to choose every now and now and now . . .

You have an effect.

The effect of you.

As with other whetstones, let's start by taking three deep breaths in and out. As you inhale breathe in your truth, your authentic self, and imagine seeing yourself filled with light. As you exhale breathe out any doubt and fear and feel a positive connection with this inner light.

Breathe in truth. Breathe out fear and doubt.

Breathe in light. Breathe out a positive connection to all.

And settle into a comfortable feeling of lightness.

Now imagine in your mind's eye a pebble dropped in water and the ripples gently moving out in circles. Each circle naturally following the next in a wave of movement that goes on and on . . .

As you think of this, find your friendly self and see yourself as you authentically are, with love and compassion, as a caring friend would see you.

Now as your friendly self consider for a moment giving yourself a gift. Does anything immediately come to mind?

Whatever comes to mind is fine, but the gift I want you to consider for yourself for this whetstone should be something that you need for your real and solid happiness. This must be something that you can give yourself, not a gift from someone else. Similarly, this is something just for you, not someone else. It can be fantastical, but it must be within the realm of possible. For instance, if you're thinking a trip to Pluto would make you happy, think of something here on planet Earth.

Really think about it . . . What do you truly need for your happiness? Of all the possibilities, what gift would bring joy for you in Mind, Body and Spirit?

- Are you holding onto some guilt or blame or a grudge about something? If you let it go would that make a difference inside? Is there something you've done for which you could give yourself forgiveness? Compassion?
- Are you a perfectionist? Do you beat yourself down? Perhaps you could give yourself a break?
- If you found a way to regularly set aside some time just for you, would that fill your soul? In silence, meditation, listening to music, taking a walk, a run, enjoying a sunset, a museum, a movie, or anything else?
- What about the gift to yourself of time with family and friends? Perhaps you could arrange to have more time, or more quality time, to spend together.
- How about the gift of better health? Eat healthier, exercise more, rest more, drink less alcohol, address any issues . . .

- Is there a creative talent you'd love to develop? The gift of music, painting, writing, drawing, design, and so on?
- If you're thinking of a tangible item, what about it is appealing for you to have? What will it do for you? Will the thrill of acquiring it wear off quickly, or will it bring lasting joy?

There's no right or wrong answer for what kind of gift this is. This is your gift to you from your kind and friendly self.

Do you know what it is?

Good.

Your task now is to give yourself this gift.

Can you do this for yourself? If not, why not?

If you need to, it's okay to choose something else. If so, think of a gift you can give yourself.

This is not an act of selfishness. This is an act of caring and honoring. The principals in the reciprocity of sharing apply to you inside as well as with others. The more you share with yourself in an accepting and humble manner, the more you have to share with others.

So give with love and generosity.

And receive in the same way.

Over time, notice the effect this has within you.

Giving to yourself is the first circle of the ripples on your pond.

So let's move to the next rippling circle.

Now think of a person you know. It can be someone you're close to, or a casual acquaintance. To make it more interesting, you can optionally select someone that you have issues with, or even feel you don't like.

Now consider doing something as a gift for them. Different than a gift you might run to the store and buy them for their birthday, this should be a gift that speaks to their deep and lasting happiness in Mind, Body, and Spirit. While a new gadget or bauble may be functionally helpful or exciting, take a moment to first think a little deeper into some other options. In thinking back through the different options for your own gift before, is there anything that would seem to resonate for this person now?

This gift should be something completely unexpected, not only in timing or occasion, but in terms of what you normally do for or with this person. It can be simple or elaborate, given over a period of time or in a moment, but it should be something meaningful and that you make a special effort to do.

What comes to mind for this person?

Does he or she need a listening ear?

A kind word or a hug?

A home-cooked meal?

Help watching his or her kids?

A shoulder to cry on?

A running partner?

A massage?

Laughter?

Forgiveness?

Understanding?

A truce?

You can choose to give this person an item as a gift, but if you do, it should be something deeply personal for his or her happiness, not just a shiny trinket that brings a fleeting smile.

Whatever comes to mind, speak it out loud or write it down and see what it feels like to think of doing this for this person. Do you have any concerns or hesitations? What are they? Is there anything that would prevent you from doing this for him or her? If so, think of something else until you find what's doable.

Now consider for a moment this person's reaction in receiving this gift. Do you find yourself anticipating his or her reaction as a reward for what you've done? If this person didn't react in a certain way, would you be disappointed? Hurt? Angry? Indifferent?

How we give and receive those things we share, whether material or not, and our expectations around them can inform you about the nature of the relationship, and yourself. Furthermore, the very act of giving or serving and the expectations and attachments that go with them in themselves will transform the relationship to another plane. Imagine for a moment the difference in receiving a gift freely given, versus one that carries obligations by your acceptance of it. There can be a world of difference between them.

Some societies in the world still operate under a traditional gift economy, where a sharing of food or other abundance becomes distributed throughout the clan and social network, such as the Native Americans of the Pacific Northwest who practice the potlatch ritual, in which leaders give away large amounts of goods during a large feast and strengthen group relations while gaining honor for the leader.

In many traditions the gift is to either be consumed or passed on, whereas holding onto the gift or turning it into a capital good is strongly prohibited. For instance, an animal received as a gift must be eaten, not bred, and nonconsumable items must be passed to another in an appropriate amount of time and not held onto.

Even in a consumer-driven economy, a gift-giving season such as Christmas has its own set of expectations for those that participate in the holiday ritual. Christmas usually involves an exchange of gifts between people at the same time, versus a birthday, where typically there are multiple givers to one person, and the return gift is exchanged in the future. There are expectations about the value of items exchanged, proper protocols for thanking, admonishment for receiving without giving, and so on.

We don't always think about it, but there can be a lot of attachments, agreements, and expectations that may go with giving and receiving. Which is fine, even great, it's simply one of many ways we reciprocate and share with one another, how we interact and get along. Understanding how we participate in the circuit back and forth can give us information and choice about what we attach and agree to.

As you think about doing something for this person, honestly consider whether you might have any expectations in doing so.

- Would you expect the favor to be returned in kind at some point in the future?
- Would you be happy giving this to that person no matter his or her reaction or return of favor? Whether yes or no, are you okay with this? About yourself or that person?
- Do you hope for any social recognition or prestige?
- What, if anything, changes in your attitude or feelings if you think of giving this anonymously, and in a way he or she would never know it's from you? If you lost the thrill of seeing that person's reaction, would this keep you from giving?

Again, there's no right or wrong here; this is simply information for you to consider about yourself and your relationships. If there's something that doesn't seem right, you can now choose to take steps to change it, as you like.

Your task now is to go about giving this to this person, and to do so with as little expectation and attachment on your part as possible. Make the time, take the effort, and share your light and love with this person.

As you do your light will grow. By passing to another it shines within them and back to you again.

The circuit between you is brighter.

And within each of you there is more to share now and now . . .

A nd now there is one last rippling circle for this whetstone, the ring of sharing with something bigger than yourself—a common cause for all.

The term "six degrees of separation" refers to the idea that all people on the planet are connected to each other through only a few steps of contact between one person they know to any other person. In moments when you may feel isolated or alone, it may not seem so, but what you do, what you think and say does make a difference simply because we are all connected—oftentimes in ways you may never know. But knowing every detail of the effect of your actions or your connection isn't the point of a hero's deeds. A hero's light shines simply by living true to their authentic self in sharing that light with others.

There are countless ways in which to make a positive difference in the world, from sharing a smile to leading a revolution against oppression.

What I'd like you to do is think of your passions and consider ways that you could share them to make a positive difference to the world and community at large. It doesn't have to be grandiose; little things can make a big difference in the life of another, and from there it ripples out. I know of a couple locally in the area where I live that are on a mission to simply hug people they meet on the street. They're respectful and not intrusive about it, but they believe a hug can make all the difference to someone. And it's true; one woman hadn't been hugged in over seven years and broke down in tears when she felt the warm kindness of strangers with their arms around her. Imagine how that effect rippled for the rest of the day through that woman's life.

Perhaps you care deeply about the environment or art in

schools, living conditions for animals, sustainable farming, health and healing, clean water, reading to a child, better education, integrity in business, honesty in government, curing a disease, caring for the elderly, green energy, or simply keeping the sidewalks clear for everyone to pass safely by.

It doesn't matter what it is, what matters is that you somehow get involved and share your light.

Who I am and your role in the world is your decision.

The nature of the force you bring the world is your creation in sharing your light.

It is up to you.

So what are you passionate about?

What ways are out there to be involved?

Perhaps there's an organization you could get involved with that is working along these same lines already. Or maybe you simply share your thoughts in writing or through your work or art— with your political leaders, in an online blog, or through charitable organizations.

While it's helpful to voice the issues, it's important to get beyond the stage of raising awareness or even just complaining, and move into doing. Create actionable things to do.

Create a life of sharing.

Share a life of creation.

Share the wisdom in the words of Bruce Lee when he said, "Real living is living for others."

The effect of Hero Living.

Living the Hero Effect.

All for One, One for All

Sometimes it may seem that the reciprocity of sharing is about big ideas and programs that reach out and affect the world at large in grandiose sweeping motions. But in fact, some of the most important, meaningful and poignant moments of sharing come in our relationships to those we are closest to. I can't tell you how many times my beautiful ex-wife said to me, "Baby, you are so cool!" For some reason that line from the movie *True Romance* stuck with us and became part of the fabric of our relationship from the time we watched it together as young adults.

We first met when my buddy invited a gal he knew from the Kansas City Art Institute to check out the kung fu class at the YMCA. I was the one with the car, so I offered to give her a ride the next time my buddy, Ceasar, Michael, and I were going to class. I stopped the car and in hopped a gal who stopped all our hearts. We were young men not quite sure of how to handle a pretty young woman, but her warmth and wonderful smile put us at ease and we all fell in love with her.

Over the next few months we were all in a motion of living, breathing, and sweating kung fu and watching martial arts movies, and we became an inseparable family. She even came with me to the comic book store every Wednesday and learned about comics, and I followed her on culinary adventures of sushi and mochi because of her Japanese heritage. In time she and I started dating and fell in love, and eventually we married.

In the first year or so we moved around to Texas to Omaha, and I announced I wanted to join the Marines and go for Recon, a choice that would spell periods of separation for us, but still my baby supported and said, "Baby, you are so cool!"

I packed my bags and headed for boot camp to train to be capable of any mission on land, sea, or air, at any time. At any time, the call to soldiering could come, and it did. And she was left to care for our home and the dog, manage her career, and handle the affairs. Affairs of discussing my burial wishes and filling out forms for the "Marine Corps Lottery"—the $200,000 she would receive if I was killed in action. The affairs of being apart.

Every homecoming became a honeymoon, every kiss a reminder of our wedding day, but with constant battles in Afghanistan and Iraq, I was deployed or preparing for deployment for five
years straight. If I have any regret at all about our past it's that I left
her alone so much during those years. Alone, and I'm certain lonely,
she still wrote me scores of beautiful letters, most of which wouldn't
even reach me until I was home, but she wrote them anyway for
her and for me. She wrote them to share the light in her heart with
her husband in dark war.

Lonely on the battlefield, I missed her terribly too, but it was
showing. My leaders strongly counseled me to keep my eye on the
ball—the Taliban in Afghanistan—so I did my best to forget the
lovely "MoonPie" face that I used to kiss good-bye in the morning
because the Marine Corps rises very early. But she never forgot
me. All the while she was sharing me with the world of black ops
and night infiltrations, she was still that blossoming rose with her
face turning to mine like I was the sun and she was soaking up my
radiance and smiling it back. She shared me.

But after so many years and wars apart, we just started drifting
apart. My baby who dreamed and prayed for my return also prepared for a somber, silent return in which there would be no embrace or kisses or ticker tape. I returned from the battlefield a
war-torn and scarred man, while she had become a fading flower.

We used to climb at a rock gym and swim together every Sat-
urday and Sunday, but after all of my wars I started to just drink on
the weekends. We used to talk in bed late at night and read comics
together and make love, but after the grinding of Recon I started
sleeping on the couch because I was uncomfortable being close to
anybody. I was falling into rage and alcoholism, and she was in a
depression because her husband was living with her but was never
home. We were falling, caught in a downward spiral of reciprocity

My comic-book-style illustration and story of my "MoonPie"
drawn while on tour of duty in Afghanistan in 2001.

of hurting back and forth, and neither of us knew how to catch each other or ourselves.

And yet the funny thing is we have. Although we struggled and eventually separated and parted as man and wife, she has still always been in my corner. Every success and victory I've had she would call or see me and give me the biggest hugs. Once we got past the pain of disappointment and failed expectations, the telltale signs of our shared love and commonality were still there to be seen.

Just recently I was out of town and I let her borrow my car while I was gone. It was a mess as usual, loaded with training clothes and equipment, coffee cups, street clothes, and protein bar wrappers everywhere. But still today, even though the marriage is no more, she loves and cares for me, and while I was gone she completely cleaned and organized my car. She laughed when she said, "Baby, you got to get organized!"

We are no longer caught in a downward spiral; we are lifting each other up in a new reciprocity of positive sharing. No longer as people who have hurt each other, but as people who love. As she is living her authentic journey of "more life," her light shines to me and mine to her, because I am behind her all the way too. We are all for one, and one for all.

She has sacrificed and saved me so many times.

She is my hero.

Baby, you are so cool!

The question of sharing takes shape gently and intuitively with nudges to listen and consider along the way. You can make mental notes or jot down ideas, but unlike most questions, it's likely you will never formulate an official reply. The hero inevitably lives their life into the answer. It chooses you.

The sensation often feels like you're plugged into something bigger than yourself—a purpose, a meaning, a calling. You have become a conduit for the message of Hero Living and no other hero can share it quite like you.

The playwright George Bernard Shaw wrote, "This is the true joy in life: The being used for a purpose recognized by yourself as a mighty one. The being a force of Nature, instead of a feverish, selfish little clod of ailments and grievances complaining that the world will not devote itself to making you happy."

He continued, "I am of the opinion that my life belongs to the whole community, and as long as I live, it is my privilege to do for it whatever I can. I want to be thoroughly used up when I die—for the harder I work, the more I live. I rejoice in life for its own sake. Life is no 'brief candle' to me; it is a sort of splendid torch which I have got hold of for the moment, and I want to make it burn as brightly as possible before handing it on to future generations."

This splendid torch is in your hands to light as you will now and now and now . . .

When we feel hurt or under the yoke of oppression it can be oh-so-easy to slide down a spiraling cycle of negativity and not care about anything besides our own pain and misery. The road to bitterness is always a choice before us. And I promise you that every hero has felt the temptation to go down that road in his or her hurt and pain. And if you've ever felt yourself on that road, you understand this yourself and how dark it can be.

Many in the world are born into a running river of generational hatred and violence. Under such a reign of meaningless chaos, it can be a challenge to even realize there are other options to a long and desolate night of bitterness. A challenge I have experienced myself. But the magic is in understanding the wisdom of Ralph Waldo Emerson, who wrote, "What lies behind you and what lies in front of you, pales in comparison to what lies inside of you."

This wisdom is so simple, so powerful; but it can be easy to miss or forget or misplace.

Simply by looking inside to see and follow the bliss of your authentic self, to love and accept and be *who I am*, a light naturally shines for yourself and to others, and in this we are all transformed out of the darkness.

No matter what has been passed down or around, no matter what pain or fear or oppression, the hero honors and keeps that which is positive and breaks through the shackles of that which weighs heavily down, transmuting the downward spiral of negativity onto a track of escalating mutual cooperation and sharing. Hearkening to the motto of the Three Musketeers, "All for one, and one for all," the hero understands that we are all part of the fabric woven by generations of ancestors through time, and that his or her role is alive as the weaver of cloth still being created on the loom of all that is now and now and now.

If you have moments where you feel tempted to participate in reciprocity with hatred and violence, consider the words of Martin Luther King Jr. who said, "If you succumb to the temptation of using violence in the struggle, unborn generations will be the recipients of a long and desolate night of bitterness, and your chief legacy to the future will be an endless reign of meaningless chaos."

We must bring our hero wisdom to bear in doing all we can to share and burn bright a hero's light. We must protect that light for all and for the one. By positively sticking to the truth of the hero, we choose and are in charge of our participation in the reciprocity circuit, by sharing the light of possibility and positive change.

Instead of viewing reciprocity as a basic circuit of back-and-forth tit for tat, the wisdom of Gandhi shines through in understanding that "an eye for an eye only ends up making the whole world blind." We can destroy our enemies in an eternal "eye for an eye" until we're all wasted away. Or we can destroy an enemy by making them our friends and work together for harmony and peace. Perhaps it seems an idyllic notion, but as the popular saying goes, "Shoot for the moon. Even if you miss, you'll land among the stars." This is living in possibility, sharing the light of possibility.

And I for one choose to shoot and land among the stars.

In doing so, one can effect a positive circuit in the reciprocity of sharing for all by simply stepping onto the hero's path and sharing the boon of truth.

That the seed of a hero lies within each of us.

We are all made of the same stardust.

Each of us is one share of one human family.

One family that shares one planet spinning around one star.

You have the joy and blessing and responsibility of taking the inheritance from those before, adding to it, and passing it to others.

That is your quest.

"To laugh often and much; to win the respect of intelligent people and the affection of children . . . to leave the world a better place . . . to know even one life has breathed easier because you have lived. This is to have succeeded."

Ralph Waldo Emerson wrote this while he was Hero Living.

Now it's your turn.

Now and now and now . . .

You are a hero.

Be the hero you wish to be living and sharing and living . . .

CONCLUSION

I am in perpetual wonder of my life.

As a kid I had no idea the effect it would have on my life's journey to "want to be Bruce Lee when I grow up." What I knew was I loved doing punches and kicks like my hero, and I just followed my bliss from there. I had never heard the words of Joseph Campbell as a kid, but I sure would've known what he meant when he said, "A hero is someone who has given his or her life to something bigger than oneself." And I just knew that was the kind of life for me. That was my bliss.

Of course, I didn't grow up to be Bruce Lee, but along the way I learned a little something about heroes and a lot about myself. I learned that when I live as a hero of my true authentic self right here and now I am more filled with happiness and wonder for our world, and of my and your and our place in it. And I know that most everyone is just like me as a kid looking up to heroes like Bruce Lee and Spider-Man, because throughout history every culture and tradition has had its own pantheon of heroes.

I think that's simply because we humans need heroes.

We need the stories and myths of heroes as an inspiration for our hopes and dreams. We need real life heroes to protect and defend and bring those dreams to life.

The beauty about the iconic mythological world of heroes is it shines a light on the path of how we, as ordinary human beings, can step into the footprints of heroes that have gone before us and live an extraordinary life.

We can see the heroes that walk beside us every day.

We can recognize the hero inside each one of us right here in the now.

And each one of us at any moment, this very moment, can step into the possibility of Hero Living now and now and now . . .

In his seminal work *The Hero with a Thousand Faces*, Campbell wrote, "A hero ventures forth from the world of common day into a region of supernatural wonder: fabulous forces are there encountered and a decisive victory is won: the hero comes back from this mysterious adventure with the power to bestow boons on his fellow man."

This sort of adventure can take place on the external and an inner level, as he continued to describe with first "a break away or departure from the local social order and context; next, a long deep retreat inward and backward, backward, as it were, in time, and inward, deep into the psyche; a chaotic series of encounters there . . . of a centering kind, fulfilling, harmonizing, giving new courage; and then finally, in such fortunate cases, a return journey of rebirth to life."

And that's what it can feel like turning inward to see *who I am*. There before you in the mirror are all the agreements with suffering, bars on your cage, quirks and foibles, successes and failures, love and compassion, all the myriad questions of "what's important" and "what's the meaning," and those negative loops and positive signs, and people who care and more. It's all there before you as "a chaotic series of encounters," all intoning a summons as a loud quiet call. An invitation always extended simply because *you are here*. The hero's invitation to accept and take hold and be *who I am*, and live joyfully in the flow of "know thyself."

No matter what, at any moment, just like Ebenezer Scrooge in Charles Dickens' *A Christmas Carol*, you can let go of your past with abandon, wake up to your true self, and simply take your next step as your first square on the hero's path. No matter your quirks and foibles, no matter where you are or where you've been, no matter what fabulous forces you encounter, even in spite of yourself, the loud quiet call and invitation into the hero adventure perpetually beckon you to dive in deep supernatural wonder to explore and know and live the treasure within, to accept the eternal gift of "know thyself" now and now . . . in acceptance and responsibility and love.

I've found this to be true whether in the quiet of solitude or the loud raucous sounds of a kung fu match or the bombs of war. But you don't have to step into a fighter's ring or join the rank and file of the military to be on the hero's journey. "Man's greatest actions are performed in minor struggles. Life, misfortune, isolation, abandonment and poverty are battlefields which have their heroes— obscure heroes who are at times greater than illustrious heroes." These words by Victor Hugo so poignantly point out the truth of the world of heroes—that they are everywhere.

So take hold the boon and stoke the fire of the hero's eternal flame to share with others—as physical deeds or the spiritual gifts of those lessons and knowledge you garner along the way. Starting with this . . .

You are a hero.

Even if it doesn't feel that way or you don't believe, the seed is there if you but welcome it to bloom and grow.

I know. Because if I can do it, you can too.

My story is your story is our story.

So now that you have the strides through which the hero dynamically moves, plus the awareness of how your body, mind, and emotions can inform and direct Hero Living, consider these questions: Where are you in the hero journey right now? Are you fighting? Are you acquiring new tools? Are you paralyzed? And if you were to look deeper into the different facets and roles of your life—spouse, parent, moneymaker, homemaker, son, daughter, victim, survivor, and so forth—where does each of these facets fall in the hero's journey?

I invite you to use the hero's seven strides as framework and friend for contemplating your life and your various roles. You will find that in some facets you are farther along while, in others, you are farther back. Keep in mind, I use the word "farther" not as a quantifier, but as a qualifier. In other words, when you get a clearer view of where you are in any given facet and stride, you get a clearer view of where you want to go.

In each stride I included various Hero's Whetstones for your use in moving along the path of your own hero's journey. You can refer back to them individually or sequentially as needed or as feels right to you as you consider the different facets of your life. These Hero's Whetstones are your whetstones to use to help your life along the hero's path. I have listed the strides at the end of this chapter with a brief description, so you can easily find them now or in the future as needed.

This is not a fitness book, so I haven't spent time on specifics for how to train and nourish your body, but as we conclude I do want to be clear about the importance of your physical health and fitness to the hero's journey.

The author and mountaineer James Ramsey Ullman once wrote, "A man climbs the mountains because he needs to climb, because that is the way he is made. Rock and ice and snow and wind and the great blue canopy of the sky are not all that he finds upon the mountain-tops. He discovers things about his own body and mind that he had almost forgotten in the day-to-day, year-to-year routine of living. He learns what his legs are for, what his lungs are for, what the wise men of old meant by refreshment of the spirit."

I know so many people who tell me they're out of shape or feel out of touch with their body, so what I love about this passage is the nudge to awaken to the elemental experience of being. To shift into a living breathing awareness of self—Mind, Body, and Spirit—through movement and doing, to feel the sun on your face and the wind in your hair, because that's what we're designed to do. Excepting any physical handicaps, injuries, or other limitations, your body is designed to move and jump and climb and play and work. And if you're not regularly training your body so you can use it for productivity and fun, you are missing a critical component of your life experience.

You'll notice that every whetstone begins with a simple movement of three breaths in and out. This is intentional, to engage the whole of you in you, because your body, mind, and emotions are the integrated vehicle of your experience. It is this holistic awareness with an attitude of exploration and adventure in the mountains and valleys of our lives that brings life to life.

What you *do*—think, move, sense, feel, eat, drink, breathe, smoke, and more—all conspire as your creation of your experience. What you put in your body affects your thought, affects your mood, affects your body, affects your thought, affects your . . . all in the infinite flow of creation. The choices you make, the attitude you take, all the doing that you do—even in doing "nothing"—you are the cocreator of your experience. You are actively creating your life in relationship with all that is.

You are a Human Doing in your creation of being.

For instance, I am an elite-level athlete. I am because that's what I create every day. I could choose to be sedentary and eat foods that don't nourish, but that does not serve the purpose of my true authentic self. My motivation for fitness training is not to merely have big muscles. In moving my body and pushing limits I am in the bliss of creating the best vehicle I can for my adventures and way of being, and the body that you see is the result.

The shape and condition of my body is never static. It changes all the time, every day. Through different stages of my life I have been stronger in some ways than in others—for instance, my legs were much bigger when I was running and swimming with heavy gear for miles and miles in Recon than they are now. But I don't care about the inches and pounds; I care that my body can do what I need it to do for my mission, so that's what I focus on and *do*!

Think for a moment about the condition of your own body. Not how attractive you think you are, but your physical condition and health. Or better yet, if there's a mirror close by, look at your reflection. What thoughts do you have about yourself because of the condition or health of your body? How do you feel about yourself? No matter what your answers, this is great as information about your current Mind, Body, and Spirit connection. It also reveals how closely linked your thoughts and feelings are to your body.

If you happen to feel any guilt, shame, embarrassment, or other negativity about it like so many people do, ask yourself if these feelings in turn also keep you from moving and using your body. If so, perhaps you are in a downward cycle. If that's the case, resist any urge to push yourself farther down with more negative thoughts, and instead consider that you are now at a moment of choice to simply shift onto an upward track and move your body in spite of your thoughts and emotions.

Think of children running, laughing, and playing and be one for yourself inside. Give yourself a break and freedom to learn about proper nutrition and getting your body in shape for the life you want, and breathe and move and laugh and *do*!

Even if your body resists moving from lack of use, or you sense some aches and pains, I promise if you make a practice of moving your body, your body condition will improve and your mind and emotions will follow. That's simply the way it works. This is simple internal circuitry that you have the ability and power to learn and manage.

I have personally experienced this and seen it in others. I read the story once of Vinu Malik, the founder and CEO of Fuel Belt, whose products for staying hydrated during endurance sports are used by top triathlon athletes around the world. By looking at his pictures today, you'd never know that in college he was bedridden with chronic fatigue syndrome. He lacked the energy to lead a normal life, but Malik would see triathletes on TV and in magazines and he became inspired to spend his free time exercising.

"You'd think exercise would make you more tired," he says. "But it helped stimulate my system, and taught me to focus on my nutrition." Before long he was training for an Ironman competition and along the way invented a hydration belt to help keep him hydrated during training and races. And years later he's now completed twenty-seven Ironman races and runs a successful business around his bliss of triathlons. Wow! That inspires *me*!

Perhaps you're in great physical condition, but your mind and emotions somehow aren't firing as you'd like or in full support of your hero's journey. Maybe your thought patterns hold you back, or you feel overwhelmed by your emotions and out of control. Whatever aspect of your Mind, Body, and Spirit connection may not be optimal or as you'd like it to be for your journey, it's okay, because all of that can change in a moment, no problem.

Getting your mind out of the habit of reasons and excuses for why not and shifting onto the track of "I can" will immediately move you into the flow of possibility. And there you will experience the flow of your dreams, where if you take a step toward them, your dreams will take a step toward you. The flow of choosing every moment as a practice of your solid and steady happiness.

If I can do it, you can too. Because my story is your story is our story. A hero's story of "I can."

The Story of Us

We, the human family, have taken many twists and turns in the story of who we are as individuals, communities, and cultures. History has played out endless versions of people in need of acceptance, honor, pride, shelter, food, and safety. People experience the gamut of experience from the thrill of victory, the agony of defeat, fighting and wars, disease and heartache, to searching for truth and curing ills, and love and caring for one another.

As I write this book from a place of relative luxury and convenience, the negative effects of global-scale prospecting on the environment and each other may seem to appear far off. But it's immediately apparent when you're in those places where others are suffering because of it, where some people are working for bare sustenance while providing the comfort and luxury of others. Where the planet is groaning warm with pollutions and toxins, rapacious mining and burning, and people and animals are unable to lead a natural, healthy life. And there is much less than six degrees of separation between all.

When I think of this I know there are many heroes out there working toward solutions, advocating for change on the one planet we all share. They are out there—beautiful living-color heroes.

At the same time it seems some must believe we have all the time in the world to address our most pressing needs, or think they are powerless to make a difference. Or perhaps there are some of us who, as individuals or as a part of institutional entities, are caught

in the mesmerizing myth of "more" and the illusion of "the top."
The mirage that if we simply have more revenue, profit, dividends,
market share, territory, turnover, expansion, control, power, and
more—or higher pay, positions, stock prices, buildings, prestige,
wealth, and on and on—that we will somehow have success and
bring about true happiness.

However, what can actually happen in this scenario, when
"more" and "the top" come at the expense of others, the individual
and the institution inculcated with an appetite for more can take on
the role of villain as oppressor or even dictator or totalitarian in a
voracious search for more and more and more. As if there's no limit
to how many "more" things we can buy and sell, no limit to the resources we deplete to make or dispose of those things, or no limit
to the amount of toxins we can take in and dish out, and remain alive
and healthy as a people and a planet. As if it doesn't matter how we
treat each other as long as the means gets us "more" in the end.

When we care more for "more" than we care for each other, all
of each other, we are caught in samsara—a loop of suffering in our
relationship. In such moments that we realize we are in samsara,
that is the loud quiet call to take stock of *who I am*, who we are, and
rally to the sound of the hero's call.

That is the moment to creatively step into Hero Living.

In this moment, as in every moment, we are all at the brink of
possibility for choosing the nature of who we are and the direction
of our step. Will we step together? Trip each other up? Find a way
to dance?

It is up to each one of us, me and you, to decide how we participate in the reciprocity and cocreation of our relationships. We
are all in relationship every moment of our lives—in connected
relationship with ourselves, other people, animals and plants, the
environment of the planet, all together moving in the constant
dynamic motion of being.

The hero is mindful of his or her responsibility to work in harmonious sustainable relationship with all in the system and environment. The hero understands that he or she is in relationship with the whole. The hero acts to defend and protect and breathe life into the life of the whole.

So here in every moment of now and now, the choice is yours.

I believe the world is fighting and telling many of our present stories in a circuit of war and fear because the hero is not showing up in a real, completely passionate and courageous way in all the places we need. The hero is hidden in the shadows of agendas and doublespeak and political correctness, and greed and power and command and control, and ratings and shock value and habituated numbing.

I mean to say that as more of us wake up to our personal power to make change in ourselves, we will create a sea change in the world around us unlike anything that has been recorded before. That we—you, me, and everyone—can make this journey the most special, empowering, and compassionate message that will continue to help, hold, and lift humanity to the next level.

To quote Campbell a last time, from *The Hero with a Thousand Faces*, "We have not even to face the adventure alone, for the heroes of all time, have gone before us: the labyrinth is thoroughly known; we have only to follow the thread of the hero path. And where we had thought to find an abomination, we shall find a god, and where we had thought to slay another, we shall slay ourselves. Where we had thought to travel outward, we shall come to the center of our own existence, and where we had thought to be alone, we shall be with all the World."

We are not alone or without guidance. We have the hero's map and the compass, mirror, and lantern to lead the way. We have the wisdom of sages and gurus who have counseled essential keys to individual and communal happiness to include respect for one another and getting along.

We have the words of Socrates who said, "The shortest and surest way to live with honor in the world, is to be in reality what we would appear to be." Simply show up and be the hero you wish to see.

Let go the trappings that keep you caged, stagnant and paralyzed, and move. Consider your life with hope and hold onto your dreams regardless of where you are. Wherever you are, that is the perfect place from which to take the next step toward your dreams as a hero. As the thirteenth-century Persian poet Rumi once wrote:

Come, come, whoever you are,
Wanderer, idolater, worshiper of fire,
Come even though you have broken your vows a thousand times,
Come, and come yet again.
Ours is not a caravan of despair.

As you ruminate, consider this truism: You don't have to pay penance. You don't have to earn. You don't have to deserve. The choice to move into a different experience is in and of itself redemptive. The choice to move is enough because you are enough; always have been. This is a heroic act of such epic, healing courage, new possibilities have no choice but to show up and meet you.

Simply continue to gift yourself the hero's path, and I promise your life will transform to "something bigger than oneself." Every moment in this big bad beautiful world is precious now and now and now . . . Every moment. Every experience is valuable. All is a gift. Unwrap every moment with wonder and delight and the unfettered pleasure of a child. To see the world with fresh eyes now and now will grant you rich treasures in every moment.

Simply start with taking a breath, checking in and opening up to the moment, to *who I am* as pure possibility. Tuck your chin a bit. Keep your hands up, ready for anything. And now move. With grace, bravery, and power . . . move!

It starts right here right now and now . . .

Hero Living starts inside and radiates out now and now . . .

Every certainty of the story of us lies behind, every possibility now lies ahead. And it is up to us.

We can all be the heroes we wish to see.

I invite you to show up for yourself this moment. This now. To awaken the hero inside, to engage the seven strides, to practice the tools you learn, and to move your life into possibility, authenticity, and reciprocity. Claim yourself. Gift yourself. And that will be enough. That will be the difference.

Life will quite literally come to life now and now . . .

The story of your life, my life, our life . . .

The living breathing hero's life of Hero Living.

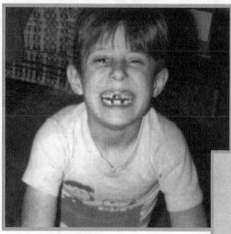

Smiling big as a kid.
Courtesy of Reyes family

With my "cowboy" brothers.
Courtesy of Reyes family

**With my brother Michael
in our apartment in Kansas City.**
Courtesy of Reyes family

Deployed in Afghanistan.
Courtesy of Rudy Reyes

With friends Dan and Sal Alvarez while filming HBO's *Generation Kill* in Africa. Much appreciation and love to "Big Dan" Mosta, who is no longer with us.
Courtesy of Rudy Reyes

With the fellow actors of my team while filming HBO's *Generation Kill* in Africa.
Courtesy of Eric Kocher

With a bunch of the fans who would constantly follow us around while filming HBO's *Generation Kill* in Africa.
Courtesy of Sal Alvarez

In Hero Living spirit.
Courtesy of Sal Alvarez

The Hero's Whetstones

STRIDE 1—STAGNANCY & PARALYSIS

The Hero's Whetstone: Tuning In. Assess your emotional landscape and identify the bars in your cage that keep you trapped or paralyzed.

The Hero's Whetstone: Using Your Inner Eye. Discover the Sisyphean agreements you have made with your suffering.

STRIDE 2—MOMENT OF MOVEMENT

The Hero's Whetstone: Be the Dreamer of Dreams. Remember, review, and identify your dreams of old and today.

The Hero's Whetstone: Reading Your Map. Build a balanced list of your assets, strengths, and areas that need improvement.

The Hero's Whetstone: Squaring the Direction of Your Step. Get real with "What do I really want?" in removing bars from your cage that keep you trapped.

STRIDE 3—FIGHTING & SURVIVING

The Hero's Whetstone: Breathe Your Flow of Power. Authorize yourself to fight for yourself and punch with your powerful exhale. Hi-yah!

The Hero's Whetstone: A Balanced Fighter Be. Assess your fighting style and find a balance to your style, resources, and assets.

STRIDE 4—TOOLS & SKILLS

The Hero's Whetstone: Honoring Your Enemy. Learn to respect your enemies as obstacles and challenges from which to grow.

The Hero's Whetstone: Packing Your Toolkit. Assess and list the tools and skills needed for a mission on your journey.

STRIDE 5—PRACTICING & HONING

The Hero's Whetstone: Your Practice. Develop a curriculum and plan for acquiring, practicing, and honing skills needed for your mission and journey.

The Hero's Whetstone: Practicing Your Destiny. Learn to find the language of your Mind, Body, Spirit connection and emotional life as a barometer and compass for your journey.

STRIDE 6—PURE UNEDITED, UNINHIBITED POTENTIAL

The Hero's Whetstone: Know Who I Am. See yourself in and through others to understand the many facets of yourself now and now.

STRIDE 7—RECIPROCITY OF SHARING

The Hero's Whetstone: Living the Hero Effect. Experience the effect of the hero *you*—in you, with others, and in the world at large.

ACKNOWLEDGMENTS

I am in vital humility as I say to all of you who have taken the time and given the energy for a smile, a kick, an argument, an embrace, and laughter, I thank and honor you. In Hero Living everyone at every time is connected to the fabric of real possibility and awareness. In this way some of those I am most grateful to are my tyrants and oppressors, as they gave me life-and-death impetus to drive on and listen to the hero's call. To listen in a way that I heard a voice inside that said, "You don't need to take this. You deserve to be valued and empowered." That voice was my voice. That voice was the hero's voice of us all. That voice is your voice.

I would like to name some names and some places for the sake of honor, respect, and love. Honor for the high esteem they hold in my heart. Respect for the sacrifices and wisdom that are shared and amplified by the hero's journey and process. And love for the simple bliss of awakening the call inside me, and guiding me in sounding the call in others.

From my childhood . . . South Texas and the barrio wonderland of preschool years, the Reyes family, the Cantu family, Grandma Carmen, the suburbs of Kansas City, MO, and its safety, bicycles, and autumn leaves. Cousin Belinda and Gary, who loved and took me and Michael and Ceasar everywhere. The fantastic films of Bruce Lee, Sylvester Stallone, Ridley Scott (*Alien*, *Blade Runner*, and *Legend*), and Michael Mann (*The Jericho Mile*, *Thief*, and *Miami Vice*), Marvel Comics (I used to be loyal to Make Mine Marvel!), the Olympics, Sean Blakemore, and snow sledding. And of course swimming pools, creeks of any sort, tadpoles, and kite flying!

Those from my adolescence . . . South Texas for its hard lessons of cruel survival, Christie and my first kiss, Michael and Ceasar for giving me a reason to live. Sickness, parasites, and disease, for their honesty at shining a light on my inner condition. Drawing comics as a way to believe in something true and honorable. All the athletes that I beat even though my hand-me-down shoes were too big, because it is never "the shoes." Daredevil, Wolverine, Spidey, Batman, and especially Elektra, because she showed me that anyone, no matter what, can be redeemed. The Omaha Home for Boys, especially Mr. Orr, the dean of boys: Sir, you absolutely made an impact, and I looked up to you so much, you will never know the difference you made in my life as a coach, as a father figure, and as a man. The old NKC gang, who I am still close to: Scottie and Jules, Tommy and Joe, Teddy and Jon. The Swedlunds—Pop, I miss you. Mr. McClain, my art teacher and track coach, and Mr. Hatfield, who introduced me to creation myths and the power of Joseph Campbell. *The Gunslinger*, by Stephen King; *The Karate Kid*; Lloyd in *Say Anything*; Sofia in *The Color Purple*; and David Lynch films. Cathy, my first love. Bobby and Larry and Don Dokken. Music and record conventions were a blissful pastime, like U2 and The Cult. My martial arts training years . . . Sifu Jon Reider, Sifu Chun Man Sit, Sifu Jeff Bolt, Sifu Yang Yang, Sensei Joe Roberts and the Nelson Atkins Museum of Art, and Michael and Ceasar as my constant training partners. Midtown KC, the Inner City, and its rumbles and its danger, also its realness. Mann films (*The Last of the*

Mohicans, *Heat*, and *The Insider*), Sheree, Clint's Comics, righteousness of discipline and chivalry, training of Mind, Body, and Spirit, Chin Woo Academy, Lucille's, Dave Otto Miller, Broadway Cafe, Mary Anne and her boys, my Venus Auto brothers, Tarantino films (especially *True Romance*), Nikki, Grimm's Tattoo, and for the luck of being a young man with a big smile and a big heart. And basically I say thanks for living to eighteen.

Recon . . . United States Marine Corps Staff Sergeant Dixon, Senior Drill Instructor; Staff Sergeant Sly, Drill Instructor; Staff Sergeant Torres, Drill Instructor; and Staff Sergeant Lumbao, Drill Instructor. Thank you. SOI and our Super Squad. Amphibious Reconnaissance School and Sergeant "Crawdaddy" Crawford, who was my Recon hero. Sergeant "Big Frog" Roger Sparks, the Jedi of Recon, I am now and forever your humble student; I cannot say enough about your talent, skill, and humbleness. The old Second Platoon. Pappy, Staff Sergeant Johnson, and Captain Dill . . . don't forget Emelio! Bravo 2, Mike Winn, Nathan Fick, Garza, Chaffin, Walt, Jacks, Espera, Brad, Ray, Budweiser, TB, Stieny, and the rest of the platoon. The best *ever*. Eric Kocher and his guys . . . heroes, every one of them. Jeff, you are my Recon brother. My last platoon in Alpha, Treadwell, Captain Von Krauss, your leadership, passion, and bravery set the tone, G Money, Aweau, Dan Weiner, Austin, and of course my little Canadian son who became a better scout sniper than myself—McCoy, Mickey C. You are my heart, little man. Alpha 1, you all brought me back home.

And my wonderful life, on and on . . . Saucie, Michael and Ceasar, my Rancho warriors and hard strikers. Big Rudy, Angela Smith, and Sal Alvarez, without whom none of this would be possible. To Evan Wright, my HBO *Generation Kill* family, I miss you "Big Dan" Motsa, and my complete failure and then a fresh start. Carmen, Gabe, and Denise, my BFFF, Charlie T, Craig Aramaki-san, Todd Scurr, and the ambassador of the quan, Jason Graves. Love. Compassion. Sharing.

Loss. Eddie Wright, you are a man among men. Sweetie Brown, for the pure heart of love. And of course all of the heroes who show up each and every moment to cocreate amazing victories and relationships, who risk it all in the face of the cosmos. Risk it all staring into red giants and nebulous seas and the darkest nights . . . and still they look with eyes unwavering. Angela, you know what I am talking about. And my brothers and sisters at Penguin Books and William Morris for helping to get this book to you, my hero.